DATE DUE		
JUL 3 1995			
OCT 0 2 1995			
OCT 0 9 1996			
NOV 1 8 1996			
1 7 NOV 1998			
0 3 DEC 1998			
1 0 DEC 1999			
2 3 FEB 2001			
2 0 FEB 2002			

The Crisis
of Socialism
in Europe

The Crisis of Socialism in Europe

Edited by

Christiane Lemke

and Gary Marks

Duke University Press

Durham and London

1992

© 1992 Duke University Press
All rights reserved
Printed in the United States of America
on acid-free paper ∞
Library of Congress Cataloging-in-Publication Data
appear on the last printed page of this book.

To Hauke, Joshua,
and Lea

Contents

Preface

The year 1989–90 marked a watershed in European politics. Revolutions in east central Europe undermined communist regimes and led an upsurge of democracy in the region. The hectic processes of institutional recasting, economic restructuring, and party-political mobilization carry the seeds of a New Europe in which one of the major threads of political development since the industrial revolution—socialism—is rejected as a regime that has been tried and failed. In western Europe, socialist parties have been on the defensive for some time. Traditional socialist emphases on the blue-collar working class, on a broad subcultural movement, and on expanding the state appear increasingly anachronistic in the most economically developed European societies. At the same time, new social movements oriented around environmentalism and feminism have challenged socialist monopoly of the discourse of dissent. Socialism in each of its facets—as a set of ideas, as a party-political movement, and as a regime type—is called into question by developments in eastern and western Europe.

What are the roots of this crisis? Is there one crisis of socialism in eastern and western Europe or two? What are the future(s) of socialism, and can those futures be influenced by socialists themselves? Is the crisis of socialism a healthy manifestation of reflection and reformulation, or does it mark the end of a particular epoch of European history?

This book is based on a series of papers prepared for the "Crisis of Socialism in Eastern and Western Europe," a conference that brought scholars from eastern and western Europe and the United States to the University of North Carolina at Chapel Hill in April 1990 with the generous support of the Lurcy Charitable Trust Fund.

In the introduction, Christiane Lemke and Gary Marks analyze the crisis of socialism in the context of some basic political developments in eastern and western Europe. The following chapter by Geoff Eley is an overview of the history of socialism in western Europe. He reminds us that socialism has a long, rich, and diverse tradition and argues that the crisis of socialism is primarily a crisis of the statist stream of the socialist movement. The following two chapters, one written by a historian, the other by a political scientist, analyze the birth and death of communism as a regime type in eastern Europe. Norman Naimark examines the way in which different forms of national communism were smothered by Sovietization in the immediate postwar period. Sharon Wolchik discusses the origins of the revolutions in Hungary, Poland, Czechoslovakia, Bulgaria, and Rumania, as well as the future prospects of socialism in the region. Iván and Szonja Szelényi investigate emerging party cleavages in Hungary and argue that an untapped potential for social democracy exists in the country.

The following three chapters address the problems socialism faces in western Europe. Andrei Markovits explores how the West German Left has responded to the fundamental changes in eastern Europe. Wolfgang Merkel empirically evaluates, and rejects, the hypothesis that socialist parties are declining across western Europe. Herbert Kitschelt analyzes the challenges to socialist problem solving in western Europe and sets out a framework for a postsocialist discourse. In his postscript Konrad Jarausch discusses potential directions for the Left from the perspective of a historian.

From Decline to Demise? The Fate of Socialism in Europe

Christiane Lemke

and Gary Marks

The growth of socialism as an ideology, party-political formation, and regime type has been one of the most important developments in European politics over the last century. A century ago socialist parties were small sects of workers and intellectuals struggling for the freedom to organize and communicate in societies where their constituency, the working class, was excluded systematically from politics. In Germany, the Social Democratic party was emerging from a period in which the dissemination of socialist ideas in meetings, through the press, and by trade unions was banned by the state. In Russia and much of eastern Europe, socialists were still hunted down by police and spies working for feudalistic authoritarian regimes. Although they had the advantage of a freer legal climate, socialist parties in northwestern Europe were small or nonexistent one hundred years ago. In Britain, the Independent Labour party and the Social Democratic Federation had but a few thousand members between them and no significant electoral support. In southern Europe, socialist parties were small sects that contended with anarchists and syndicalists for influence within weakly institutionalized labor movements. Before World War I many socialist parties underwent a crisis of strategy as they grappled with the issue of revolution or reform, but there were never serious doubts that support for socialism was growing and would continue to grow.

1

Once we step back from the turmoil of events of 1989–90 and look at socialism from the perspective of the development of European politics between the nineteenth century and the present, it is clear that we have come to the end of a major transformation. After World War II, socialism was a growing and dynamic force. The Soviet Union, by virtue of its victories in World War II and its growing military might, dominated eastern Europe. In western Europe, socialist parties changed the boundaries of political life as they demanded the extension of basic political rights and brought previously unrepresented groups into the political system, reshaped party systems along a new employee-employer cleavage as they grew into major electoral contenders, and extended the role of the state to fulfill their extensive economic and social welfare agendas.

To state the impressive growth and influence of socialism over the past century is to see how different things are now. This is true in the obvious sense that the revolutions of eastern Europe have destroyed, presumably forever, the legitimacy of authoritarian socialism as a regime type. But the dynamism and influence of socialism in western Europe has changed just as fundamentally. The very success of socialist parties over the past century in shaping democracies based on social democratic principles of welfare, educational provision, and state intervention in the economy has meant that socialists find themselves as defenders of the status quo, not radical reformers. But the crisis of socialism is not simply a function of its success. Basic characteristics of socialist parties over the last century—characteristics that hang together in a logically coherent ideal type that we describe as "traditional socialism" (a blue-collar constituency, extensive subcultural organization, and emphasis on state regulation)—are increasingly anachronistic in the most economically developed societies.

From the perspective of the development of socialism over the last century, several strands of change, including the failure of socialism as a regime type in the Soviet Union and eastern Europe, the decline of traditional socialism in western Europe, and the rise of environmental movements, constitute a "crisis" of socialism.[1] The collapse of state socialism in the East and the decline of traditional socialism in the West complement and reinforce each other. Strong social democratic parties persist across western Europe, but socialists no longer monopolize the discourse of dissent. The traditional pillars of these parties in western Europe are weakening visibly. Their core constituency, the blue-collar working class, is declining; their organizational

Christiane Lemke and Gary Marks

base as encompassing movement parties is eroding; their traditional commitment to the expansion of state control of the economy and society is viewed as a liability. In a growing number of countries, environmentalists, women's groups, and greens challenge the traditional socialist monopoly of the discourse of dissent on a variety of new social issues including equal status for women and minorities, reproductive rights, quality of life issues, and opposition to nuclear weapons.

Our aim in the following pages is to chart the most decisive influences on socialism in Europe as far as they can be evaluated at the beginning of the last decade of the twentieth century and discuss how they constrain the future of socialism. We use the word *constrain* advisedly. Although it is certainly not possible to predict such specific political outcomes as elections or policy shifts, we believe that it is worth trying to think through the logic of the past for the structure of political alternatives in the future. While it is usually impossible to predict the actual choices that people make, it is sometimes possible to discuss sensibly the range of choice available. In this more open-textured sense we attempt to analyze the essential elements of the current situation and their implications for the future.

The End of Communism in Eastern Europe

Communism Is Dead

With the collapse of communist regimes across eastern Europe, an epoch has come to an end.[2] Revolutionary changes have transformed East Germany, Czechoslovakia, Hungary, and Poland. Even in the countries of southeastern Europe, where communists have been able to cling tenuously to power, Soviet hegemony no longer exists.[3] The starting point for the analysis of postrevolutionary developments in east central Europe is that communism as a regime type is a historical phenomenon rather than a viable political alternative.[4]

Socialist command economies failed not only to catch up with their western capitalist competitors, but were also unable to meet the most basic demands of their populations. Centralized bureaucracies stifled innovative adaption, production quotas displaced attention from fulfilling human wants, human and natural resources were wasted on an enormous scale, and the environment was so neglected that it became life threatening. These failures were politically corrosive for regimes that staked their legitimacy on their ability to organize production rationally. Command economies nurtured the very crises that led to the downfall of communism.

The suddenness with which these regimes fell revealed just how illegitimate and inept they were.[5] The degree to which political elites had lost both popular support and their will to rule surprised even those who opposed them. These regimes had more than four decades in which to entrench themselves, but once the threat of Soviet coercion was withdrawn they crumbled. Not only did communist parties alienate the intelligentsia, but they also managed to estrange their core constituency, workers and farmers, in whose name they claimed to speak. These regimes began with the goal of molding a socialist culture, but they created an ethical vacuum, an ever-widening gap between official discourse and the realities of everyday life.[6] In their effort to perpetuate their rule, communist elites forged an iron cage of rigid bureaucracy that sapped their political will and even their belief in their own legitimacy.

Reformed communist parties have contested the first free elections in east central Europe, but they have done so as marginal parties struggling to throw off the negative weight of the past without a natural constituency except present and former employees of the declining state apparatus.[7] These parties have rapidly lost membership. In East Germany, membership of the PDS, the former East German Communist party, fell from 2.3 million to 300,000 within a year after the November 1989 revolution. In Czechoslovakia, Communist party membership declined from 1.7 million in October 1989 to around 400,000 a year later. Former communist parties have performed poorly in national elections. In Czechoslovakia and East Germany, Communist parties received 13 and 16 percent of the national vote in the 1990 elections. In Poland, the only completely competitive parliamentary elections have been the 1990 local elections in which the Communist party received less than 1 percent of the vote. In the presidential election of 1990 the Communist party candidate received virtually no support. Even in Hungary, where a strong reform wing emerged within the Communist party from the late 1980s, the reform-oriented successor of the party, the Hungarian Socialist party, received only 10.5 percent of the vote, while the orthodox wing did not surpass the 4 percent necessary for representation in the National Assembly. In retrospect, it is clear that repeated attempts by ruling communist parties in Hungary and Poland to adjust to their declining legitimacy did not enhance their electoral competitiveness. Instead, the willingness of these parties to enter into a dialog with their oppositions provided breathing space for competing political groupings to organize and may, in fact, have accelerated communist decline.

The legacy of communist rule is a heavy burden for the political Left in east central Europe. Vaclav Havel has noted that in the popular imagination socialism connoted "an ordinary billy-club" used to hit free-minded people. Democratic socialism has suffered from guilt by association. In several countries communist parties have taken the socialist label, and noncommunist leftists have sought to differentiate themselves by calling themselves social democrats. Despite their attempts to draw a line between themselves and former communists, social democrats find themselves tainted by the legacy of communist rule. In Hungary and Czechoslovakia, social democratic parties were unable to overcome the 4 and 5 percent barriers necessary to gain representation. Even in East Germany, where social democracy has a long tradition and the Social Democratic party was expected to become the largest party in the first free elections in March 1990, the party received just 21.8 percent of the vote compared to the 48.1 percent for the Christian Democratic-led coalition.

There Is No Third Way

One of the major conclusions to be drawn from the experience of east central Europe in the months following the revolutions is that there is no practicable third way combining market reforms and private property in the context of a national planned economy. Yet the polarized options of laissez-faire capitalism versus state socialism—the so-called first and second ways—are too crude to serve as useful blueprints for reform and too simplistic to conceptualize even the most basic variations across developed political economies.

The aspirations of many intellectuals of the Left across east central and western Europe for a third way as an alternative to western capitalism have been shattered. There are both economic and political reasons for this. Economic reformers are generally convinced that it is impossible to combine centralized state control of the economy alongside an innovative and robust entrepreneurial sector.[8] In a shrinking state sector with fewer lucrative administrative positions there are dwindling incentives for state managers or workers to make enterprises more efficient. At the same time the market itself remains undeveloped. Moreover, the assumption that one could manage these economies by developing centralized national plans cannot overcome the fact that these economies are rapidly becoming intertwined in an international economic system in which many of the most decisive economic influences lie beyond national control.[9] Given a series of unsuccessful attempts to reform state socialism, the new reformers have been driven to the conclusion that a combination of plan and market is the worst of both worlds. The failure of the third way is as much political as economic. Proponents of various third-way options were sensitive to the problems that would be generated by the wholesale introduction of market reforms, yet they did not take up the immediate political challenge of creating a democratic society in the postrevolutionary situations that confronted these societies. The piecemeal changes they conceived were out of touch with demands for political and economic transformation to create a civil society based on individual property ownership. The notion of piecemeal adaption as part of a third way was undercut because it appeared to compromise with state planning and bureaucratic corruption. There are strong pressures to sweep away the remnants of the old system and to prosecute those responsible for fraud, corruption, and the misallocation of resources, pressures that are intensified because many former communist cadres managed to transform their positions of privilege under the old system into ownership of plants and factories in the new.[10]

This is not to say that pure capitalism will be introduced. Those who celebrate a victory of laissez-faire capitalism overlook the fact that all European countries have mixed economies characterized by extensive welfare states, government regulation of industry and the labor market, and the redirection of resources to poor regions and to agriculture. In eastern Europe the state will continue to play a major role in the economy even after market mechanisms have been established. None of these societies have strong laissez-faire traditions; the state has always been centrally involved in the economy, particularly the labor market. In Poland, for example, the "crash course" introduced in January 1990 emphasized state provision of welfare and included economic subsidies, national unemployment insurance, and a retraining program for the unemployed. In Czechoslovakia, state ownership is being dismantled only gradually, and foreign ownership remains under strict state control.

The demise of state socialism in eastern Europe has actually undermined the utility of conceptions of political economy framed in terms of a polarity between laissez-faire capitalism on the one hand and statism on the other. While simplistic conceptions of market versus state have served effectively as ideological guideposts, they are blunt instruments for analyzing concrete choices in the New Europe. With the collapse of state socialism, variations among capitalist political economies are likely to be more significant. To be sure, competitive capital and labor markets will be created in east central Europe, but the extent and character of state regulation will reflect choices that cannot be reduced to an overall preference for the creation of a market society.

Class Is Unlikely to Be the Dominant Cleavage in Eastern Europe

Democratic socialist parties gained little support in the first free elections across eastern Europe, but it is uncertain whether these early results can be extrapolated into the future.[11] The contamination that democratic socialist parties suffered as a result of the extreme unpopularity of communism may erode over time. Socialist parties might gain support from the unemployed and those who suffer economically as a result of market reforms. A new underclass is already forming, partly as a result of mass migration from poorer eastern European countries. In societies where the basic framework of western social democracy is absent one might assume that socialist parties have a clear mission that would attract mass support.

However, good reasons exist for believing that the crisis of socialism in eastern Europe goes beyond the negative legacy of communism and is rooted, more profoundly, in the weakness of class as a decisive cleavage in the foreseeable future. The cleavage between workers and employers, central to socialist party mobilization in the past, is only one of a number of competing sources of political identity across eastern Europe and is unlikely to become dominant. Over the past forty years political conflict in eastern European societies has not been structured along class lines because there were no capitalists for workers to mobilize against. When workers did mobilize, as in Poland from 1980 on, they did so as part of a larger movement that stretched across class lines. The nonclass character of political mobilization was reinforced by the revolutions of 1989. The basic conflict concerned communist domination, and this was fought in the name of national self-determination and moral self-regeneration rather than any particular class or group.

Will class emerge as a fulcrum of political organization in the post-revolutionary era? The forums that mobilized revolution across east central Europe were aggregations of those opposed to communism and represented a wide range of social groupings. As one would expect, they are becoming unglued as the struggle against communism is replaced by the complex task of creating and sustaining a new political and economic order. The emerging political organizations are based on diverse crosscutting cleavages: religious versus secular, regional versus national, communist versus anticommunist, populism versus cosmopolitanism, native versus immigrant, and cleavages based on ethnicity.[12] Class may emerge as one basis of cleavage, but there are several reasons for expecting that it will not become a dominant cleavage.

First, in countries where class has competed with religious and ethnic identities, the salience of class has been relatively weak. Whereas traditional labor organizations, including unions, were coordinated as proletarian organizations under communist control, religious and ethnic identities withstood the monopoly of communist power. Civil society was weak, yet religion and ethnicity continued to be rooted in everyday life and will remain powerful foci of identification in the postrevolutionary era.

Moreover, workers in heavy industry, the core socialist constituency, are likely to decline in number because these industries are among the least competitive in Europe. At the same time, the undeveloped service sector is likely to grow sharply as East European economies modernize. Workers in the service sector are difficult to organize into unions and are less likely than blue-collar workers to be attracted to social democracy.

The infusion of foreign capital will further complicate the political expression of economic conflicts along class lines. Exploitation of workers can be attributed not only to capitalism but also to foreign control of the economy. Socialists themselves have in many cases been divided over the issue of foreign investment, while populists have exploited resentment against foreign economic domination in an effort to appeal to nationalist sympathies. Thus even in the economy a class conception of conflict is blurred by political appeals framed in terms of nationalism.

The Decline of Traditional Socialism
in Western Europe

Even before the collapse of communist regimes in eastern Europe, socialist parties in western Europe were undergoing a fundamental transformation encompassing their constituency, their organization, and their policies. Traditionally, these parties were mainly proletarian, that is, blue-collar working class; they were the political expression of a deeply rooted working-class movement and subculture; and they emphasized the state as the key instrument of reform.[13] Since the 1970s these elements have eroded in the old heartland of socialism, central and northern Europe. In the newly democratized countries of southern Europe—Greece, Portugal, and Spain—socialist parties have been reconstituted along nontraditional lines. They are broad-based parties only diffusely rooted in the blue-collar working class; they are not an expression of a working-class subculture, nor do they have strong union ties; and, finally, they tend to reject traditional measures of state ownership or control of the economy in favor of market-oriented approaches.[14]

While the future of socialism depends on choices that are difficult, even in principle, to predict, we believe that the range of choice and the trade-offs between different courses of action are more accessible to analysis. Socialists have reached a crossroad at which they face a difficult choice. If they shift away from their traditional moorings, they risk alienating their core constituency; if they remain in the traditional socialist mold, they almost certainly face political marginalization.[15]

Socialists Have Lost Their Monopoly
of the Discourse of Dissent

For more than a century socialism has been the dominant source of ideas for purposeful change in society. The content of the programs for change has varied greatly, both through time and across countries and continents, but socialists were consistently in the vanguard of those with universal visions of the future. This monopoly of the discourse of dissent was the outcome of fierce competition from anarchists and later from syndicalists, but both were defeated or co-opted by socialists even in the southern periphery of Europe where they were most entrenched. Laborism based on strong, politically independent unions was another competitor, particularly in Britain in the late-nineteenth century, but this too was drawn into the orbit of socialist influence. Fascism, which corrupted socialist ideas and hinged them to a force perennially underestimated by socialists—nationalism—threatened the monopoly of socialism across the whole of central Europe before it was delegitimized in the aftermath of World War II. Only in the United States did the major union movement sustain its independence from socialism. From the end of World War I to the 1960s, socialist ideas—founded on the role of the state as the chief instrument of reform, the demand for universal political, social, and economic rights, and the notions that class conflict was the most basic conflict in society and socialist parties were the natural representatives of the working class—constituted the basic points of departure for organized dissent across European societies. There were continuing, intense, and sometimes violent fratricidal disputes among radicals about the possibility of meaningful reform under capitalism and the place of parliamentary democracy, but the parameters of discourse were those within the broad tradition of socialism.

In the post-World War II decades, the claim that socialism was the ideology of progress was so strong that it influenced even parties in direct competition. In Britain, a strong and sometimes dominant tendency within the Conservative party, led in the 1950s and early 1960s by R. A. Butler and Harold Macmillan, shared a number of socialist prescriptions, albeit in diluted form, about the role of the state in economic planning and universal welfare rights. In West Germany, center-right governments under Konrad Adenauer incorporated aspects of the welfare state in building a social market economy. In several West European societies both social democratic parties and their opponents agreed on the need for a greater state role in the economy and for progressive extensions of welfare rights, while disagreeing primarily on the pace of reform and on more distant goals. The social contracts bargained between governing parties and the major functional interests, particularly trade unions, in several central and northern European countries were derived from the efforts of socialists, particularly in Sweden, to reform capitalist societies in a socialist direction. Such efforts were always vulnerable to the charge from the Left that although they affected distribution, social contracts did not change the character of capitalist production, exploitative wage labor. The remarkable thing was, however, that even the radical critique of social democratic social contracts was driven in the realm of socialist discourse.

Christiane Lemke and Gary Marks

No longer is this the case. Strong social democratic parties persist across western Europe, but socialists no longer monopolize the discourse of dissent. They must compete with a variety of New Left groups including environmentalists, women's groups, antinuclear groups, and "greens" who raise issues concerning the quality of life, the role of gender, participation, and decentralization that cut across traditional socialist issues and divide the socialist electorate.[16] Although their aggregate electoral support remains high, for the first time ever socialist parties are losing support among young people to radical parties that reject socialism.

The socialist monopoly of dissent had a subtle influence on its adversaries on the political Right that is, in retrospect, all the more obvious now that it is declining. In this case, as in others, few things aid an understanding of the causality of a complex social formation so much as its collapse. After World War II many conservatives as well as socialists assumed that basic elements of socialism, particularly economic planning and an expanded welfare state, were an inevitable part of the future of capitalist society. Even those on the Right who opposed such reforms believed that they were part of the tide of history, that they could be resisted but not turned back. This view has conspicuously disappeared since the late 1960s. Socialism no longer has a silent hold over conceptions of the future, as is testified by the energetic revival on the Right of notions of liberalism and laissez-faire that predate socialism.

Working-class Roots Are Weakening

Socialist parties have traditionally been working-class parties, targeting the proletariat as their chief recruiting ground. This was true not only of Marxist socialist parties, but also of labor parties in English-speaking societies, which were, if anything, even more confined to blue-collar workers than socialist parties on the Continent. Second, socialists traditionally viewed the working class as the universal class. For orthodox Marxist parties this meant that the triumph of the proletariat through revolution or elections would herald a socialist society in which classes themselves would eventually disappear and all would enjoy freedom. As orthodox Marxism receded and it became clear that the traditional proletariat would never constitute a majority of the society, the notion of the proletariat shifted so that diverse groups of white-collar workers were included, although the blue-collar worker remained the quintessential worker. What benefits such workers, socialists argued, benefits society as a whole.

These working-class roots are dissolving. The proletariat, by virtually any definition, has been in relative decline for about half a century or more in advanced industrial societies. In more recent years, the absolute number of blue-collar workers has been shrinking in several western European societies.

The working-class character of socialist parties has been corroded in a more subtle, but equally fundamental, way by the declining influence of social class in shaping political choices across western democracies.[17] Social democratic parties have campaigned for universal political rights, universal welfare programs, and the redistribution of income so that class inequalities of consumption would be diminished. To the extent that they have been successful they have undermined the classness of society and reduced the salience of the class cleavage on which they are based. In this respect the problems facing socialist parties have been generated not by their failure, but by their success.

The Socialist Movement Subculture Is Shrinking

Socialist parties were the first mass parties in western Europe. To compete politically, workers and their allies had to use force of numbers because they lacked economic resources or status. Socialist parties became huge organizations demanding a new principle, one man (subsequently one person) one vote, to counter and transform an economic system determined by the concentrated private ownership of the means of production. These socialist parties represented a broader social movement of unions, clubs, pubs, presses, libraries, and so on, encompassing the whole range of working-class life. Socialist parties were part of a multifaceted subculture that aimed to foster socialist values in an enclave within capitalism, to build a new society in the womb of the old.

The socialist subculture was a valuable political resource for socialist parties. It helped them weather state repression, as during the "heroic" years under the antisocialist laws in Germany between 1878 and 1890. It linked socialist parties to large trade union movements that provided them with a level of organizational and financial support to which they could not otherwise have aspired. It provided socialist parties with a core constituency of individuals who defined themselves as socialists regardless of their support or opposition to the particular programs that the party espoused at any one time. Such people were relatively immune to the appeal of bourgeois parties as they struggled to compete with socialist parties under manhood suffrage. Paradoxically, the existence of a strong working-class subculture allowed socialist parties to appeal to white-collar workers and other nonproletarians more effectively because they did not fear alienating workers by making cross-class appeals.[18]

In recent decades working-class subculture and the socialist movement have weakened and fragmented. The reasons for this are rooted in economic and social developments common to advanced industrialized societies. With the decline of traditional heavy industry and coal mining across western societies, working-class communities that were formerly the core of the socialist movement have been dismantled. Those that remain are far less insulated from diverse influences of the society at large. More frequent commuting has weakened the nexus between work and home; increased geographical mobility has eroded the sense of collective identity within working-class communities grounded in loyalty built over generations; and the growth of mass media, particularly television, has weakened the role of socialist parties as purveyors of political information. What these and other developments have done is to instill a greater sense of choice of life-styles and political orientations; they have reduced the normative coherence of working-class communities and the political cues they offer. As a consequence they have undermined the cultural embeddedness of socialist movements.

Socialist parties have not stood on the sidelines as passive onlookers. They have, in fact, pressed forward reforms that reinforce some of the developments noted previously. As parties based on the class divide, they have continually tried to gain improvements in workers' lives, and to the extent that they have succeeded they have negated class and status inequalities. The development of the welfare state, a major goal and accomplishment of socialist parties, has actually reduced the reliance of individual workers on their extended families and larger communities. Socialist parties have sought consistently to enhance individual opportunities and life chances although their programs have been formulated in the language of social welfare, economic planning, trade union rights, and the role of the state.

Trade union movements, at the center of the socialist subculture, have become significantly more fragmented over recent decades.[19] The great debate over the future of trade unions and whether declines in the level of unionization that have taken place in several (but by no means all) countries are irreversible has drawn attention away from some developments critical for the future of industrial relations and socialist parties. Trade unions, the largest working-class organizations in every western society, have become noticeably more heterogeneous in membership, more organizationally incoherent and politically disunited. The chief reason for this is that the old core of union movements, as they expanded from the last decades of the nineteenth-century, blue-collar workers in heavy industry and mineral extraction, have lost their predominance to a variety of newer groups with diverse interests.

Unions are also facing decentralization of industrial relations threatening their coherence from below. There has been a general pressure on the part of employers toward factory-level negotiations, often encompassing factory-specific bonuses, in the name of labor market flexibility, and this makes it difficult for unions to sustain worker identity within the work force as a whole.[20]

It has been very hard for unions, historically dominated by blue-collar male workers, to adjust to the growing proportion of women and white-collar workers in the labor force. Women now account for around 40 percent of the entire labor force in the most advanced West European economies yet remain poorly organized, partly because unions have not succeeded in tailoring their appeal to the particular needs and demands of women. Women are hardly represented in the ranks of union leaders.

White-collar and professional workers have become a major grouping within union movements. In Britain, where the union federation, the Trades Union Congress, was never centralized or coherent, white-collar unions have been encompassed within the organization. In Sweden, where the union movement developed along explicit socialist industrial lines, with the goal of one and only one union for any particular industry, the organization of white-collar and professional workers has drastically reduced the coherence of the union movement. The main blue-collar-dominated federation, the LO, the industrial wing of the Swedish Social Democratic party, is faced by rapidly growing autonomous white-collar union federations. In general, the mobilization of white-collar and professional workers into unions has created the greatest fragmentation in union movements that were the most cohesive previously. Unions remain large and powerful organizations, but whether or not they are in a process of inexorable decline, they are certainly becoming less coherent.

European Integration Is Antithetical to Social Democracy

Socialist parties performed relatively well in recent elections to the European Parliament. They form the largest group in the European Parliament and, for the first time, socialists along with communists and greens have a slim majority of total seats. Yet the process of European integration and, in particular the creation of a common market as an outcome of the 1992 project, threaten key elements of socialism in western Europe. The thrust of reform has been to open western Europe as an integrated market without providing any coherent framework for social or industrial regulation. The results of this for labor are clear, compelling, and dismal.[21] First, unions find it difficult to bargain effectively with employers and sustain their organizational density in the international division of labor. Second, societies with extensive welfare systems and industrial regulations face social dumping, intensified "unfair" competition from societies in which business is not so constrained.

Before the logic of this is outlined in more detail, it is important to emphasize that there is nothing essentially antisocialist about European integration. Visions of a united Europe have been deeply influenced by socialist ideals of internationalism, and socialists themselves have been among the most active in pressing for integration. Moreover, it is also worth stressing that some of the reforms run parallel to socialism, for example, structural reforms have been introduced to increase economic equality within the European Community (EC) by aiding the poorer regions. These reforms combine two interesting principles: intensive economic planning in an attempt to improve economic prospects in the poorest regions, and concertation in creating plans on the part of governments at all levels of the European polity: the European Commission in Brussels, member states, and local governments. Other reforms consonant with socialism include tentative steps enlarging the role of the European Parliament and some EC directives strengthening equal treatment for women.

However, the main thrust of reform so far has been in creating a European-wide economic space rather than regulating that space through coherent social policies or building strong supranational institutions of European governance. This two-track development of

European integration appears to have some profoundly negative consequences for organized labor and social democracy. Trade unions are particularly hard hit. To the extent that unionized employers face competition from nonunionized employers, so they are all the more determined to resist union demands. In addition, unions face the threat of being outflanked by European-wide corporations that can relocate to countries where the work force is unorganized.

Neither of these possibilities would be a problem if unions were able to duplicate the supranational character of their adversaries. But it is one thing for a company to span Europe and quite another thing for a union. Companies are minimally based on the pursuit of material gain, and this logic travels without difficulty across western borders. Unions, by contrast, provide a collective good, and they are unable to do this simply by appealing to individual economic interest. Instead, they use a variety of incentives: from social norms, to ideological appeals, to various forms of legal compulsion tailored to the particular circumstances of their society and the groups of workers they target. Unions are more intensively nationally rooted than corporations, and as a result they find it far more difficult to develop supranational organization.

The incoherence of unions in the EC severely constrains the possibility of social democracy based on institutionalized class compromise as it was practiced in central and northern Europe in the decades since World War II. In these countries social democracy was strengthened by the existence of centralized and encompassing national union federations that exchanged wage restraint for social, industrial, and welfare reforms.[22] Socialist parties were able to solidify their rule by mediating class compromise, integrating labor into the policymaking process in the context of effective economic policies.

The European economic and political system as it has emerged in the 1992 project is antithetical to institutionalized social democracy based on the Swedish or Austrian models.[23] Not only is a coherent union movement absent, but the European polity is also extremely fragmented, reflecting both diverse member-state interests and an institutional structure based on a complex distribution of power across the European Council, Commission, Court, and Parliament. Even if unions were strong and united, no coherent European government could engage them in national bargaining.

Socialism Is Dead. Long Live Socialism!

We have observed that communism as a regime type has disintegrated and that the traditional bases of social democratic parties are declining. But this is very different from saying that socialism itself, or even presently existing socialist parties, must decline.[24] First, socialism as a set of values concerned with humanization of work, extension of democracy, social and economic equality, and universal rights will continue to be a powerful critique of capitalist society. The introduction of market economies in eastern Europe will create new inequalities that may give rise to radical movements drawing on traditional socialist themes. In western Europe, skepticism about further extension of the state has already drawn socialists to reevaluate the old, although neglected, communitarian stream of socialist thinking.[25]

Second, we are dealing with self-conscious political actors who attempt to adapt to, and indeed to shape, external circumstances. The responses of present and future political actors are critical because the trends diagnosed are *self-reflexive*, that is, understanding the process actually changes the process itself. This is true of any social phenomenon that involves individual or collective decision making. However, there are strong indications that the strategic room for maneuver by party leaders has actually widened. In western Europe, the structural determinants of party affiliation and voting have weakened since the 1970s. The causal power of inherited or involuntary characteristics, particularly social class and religion, in determining voting decisions has declined while the role of prospective and retrospective evaluation of parties, leaders, programs, and governmental performance has increased. This has intensified party competition, a development reflected in the emergence of a new industry, political consulting, to satisfy the demands of party elites for information and advice. These developments have gone hand in hand with the decline of parties as monopolistic purveyors of political information, the enhanced role of television, and the intensified focus on the personality of competing party leaders.

In eastern Europe the significance of political elites is as great, or even greater. As in any postrevolutionary phase the political situation is extremely fluid: vital choices are being made not only on policy, but also on the most basic elements of institutional structure. Political institutions are being recast, political parties themselves are in the process of formation, party cleavages are being created, property rights are being formulated, and the system of production is being reorganized. In such a fluid political context party performance is largely independent of changes in economic or social structure. While the bases of traditional socialism are eroding in eastern and western Europe, we cannot predict how socialists will respond to these challenges, or how socialism itself may be reshaped.

Notes

1. There is a well-established crisis literature. See, for example, Alan Wolfe, "Has Social Democracy a Future?" *Comparative Politics* 11 (October 1978): 100–125; Martin Jacques and Francis Mulhern, eds., *The Forward March of Labour Halted?* (London: Verso, 1981); Graeme Duncan, "A Crisis of Social Democracy?" *Parliamentary Affairs* 38 (Summer 1985): 267–81; William E. Paterson and Alastair H. Thomas, eds., *The Future of Social Democracy: Problems and Prospects of Social Democratic Parties in Western Europe* (Oxford: Clarendon Press, 1986); and Michael Waller, "Radical Sources of the Crisis in West European Communist Parties," *Political Studies* 37 (1989): 39–61.

2. A new body of literature analyzes the transition from communist rule in the region. See, for example, Elemér Hankiss, "In Search of a Paradigm," *Daedalus* 119 (Winter 1990): 183–214; George Schoepflin, "The End of Communism in Eastern Europe," *International Affairs* 66 (1990): 3–16; and Jadwiga Staniszkis, "Patterns of Change in Eastern Europe," *Eastern European Politics and Society* 4 (Winter 1990): 77–97.

3. As Norman Naimark argues in this volume, Soviet hegemony was the major reason not only for the formation of rigid communist regimes but also for the deformation of national brands of socialism in eastern and central Europe.

4. While much of what we write is relevant across eastern Europe, our focus is on the countries of east central Europe—Czechoslovakia, East Germany, Hungary, and Poland.

5. Most experts were surprised about the rapid pace of disintegration of communist rule in eastern and central Europe. Nevertheless, an entire body of literature analyzes the lack of legitimacy and the failure of the regimes to modernize. See, for example, Walter Connor, *Socialism's Dilemmas: State and Society in the Soviet Bloc* (New York: Columbia University Press, 1988); Joni Lovenduski and Jean Woodall, *Politics and Society in Eastern Europe* (Bloomington: Indiana University Press, 1987); and William E. Griffith, ed., *Central and Eastern Europe: The Opening Curtain?* (Boulder: Westview Press, 1989).

6. See Christiane Lemke, *Die Ursachen des Umbruchs: Politische Sozialisation in der DDR* (Opladen: Westdeutscher Verlag, 1991). The schizophrenia resulting from this gap is depicted brilliantly in Vaclav Havel, *Power of the Powerless* (New York: Sharpe, 1985), pp. 23–96.

7. See also Sharon Wolchik's chapter in this volume.

8. So far the most far-reaching reforms have been launched in Poland and Czechoslovakia. Leszek Balcerowicz, deputy prime minister in the Mazowiecki government, and Vaclav Klaus, the Czechoslovakian finance minister, have been the principal proponents for bold reform. See "Poland's Parliament hears Plans for Radical Changes in Economy," *New York Times*, December 18, 1989; and Vaclav Klaus, "Monetary Policy in Czechoslovakia in the 1970's and 1980's and the Nature and Problems of the Current Economic Reforms," *Communist Economies* 2 (1990): 61–71. A radical free-market approach to reforms is put forward by the American economists Jeffrey Sachs and David Lipton in "Poland's Economic Reforms," *Foreign Affairs* 69 (Summer 1990): 47–67.

9. Ellen Comisso rightly argues that the crisis of socialism is linked to the internationalization of markets. See Ellen Comisso, "Crisis in Socialism or Crisis of Socialism?" *World Politics* 42 (1990): 563–96.

10. Previous institutions have proven to be serious constraints in the transition to a market economy. See, for example, Gregorz Ekiert, "Prospects and Dilemmas of the Transition to a Market Economy in East Central Europe," paper presented at the American Political Science Association, San Francisco, August 31, 1990; and Janos Kornai, *The Road to a Free Economy* (New York: Norton, 1990).

11. In fact, as Szelényi and Szelényi argue in this volume, there is a large "social democratic field" in the Hungarian case that has not yet been mobilized electorally.

12. The political diversity in the region has been described well by Timothy G. Ash, *The Magic Lantern: The Revolution of '89 Witnessed in Warsaw, Budapest, Berlin, and Prague* (New York: Random House, 1990), and "Eastern Europe: Après Le Déluge," *New York Review of Books*, August 16, 1990.

13. In this chapter we focus on the first two characteristics; for a discussion of statism in the context of West Germany see chapter 7 by Andrei Markovits.

14. The French Socialist party shares, to some extent, these characteristics. On Spanish socialism see Donald Share, *Dilemmas of Social Democracy: The Spanish Socialist Workers Party in the 1980s* (New York: Greenwood Press, 1989); and Richard Gunther, Giacomo Sani, and Goldie Shabard, *Spain After Franco: The Making of a Competitive Party System* (Berkeley: University of California Press, 1986), especially pp. 202–20 on union-party links. As Wolfgang Merkel observes in his chapter in this volume, the southern "ambivalent" parties have been by far the most successful electorally since the mid-1970s.

15. On this trade-off see Adam Przeworski and John Sprague, *Paper Stones: A History of Electoral Socialism* (Chicago: Chicago University Press, 1986); and Mark Lichback, "Optimal Electoral Strategies for Socialist Parties: Does Social Class Matter to Party Fortunes?" *Comparative Political Studies* 16 (January 1984): 419–55.

16. Ronald Inglehart, *The Silent Revolution: Changing Values and Political Styles among Western Publics* (Princeton: Princeton University Press, 1977), and *Culture Shift in Advanced Industrial Society* (Princeton: Princeton University Press, 1990); Russel J. Dalton and Manfred Kuechler, *Challenging the Political Order: New Social and Political Movements in Western Democracies* (New York: Oxford University Press, 1990).

17. See Ivor Crewe, "On the Death and Resurrection of Class Voting: Some Comments on How Britain Votes," *Political Studies* 34 (1986): 620–83; and Russel J. Dalton, Scott C. Flanagan, and Paul Allen Beck, eds., *Electoral Change in Advanced Industrial Democracies: Realignment or Dealignment?* (Princeton: Princeton University Press, 1984).

18. Przeworski and Sprague, *Paper Stones.*

19. Guido Baglioni and Colin Crouch, eds., *European Industrial Relations: The Challenge of Flexibility* (London: Sage, 1990).

20. See Richard M. Locke, "The Resurgence of the Local Union: Industrial Restructuring and Industrial Relations in Italy," *Politics and Society* 18 (1990): 347–75.

21. See, for example, George Ross, "French Labor and the 1992 Process," *French Politics and Society* 8 (Summer 1990): 54–64; and Wolfgang Streek, "More Uncertainties: German Unions Facing 1992," *Industrial Relations*, in press.

22. See Gary Marks, "Neocorporatism and Incomes Policy in Western Europe and North America 1950–1980," *Comparative Politics* 17 (April 1986): 253–77; and David Cameron, "Social Democracy, Corporatism and Labor Quiescence: The Representation of Economic Interests in Advanced Capitalist Societies," in *Order and Conflict in Contemporary Capitalism*, ed. John H. Goldthorpe (New York: Oxford University Press, 1984).

23. See Wolfgang Streek and Philippe C. Schmitter, "From National Corporatism to Transnational Pluralism: Organized Interests in the Single European Market," unpublished paper.

24. Socialist parties held up well electorally during the 1980s although it is worth noting that the best performance was in southwestern Europe where traditional socialism is weakest. See Wolfgang Merkel's chapter in this volume and Klaus Armingeon, "Sozialdemokratie am Ende? Die Entwicklung der Macht sozialdemokratischer Parteien im internationalen Vergleich, 1945–1988," *Oesterreische Zeitschrift fuer Politikwissenschaft* 18 (1989).

25. This stream of socialism is the topic of Geoff Eley's chapter in this volume; arguments for future development in this direction are examined in Herbert Kitschelt's chapter.

Reviewing the
Socialist Tradition

Geoff Eley

We are in a remarkable moment of historical change—the most re-markable since the mid-1940s, in fact. Like that earlier moment—which I'll call the moment of antifascist unity—the present is marked by the radical openness of its politics—dramatic events have com-pletely overturned existing structures, dislodging previously en-trenched assumptions of the possible, and calling into question apparently reliable certainties. Moreover, as in the 1940s, change has come from the East. It is worth remembering (because the organized forgetting of the last forty years has so successfully removed it from mind) that the war against Nazism was fought and won on the Eastern Front, that the antifascist resistance in continental occupied Europe imparted a dynamic of reconstruction that briefly effaced many of the prewar distinctions of Left and Right, and that this dynamic brought the unprecedented emergence of national communist parties as pop-ular and legitimate participants—and sometimes the leaders—in broadly based, reform-oriented coalitions. By contrast with the mid-1940s, however, the main logic of international alignment is working powerfully in favor of such openness rather than against it. Whereas the Cold War brutally repolarized the political imagination by 1947–48 and destroyed the autonomy of national roads, the end of the Cold War in the later 1980s restored the claims of national history. Indeed, Gorbachev has continuously radicalized the openness of the East Central European, and tendentially of the West European, situation. And, of course, West European politics has been experiencing its own kind of flux since the mid-1970s, in some countries (e.g., Britain) more dramatically than in others, as the effects of recession, resurgent social and political conflict, and capitalist restructuring brought the terms of the postwar settlement into crisis.

Given the triumphal antisocialism with which events in east central Europe have been greeted in the West, and the laundering of their significance through the well-tried categories of Cold War discourse, particularly in the United States—given the imaginative rigidifying of most eastern political commentary within the closed circle of democracy and the market, it is important to uphold the radical openness of this present situation. The "end of communism" also means the end of anticommunism, in the sense that the imaginative possibilities for politics in Europe as a whole are being redrawn. The transformation-in-progress in the Soviet Union and the democratic revolutions to its west increasingly remove the purchase of anticommunist injunctions in western political discourse, particularly as substantial majorities in West European societies seem to appreciate that in the international dismantlement of Cold War militarism it is precisely Gorbachev who has been setting the pace. As western political cultures were constituted between the late-1940s and the 1960s, anticommunism has been a powerful internalized constraint, and once it is taken away, new things can begin to happen. At least, we can begin to think more plausibly in new ways.

It is not my brief to reflect extensively on the coordinates of the present situation, but if we're to bring "historical perspectives" fruitfully to bear, certain aspects of the present conjuncture's specificity need to be upheld.

First, it's important to remember that "new times" are arriving not just in the East, but also in the West of the continent, marked not only by the democratic revolutions against Stalinism, but also by the crisis of social democracy in its Keynesian/welfare-statist form, by capitalist restructuring, and by a stronger move toward West European economic integration. Together the East European processes of democratization and the strengthening of the EC through 1992 make the years from 1989 to 1992 one of the few times when fundamental political and constitutional changes are occurring on a genuinely European-wide scale. I would describe 1989–92 as one of the several great constitution-making moments of modern European history, in a sequence including 1789–

1815, the 1860s, 1917–23, and 1945–49. By this I mean a moment of concentrated political and constitutional upheaval through which the entire legal and institutional landscape of the continent is redrawn, and one framework of practice and belief replaced by another. Over the longer term single-market legislation may well have just as much significance for the possible bases on which political (and not just economic) life can take place as the current events in East Europe. Moreover, the two processes are not completely unconnected because the loosening of Soviet political control in the East and simultaneous liberalizing of the eastern economies has placed the question of East-West economic relations urgently on the agenda, both as the question of economic aid and in relation to the possible forms of East European integration within the EC. In other words, how far will the existing forms of commercial interpenetration of the GDR and Hungarian economies with those of West Germany and other western economies now be strengthened, and how far will the EC now be extended to incorporate the East of the continent too? It's hard to see how the existing project of 1992 can simply proceed in its present form without some further extension of its terms to the East. The apparently unstoppable logic of German unification presents the strongest and most obvious challenge to 1992 in this respect. But however this question works itself out in the first half of the 1990s, the general point still stands: in 1989–92 we are experiencing one of the five great constitution-making moments of modern European history, through which the basic context of political action is being fundamentally reshaped, in the West no less than in the East.

Second, an important question is, What kind of political vision will guide the process of European integration? The tendency in the United States is to see 1992 mainly as a technical event with major implications for the behavior and access to markets of U.S. business, whereas in reality there's active discussion in Europe itself of the so-called social dimension and the type of social policies that should also be incorporated into the 1992 package, or at least into the future agenda. At its simplest, any restructuring of markets has enormous implications for labor, and one thing we may expect in the 1990s is a much stronger focusing of national labor movements on the transnational European level of policymaking and action. Moreover, if European socialist movements are going to be pulled increasingly into a European arena of policymaking, in practice that will mean trying to strengthen the powers of the European Parliament. Given the emergence of the socialists as the largest single grouping in the parliament during the 1989 Euro-elections, and the simultaneous appearance of a significant Green electorate in all parts of Europe, this creates an interesting potential. Again, this is not irrelevant to the situation in eastern Europe, given the likely long-term emergence of strong social democratic currents in the GDR, Czechoslovakia, Hungary, and Bulgaria (not to speak of the Soviet Union itself, particularly on the Baltic and Ukrainian periphery, providing the move to democratic pluralism is maintained in reasonable equilibrium). A return of social democratic parties to government in countries such as the FRG/Germany and Britain, Left-tending coalitions in the Low Countries and Scandinavia, modification of the rampant PCOE technocracy in Spain, and a refiguring of the Left in Italy which finally brought a social-democratized PCI into government—an aggregation of these national developments would make the pressure very great for strong social policies in the 1992 framework together with a strengthening of the European Parliament into a genuine legislature. Then it would be easier to imagine stronger forms of transnational European cooperation on the part of the Left. Of course, this may not be a very likely outcome in 1992 itself, and at present it has to be a fairly speculative possibility, an abstraction of the appropriate point from which effective Left politics will have to begin. But this scenario becomes critical for the future of eastern Europe, given the structural vulnerability of the region's economies to exploitative forms of integration with the West.

Third, I began by calling present events the most remarkable concentration of change since the mid-1940s. But a couple of intermediate points also deserve mention, not least for the ways in which they mark the declining hold of the extreme Cold War polarization on the political imagination: I am thinking of 1956 and 1968. In both years combinations of events occurred that undermined the credibility and legitimacy of both sides of the Cold War confrontation. In 1956 the Twentieth Congress and the Soviet invasion of Hungary were matched by the debacle of Suez; in 1968 the Soviet invasion of Czechoslovakia was matched by the Tet Offensive, the May events, and the Chicago Democratic Convention. To them might be added 1981, when the declaration of martial law in Poland finally laid to rest the possibility of communist self-reform. It is important to make this point because the politics of 1989 were in a very real sense the resumption of an agenda strongly articulated in 1968, with anticipations in 1956 (and, one should add, also in the mid-1940s)—although it's an agenda from which the communist political tradition is now authoritatively excluded, and in which the socialist tradition has to fight harder than one might ever have anticipated for its place. In other words, the crude polarity of "actually existing socialism" versus the triumph of market capitalism into which we are being encouraged by the vast weight of official and media commentary in the West ("the West has won"/ "death of socialism" kind of rhetoric) is not the only legitimate framework for viewing the events in eastern Europe. In fact, the dual crisis of 1956 demarcated an independent space—a "third space," as Stuart Hall has called it—from which a dual critique of established forms (Stalinism and the terms of the postwar settlement in the capitalist West) could be developed.

In the politics of the "first New Left" a series of positions were developed that are fully continuous with the discourse of democratic revolution in 1989:

> A deep suspicion of the all-encompassing state, without entrenched protection for minorities and indeed majorities, no matter in whose name it was established. A scepticism about the capacity of the centralized, command economy to meet the rapidly diversifying and expanding needs of modern societies. A fear of the collapse of politics and the economy, of state and class, class and party. A reappraisal of certain features which, in the revolutionary scenario, were always scorned as "bourgeois liberties." Above all, a conviction that "actually existing socialism" had got the relationship between socialism and democracy dead wrong. And that, in the second half of the 20th century—in the First, Second and Third Worlds—democracy would turn out to be the really revolutionary—not the "reformist"—element in the socialist tradition.[1]

As Hall insists, this part of the Left should have no embarrassment or hesitation about the collapse of the eastern communist tradition because it "has, for decades, been trying to define a socialist alternative which was rooted in a profound and unequivocal repudiation of 'the state socialist model.'" Justified forebodings about the successor situations there may be, for, as the earlier departures of the mid-1940s and 1917–23 have taught us, there are no revolutionary transitions without risks and outcomes that can't be ordained. However, over the question of principle there should be no doubt: "We should not be alarmed by the collapse of 'actually existing socialism' since, as socialists, we have been waiting for it to happen for three decades" (p. 25).

Before turning to the past, therefore, it is important to keep the history of the present in view. But at the same time, current events take their meaning not just from the ways they're shaping the possible future, but from how they relate to the given past, and the construction of the latter relationship is my main concern here. In what follows I'll proceed in two steps: first, by saying something about the specific significance of the Bolshevik Revolution and the communist tradition, now that the latter may be said to have run its European course; and second, by returning more broadly to the deeper context of the socialist tradition in the nineteenth and twentieth centuries. To anticipate the main line of argument—or, rather, to state my implicit assumption—I see no reason to accept the political invitation of the "death of socialism" rhetoric. To do so would be profoundly unhistorical. Such a verdict persuades only if we accept the sufficiency of the crude Cold War opposition between East European state socialism and West European Keynesian-welfare statist social democracy, as if "between them, stalinism and Neil Kinnock exhaust the whole of human history."[2] In fact, the most exciting aspect of current events is the final destruction of that straightjacket of understanding, although it will doubtless be some time before we get used to the unaccustomed freedom of the imagination. "Socialism" may be in "crisis," but for many of us this is old news. Indeed, it was already in crisis when I came of age politically. As then, the point is to broaden the space for experiment, diversity, and a genuine pluralism of understanding. In 1956, and then more hopefully in 1968, such opportunities were briefly opened before the fronts were brutally clamped shut. As we enter the 1990s, the space is back. Taken as a whole, the socialist tradition is a rich source of possibilities, and the purpose of this chapter is to bring this back to our attention.

Bolshevism, National Revolution, and the Meaning of October

The Bolshevik Revolution and the launching of the Third International in 1919 are usually considered in their relationship to the broader revolutionary turbulence engulfing central and southern Europe in the immediate aftermath of World War I. It would be foolish to contest the basic sovereignty of this context. But from a vantage point late in the twentieth century, the revolutionary confrontationism of the years from 1914 to 1923 appears increasingly as an exceptional—perhaps the exceptional—moment of left-wing politics in Europe in relation to the periods before and since, certainly produced by powerful social and political determinations and leaving powerful legacies for the future but with surprisingly little subsequent recurrence as a mass-based phenomenon in Europe itself. There are many localized flash points of popular revolutionary politics after the 1920s—witness the French and Spanish Popular Fronts, the aspirations accompanying the anti-fascist resistance in various parts of Europe, the radicalism of 1968, and so forth. But the much commoner experience of radical or socialist politics has been one stressing change from within the existing institutional framework of European society. At the same time, the extra-European world has provided major examples of revolutionary success, if that is defined as military or insurrectionary seizures of power linked to mass-based social and political mobilization. Moreover, in this latter context it has become conventional to stress the national parameters and determinants of communist politics and popular mobilization. Thus, within this longer global perspective, the element of 1917 that has proved most relevant and inspirational has been less the Bolshevik call for confrontation with "bourgeois democracy" than the affirmation of the rights of people to national self-determination. This was true from 1917 to 1919, not only in the immediate context of the Russian Empire and the wider extra-European world (especially Asia), but also in the East Central European region of Europe.

In other words, I'm arguing for a shift of perspective in the meaning of October. How should we view the significance of the Russian Revolution in general political and comparative international terms from a vantage point at the end of the twentieth century, particularly in the light of current events in the Soviet Union and eastern Europe, now that the dominance of the communist tradition has been dislodged in the very societies where its legacy was most powerfully institutionalized? How do we historicize the place of 1917? How do we delimit the context it helps to define, but that simultaneously specifies and limits the resonance and effectivity of the ideas the Bolshevik experience bequeathes to the Left elsewhere? How do we begin to relativize the significance of the Bolshevik model within the history and outlook of the communist Left now that the actuality of that model has increasingly run its course? Even before the events between 1985 and 1989, it was clear that we were in a major transition in that respect, a transition that began dramatically in 1956, proceeded gradually and unevenly for the next decade, became propelled even more dramatically forward in 1968, and then worked itself out during the subsequent two decades, generating fresh constructive potentials and reaching a major point of negative resolution, for which December 13, 1981, is as good a date as any. As the PCI said in its response to the Jaruzelski coup, thereby drawing the conclusion from the experiences of 1968, 1956, and 1947–48: "We must accept that this phase of socialist development (which began with the October Revolution) has exhausted its driving force, just as the phase that saw the birth and development of socialist parties and trade union movements mustered around the Second International also ran out of steam. The world has moved on, it has changed, thanks, also, to this turn that history took. The point is to overcome the present by looking ahead."[3]

How, then, do we construct the meaning of October? For our purposes, I will concentrate on three main points, each of which concerns an aspect of the international revolutionary conjuncture that subsequent developments (and retroactive communist and social democratic orthodoxies) have tended to erase, but which connect importantly to dimensions of the now-emerging new times:

First, between the decomposition of the united parties of the pre-1914 Second International and the consolidation of new communist parties in the Third (which didn't really happen until the aftermath of the Second Congress of Comintern in July 1920, in a process driven by the implementation of the Twenty-one Points during the autumn and winter of 1920–21) was an important but indeterminate space for left-wing socialisms of various kinds. In fact, a substantial body of organized socialism—essentially the old Zimmerwald majority, greatly expanded in popular support and national resonance once legal politics in individual countries had been resumed—was strongly aligned with neither the Second nor Third Internationals. Such parties had not yet affiliated with the new Communist International, but neither had they resumed a place in the Second. When the latter was relaunched at Berne in February 1919, such parties either boycotted the meeting (the large parties of the Italians and the Swiss), or else went to Berne and then withdrew. Between the First and Second Congresses of Comintern (March 1919–July 1920) a chain of secessions converted the Second International into a mainly North European affair, carried by the majority parties of Britain, Germany, Sweden, Denmark, the Netherlands, and Belgium. The first to leave was the Italian party (March 1919), followed by the parties in Norway (May), Greece (June), Hungary (June, when the social democrats merged with the communists in the Hungarian Soviet), Switzerland (August), Spain (December), the German USPD (December), the French SFIO (February 1920), the British ILP (April), and the social democrats of Austria (May).

While some of these parties moved toward Moscow, the breakup of the Second International didn't redound immediately to the advantage of the Third. It was the Twenty-One Points that produced the communist parties as really distinct formations affiliated with the Third International, and even then the splits left substantial national groupings with nowhere to go in international terms. Thus a third international body emerged in early 1921, the International Working Union of Socialist Parties, also known as the "Vienna Union" or "Two-and-a-Half International." This brought together the socialist rumps left by the Twenty-One Points (USPD, Czech social democrats, SFIO, and the Balkan social democratic groups), the Swiss social democrats (who first affiliated and then disaffiliated with the Third International in the summer of 1919), the anti-Bolshevik Russians (Mensheviks and Left SRs), and the ILP, under the effective leadership of the Austrian social democrats, who had consistently kept an independent stance between the two main camps during 1919 and 1920. Friedrich Adler, its secretary and moving spirit, saw the Vienna Union as a bridge to socialist reunification, to the kind of international umbrella in which the opposing tendencies of the workers' movement (parliamentary and sovietist) could agree to differ, but within the kind of all-encompassing unity that had characterized the Second International before 1914. But despite a unity conference in Berlin in April 1922, this possibility soon dissolved amid the violent recriminations that had become such a familiar feature of Left political exchange. By May 1923 the Second and Two-and-a-Half internationals had merged in the anticommunist Labor and Socialist International.

This universalizing of the socialist split was now to dominate Left politics (with a major exception in the mid-1940s and to a lesser extent during the Popular Front ten years before) right up to the flux of 1956 to 1968 and beyond. Two camps—communist and socialist/social democratic—faced each other cross a minefield of polemical difference. But nonetheless, we should not forget the importance of the non-aligned center grouped in the Vienna Union, which far more than the infant communist parties had carried the hopes of the Left in much of Europe from 1917 to 1923. There was, in fact, a large amount of generously disposed opinion, easily dismissed as ineffectual by the hard-nosed realists on the extreme Left and Right, but which in various ways sought to escape the polarized outcomes imposed by the Second and Third internationals. This was the centrism Lenin reviled, which bogged down the process of revolutionary clarification between Zimmerwald and the Twenty-One Points—that is, the moral voice and socialist conscience of prewar social democracy, which provided so much of the original impetus for Zimmerwald, fueled the critique of the revived Second International, and affirmed its solidarity with the Russian Revolution while refusing the disciplined centralism increasingly required by the Third International. It was borne by a Central-Southern European core, as opposed to the North Central European core of parliamentary socialism before 1914: the Zimmerwald bloc of Swiss social democrats, PSI and USPD, the admixture of Mensheviks and SFIO, and the major postwar accession of the SPÖ. Its leading voices—Friedrich Adler, Giancinto Serrati, Jean Longuet, and in a different way Karl Kautsky—could be infuriatingly wishy-washy when it came to acting on their revolutionary principles, and by Bolshevik standards parties like the USPD and SPÖ were definitely no advertisement for revolutionary decisiveness. But in the light of the intervening history—not just the degeneration of the Russian Revolution and the disfiguring stain of Stalinism, but even more the return of the Left in the 1970s and 1980s to classical democratic perspectives—their scruples need to be taken seriously. However ineffectual its bearers on a plane of revolutionary success, the line from Zimmerwald to the Vienna Union-Two-and-a-Half International described a body of principle—of national diversity and classical democracy—that the Third International disregarded to its cost.[4]

Second, if the Third International deliberately repudiated a substantial body of Left socialist opinion inside Europe itself, it had an often neglected resonance outside the continent in the colonial and semicolonial periphery, especially the Middle East and Central Asia, China, India, and over the longer term Latin America, Southeast Asia, South Africa, and so on. Here it was the fact that the Bolshevik Revolution had occurred in a backward and overwhelmingly agrarian society, combined with the Bolsheviks' emphasis in 1917 and 1918 on the principle of national self-determination, that proved most inspirational for the various extra-European movements. Taking the longer view, we can see this as just as—perhaps even more—important as the resonance of the revolution in Europe itself. For the first time, between the February and October Revolutions, the delegations of the non-Russian nationalities and various extra-European peoples began appearing at the international gatherings of the Left as separately organized and distinctive groups. It is enormously significant that among the major categories of delegates to the founding Congress of the Communist International in March 1919 were those from the non-Russian nationalities of the Old Empire (Finland, Estonia, Latvia, Lithuania and Belorussia, Poland, the Ukraine, Georgia, and Armenia) and areas of Central Asia and the Far East (China, Korea, Persia, Turkestan, Azerbaijan, and the "United Group of the Eastern Peoples of Russia").

This opening to the extra-European world was a decided strength. One of the Russian Revolution's most powerful effects, in conjunction with the collapse of the multinational empires and the triumph of national self-determination, was to bring anticolonialism and national liberation to the center of Left political discourse. When eastern Europe's subordinate people were acquiring statehood with the help of the Allies, it was hard for colonial people outside Europe not to see this as a cue. Moreover, Lenin's "Theses on the Socialist Revolution and the Right of Nations to Self-Determination" (March 1916) had preceded Woodrow Wilson's Fourteen Points, and the Bolshevik stance of national self-determination at Brest-Litovsk in December 1917 had decisively upped the ante for the western Allies in this respect.[5] The Bolshevik government's early international policy included an audacious attempt to revolutionize the extra-European and colonial world, and in this sense the Third International turned its sights deliberately "toward the Orient, Asia, Africa, the colonies, where this movement [for national self-determination] is not a thing of the past but of the present and the future."[6] Thus the large Asian contingent at the founding congress—almost a quarter of the delegates (twelve out of fifty-two)—was a major departure from the Second International's prewar record. As Bukharin observed, this was the first time such a gathering had heard a speech in Chinese.[7] In this respect, the congress inaugurated a vital future tradition, to which the Baku "Congress of the Peoples of the East" in September 1920 was to become the bridge.

Third, it is important to recognize the limited success of the Bolshevik example elsewhere in Europe itself during the revolutionary period from 1917 to 1923. As we know, a popular working-class revolution comparable to the one in Russia had not succeeded anywhere else in Europe—despite the dramatic breakthroughs in east central Europe in October and November 1918, the massive Central European and Italian radicalization of 1919, and the further turbulence of 1920. Even more, some national movements had gone down to crushing defeat in a sequence of repressive stabilizations running through Hungary, Italy,

Bulgaria, and Spain. Yet the plentiful incidence of insurrectionary outbreaks and their failures should not be allowed to exhaust the variety of revolutionary experience in the 1917–23 conjuncture. The Bolshevik model of social polarization and successful insurrection was not the only form in which a revolutionary politics could come to fruition in Europe as a whole. In fact, the commoner pattern was one in which insurrectionary turbulence (or just the chance that it might develop) elicited a major reformist departure, either by forcing the hand of a nervous government or by encouraging farsighted nonsocialist governments into a large-scale preemptive gesture.

Even where the revolutionary Left was at its weakest and socialist parties recorded relatively few gains in the postwar elections, this effect could be clearly seen—as in France (with a law on collective agreements, the eight-hour day, and an electoral reform between March and July 1919); in Belgium (the eight-hour day, a progressive tax reform, social insurance legislation, and an electoral reform during 1918–21); and the Netherlands (the eight-hour day and forty-five-hour week, social insurance legislation, public housing, corporative involvement of trade unions in the new Ministry of Social Affairs, and votes for women during 1918–20). Similar effects could be seen in Britain and Scandinavia. In all these cases a local chemistry of shopfloor militancy, union growth, and government anxiety combined with antirevolutionary paranoia fed by Bolshevik efforts at spreading the international revolution and the real explosions in Germany and Italy to produce packages of significant reform. The strength of the desire to accommodate labor movements and appease the workers was also due to the unusually favorable labor market between spring 1919 and summer 1920 (longer in central Europe), which gave organized workers a transitory political strength. Neither the reform-proneness of governments, nor the scale of militancy, nor the massive trade-union expansions were possible outside this economic context of short-lived boom. And when it abruptly passed, unemployment quickly rose to quite alarming levels, and workers were cast unceremoniously onto the defensive.

However, the net effect of the political interaction among militancy, union growth, and government anxiety was a major increment of reform, and the interesting question is the degree to which a coherent socialist political strategy was at work in this departure. Arguably the strongest reformisms in this respect—the ones capable of further incremental growth in the 1920s and 1930s—were precisely the ones with some guiding social democratic vision or intelligence, in which the parties involved could build on a prewar parliamentary position of some strength, and where the socialist leadership could act as brokers between government and mass. The weakest or most fragile reformisms, on the other hand, were those without this coherent mediating intelligence, where the foundations of a corporative settlement were built more exclusively from the transitory salience of a trade-union bloc. Examples of the former would be especially Sweden, and more ambiguously (if only because they ran violently aground from 1928 to 1934) Germany and Austria; a main example of the latter would be Britain. A further major category of reform involved land reform in key instances in Romania, Yugoslavia, Bulgaria, Greece, Czechoslovakia, Poland, the Baltic States, and Finland (Hungary is a special case due to the rapid succession of liberal, soviet, and counterrevolutionary regimes). But here both the socialist and communist Left were notable for their disastrous indifference to this regional priority, thereby denying themselves a major political constituency in the peasantry (in contrast with the openness of the Left to the farming interests in Sweden and elsewhere in Scandinavia).

Leaving aside the question of the land, the significance of this reformist increment was that in a large part of Europe—essentially the prewar Central and North European "social democratic core" (Austria, Germany, Czechoslovakia, Switzerland, and Scandinavia), together with France, the Low Countries, and Britain—the position of the Left had become much stronger than before. The strengthening took a specific form. Although in some cases (Germany, Austria, and Czechoslovakia) improvement came from the collapse of the old imperial regimes amid popular revolutionary upheaval, and in all the others from the application of large-scale popular pressures, nonetheless it did not amount to any specifically socialist advance. Specifically, socialist demands were certainly at the forefront of activity in the labor movements themselves. But with very few exceptions these weren't incorporated into any lasting settlement. Instead, the reformist advance took the form of a strengthening of parliamentary democracy, the expansion of workers' rights under the law, further recognition of trade unions, growth of civil liberties, and significant social legislation, which in some cases amounted to the beginnings of a welfare state. In particular, the enhancement of the public sphere—in parliamentary, publicistic, and cultural terms—was a major strategic gain, especially in countries where public freedoms had been cramped and harassed before 1914.

Such gains were not the direct expression of successful socialist revolution, but they were the outcomes of revolutionary situations, and a single-minded concentration on the Bolshevik experience as the main measure of revolutionary authenticity disables us from appreciating this more complex configuration of revolutionary possibility. Moreover, there was a further pattern of revolutionary politics in 1917–23, which is likewise inadequately grasped by focusing on the Bolshevik model, and that was a type of transformation in which new states were formed (or postulated) and popular aspirations were mainly canalized by a process of "national revolution." There were perhaps four senses in which this was so.

First, on the western and southern peripheries of the old Russian Empire—Finland, the Baltic, Ukraine, Transcaucasia, and even Belorussia—we should think in terms of distinct regional experiences apart from the main Moscow-Petrograd axis of the Bolshevik Revolution, that is, separate processes of revolutionary upheaval that were certainly articulated with the central Russian one in complicated ways but also possessed their own dynamism and integrity (and outcomes, if the international conjuncture of the Russian Civil War had ever allowed them the chance).

Second, between October 28 and November 9, 1918, there was a distinct East Central European sequence of revolution that was collectively scarcely less significant than the February Revolution of 1917 in Russia. These events basically erected new republican sovereignties on the ruins of the Habsburg and Hohenzollern empires in a chain which included: Czechoslovakia (October 28), Yugoslavia (October 29), "German-Austria" (October 30), Hungary (October 31), Poland (between October 28 and November 14), West Ukraine (October 31), and Germany (November 8 and 9). The socialist Left were major actors in each of these cases, and the predominant pattern of the "successor states" during the immediate founding period from 1918 to 1920 was one of parliamentary states with a strong Left presence.

Third, we should also remember the resonance of the Bolshevik Revolution in the extra-European world mentioned previously, which became manifest in the first stirrings of national-revolutionary oppositions in the colonial world.

Fourth, the toughening of civil society through the enhancement of the public sphere was also an aspect of national revolution, for in the newly created sovereignties of east central Europe the legal constitution of the public sphere was a vital process in the overall project of nation-forming.

If we focus on these three points—on the independent space for a third "Left-socialist" force between Bolshevism and right-wing social democracy from 1918 to 1920, on the Bolshevik Revolution as the inspiration for revolutionary nationalism among Third World peoples, and on the wider range of revolutionary experiences in the European-wide conjuncture of 1917–23—if we focus on these three points, we can see just how limiting the subsuming of revolutionary possibilities into the reified version of the "Bolshevik model" (and the later Moscow-dominated communist tradition) actually is. In fact, to understand both the specificity of the Bolshevik Revolution/model and the real political tasks facing an international communist strategy in the 1920s, it's vital to broaden the perspective to take in the much richer configuration of revolutionary possibilities of the European-wide scale. Once we do that, whether in the context of the East Central European national revolutions or in the parts of northern and western Europe which already possessed parliamentary systems, we're dealing not with social polarization and insurrectionary confrontation as the exclusive logic of socialist politics, but with histories in which the impact of the Left on much broader social and political coalitions becomes the defining thing. In other words, we're dealing with more prosaic but extraordinarily important institutional gains of the kind conventionally dismissed as reformism until recently by the Marxist tradition—the full array of democratic gains in the franchise, trade-union rights and labor legislation, welfare measures, the strengthening of the public sphere, and so on. Given the national and democratic qualities of the current revolutionary events on eastern Europe and the Soviet Union, this richer context of socialist politics during the 1917–23 conjuncture speaks very eloquently to the character of the present, whether or not the more specifically communist or state-socialist tradition of the post-1947 era is dead.

Social Democracy and the Alternatives

If we differentiate the "meaning of October" in this way, and step back from the dichotomous framework of Marxism-Leninism versus right-wing social democracy (or Stalin versus Neil Kinnock), what can we say more specifically about the alternative strands of the socialist tradition? To do this, it's necessary to say something first about the character of the classical social democratic tradition in the period before World War I, when democracy as we have come to know it in the West since the defeat of fascism was largely pioneered in the earlier oppositional culture of the labor movements and their demands for reform. In this respect, there are three dimensions of the organizational question: (1) the constitutional question in the conventional sense (the regulation of democracy at the level of the state and its system of law); (2) the Left's own internal organization (democracy within movements); and (3) the forms of popular political mobilization (democracy in motion).

Social democratic politics, as they emerged between the 1860s and 1914, were a reckoning with two earlier traditions of popular activity, radical democracy focused on the franchise, frequently articulated through liberal coalitions, and the various forms of utopian socialism and other early nineteenth-century communitarian traditions. Beginning in the 1860s, a distinct form of socialist parliamentarianism sharply separated itself from both liberalism and the utopian pioneers. It substituted popular sovereignty for the free and sovereign individual, and simultaneously turned its back on the locally organized cooperative utopia. On the one hand, social democrats pursued a program of maximum parliamentary democracy on a basis usually resembling the six points of the 1838 People's Charter in Britain; on the other hand, this shaped their overall approach to the problem of democratizing the state, producing a socialist constitutionalism that kept little in common with the local projects of cooperative and communal self-administration that gave birth to socialist thinking earlier in the nineteenth century. The contrast with the earlier period is clear. Either socialists had functioned as junior elements in broadly liberal coalitions, occasionally rising to separate prominence in the radicalizing circumstances of a revolutionary crisis, as in 1848–49, or else they lobbied for intermediate forms of producer cooperation backed by a reforming government (e.g., through national workshops or a people's credit bank), bordering on the more ambitious schemes of Proudhon, Cabet, and other utopians.

In both respects, the 1860s were a decisive departure. In most of Europe the dominant Left politics henceforth became the centrally directed party of parliamentary social democracy in close combination with a nationally federated trade-union movement. This new political model was centralist because it stressed national rather than local forms of action, parliamentarist because it privileged the parliamentary arena as the source of sovereignty, and constitutionalist in the given meaning of the term because it preferred representative to direct forms of democracy. This preference for strongly centralized forms of organization over the looser federated modes prevalent between the 1820s and 1860s, brought a new motif into the discourse of the Left, the centrality of the party. The case for this motif—or at least, for systems of priority that made the idea of the party seem unavoidable—was argued through in a series of bitterly contested debates that dominated the European Left from the early-1860s to mid-1870s. The main forum was the First International, a new coordinating agency created in 1864 and eventually wound up in 1876. The general setting was the European-wide process of constitutional upheaval extending from the emancipation of the serfs in Russia to the foundation of the Third Republic in France, and given most dramatic shape in the German and Italian unifications and the rising of the Paris Commune. It was during these debates that Karl Marx rose to European prominence as a central authority of socialist thinking.

Throughout these debates, the arguments for different types of state organization (the constitution of the future socialist government) and for different types of movement (the preferred mode of the Left's own internal organization) were basically homologous. Again, the contrast with what came before is instructive. The locally based associational activity of radical democrats and early socialists had tended to achieve regional and national resonance mainly through the unifying effects of certain common aspirations, focused by the work of newspapers, pamphlets, itinerant lecturers, and a few national parliamentarians and other charismatic figures, which coalesced into a national movement mainly through the impetus of particular campaigns that left little permanent framework of central organization. Correspondingly, the envisaged democratic state presupposed similar principles of decentralized organization, commonly expressed through an ideal of loosely federated, self-governing units of cooperatively organized small producers. An analogous continuity of action and organization characterized the social democratic tradition after the 1860s, with the form of the future socialist constitution being basically abstracted from the social democrats' organizational experience under capitalism. First, the preference for representative forms of national organization in both the social democratic parties and their affiliated trade unions, as opposed to direct-democratic models of decision making that left greater authority with the rank and file at the branch level of the movement, on the shopfloor, and in the localities, was replicated in the preference for a parliamentary type of constitution. Second, the strong commitment to a central bureaucratic form of organization for both party and unions, both to concentrate the movement's strengths and to equalize resources among its stronger and weaker sections, was reflected in the support for central institutions of economic planning which would allow the future state maximum potential for socialist construction.

In other words, there was little interest in the official counsels of the pre-1914 socialist parties in decentralized forms, whether in the shape of cooperative and communitarian self-management schemes pioneered by their early socialist predecessors, or in that of the soviets and workers' councils that emerged from 1917 to 1921. Indeed, Kautsky and other leading voices were highly skeptical of demands for industrial democracy and workers' control, arguing that the advanced industrial economy and the complexities of the modern enterprise precluded the introduction of democratic procedures directly into the economy itself. Instead, only a strong parliament could act as an effective democratic watchdog on the managerial bureaucracies of the economy as well as on the civil bureaucracy of the state. In this way, the model of democratic responsibility fashioned by the labor movement for the conduct of its own affairs—of a permanent officialdom held accountable to the constitutional authority of an elected assembly of trade-union or party delegates—was basically transposed to the broader arena of government in the form of a socialist parliamentary state.

This, then, was the main pattern between the 1860s and World War I—one of centralized national organization aimed at influencing the state in the parliamentary arena or, in the case of the trade unions, at securing the best deal from the employers on a trade or industrywide basis. However, we should be aware of the exceptions. Socialist parliamentarianism flourished best, not surprisingly, with a relatively free public life, where the parliamentary framework was fairly well established: Britain, German-speaking central Europe, Scandinavia, and the Low Countries.[8] It proved much weaker, equally obviously, where the political system remained repressive: preeminently Imperial Russia, together with the Slavic regions of the Habsburg Empire and the independent states of southeastern Europe (apart from Bulgaria); in these cases there was understandably a strong pull toward extra-parliamentary forms of action. We should also mention the widespread popularity of anarcho-syndicalist ideas in southern Europe, not only in Spain, where they are usually held to have constituted the dominant force in the labor movement, but also in Switzerland, Italy, and France, where they contested the leading claims of social democracy right into the revolutionary years from 1917 to 1921. Anarchist ideas provided the major alternative vision of the Left in the founding period of the social democratic tradition under the First International. In a transmuted form, they resurfaced in the syndicalist agitation between the 1890s and 1914, which raised the next significant challenge to the established mode of socialist politics represented by the parties of the Second International (1889–1914), mainly founded between 1875 and the 1890s. Moreover, in this phase syndicalist ideas migrated from the Southern European baselands to Britain, parts of the Low Countries, and even Germany. Finally, democratic nationalism provides a further continuity with the earlier nineteenth century, which doesn't fit exactly into the dominant social democratic typology. The networks of migrant artisans and political exiles linking Paris, London, and Brussels in the 1840s and 1850s were fertile ground for the early activity of Marx and Engels and linked the causes of Polish, Hungarian, and Italian self-determination to those of Chartism and the French republicans. An older kind of radical democracy continued to resonate through the international popularity of Lajos Kossuth and Giuseppe Mazzini and remained current in southern and eastern Europe well into the 1880s and beyond. The subterranean influence of Rousseau, with its celebration of direct participatory democracy and local self-government, should also be noted, although its concrete lines may be traced less easily through the popular radicalism of the West than in the democratic projects of mid-century Southern and Eastern European nationalist intelligentsias, where the image of the citizen-democrat became subtly displaced onto the collective idea of the oppressed patriot people struggling for national liberation.

Thus, having distinguished the main pattern before 1914 as being one of centrally organized parliamentarian social democracy, it is also possible to write the history of the socialist tradition in terms of these other—that is, alternative or suppressed—traditions. The dominant social democratic model was stronger in the center and northwest of the continent (allowing us to speak reasonably of a German-speaking and Scandinavian social democratic "core"), weaker for varying reasons in the South and East, with French-speaking Europe somewhere in between. The other side of the story can be supplied only partially by relating the major alternative traditions—populism of various kinds in Tsarist Russia, anarcho-syndicalism in the Mediterranean South. Differences of context played a key part, from repressive illegality under tsarism to the narrowly oligarchic liberal polities of Italy and Spain. The size and backwardness of the agricultural sector in those three countries, with glaring inequalities in the rural social structure and the existence of a land-hungry peasantry and an unusually exploited agricultural working class, also determined a different pattern of left-wing politics from the industrial northwest. Yet the sources of an alternative vision to the centralizing political socialism that dominated the Second International should not be displaced to the geographical margins, to Europe's economically backward periphery.

If the last three decades of social history have taught us anything in this respect, it is the nigh-universal origins of socialist activity among workers of a particular type: skilled workmen in small to medium-sized workshops, with a strong sense of identity in their craft or trade and a finely developed pride in its culture, who became radicalized through defending their skill and affirming their dignity against proletarianization. In this sense, we can speak of certain patterns of practical socialism among such workers, who may certainly have been familiar with formal socialist ideas at varying levels of sophistication, but who formed their basic commitments from a definite set of experiences in production. While this oppositional culture was clearly hospitable to the various intellectual projects of utopian socialists and others, it did not owe its existence to them. In fact, to see the origins of socialism as an intellectual problem—as ideas seeking a constituency—is to put the cart before the horse. Early socialist activity—as a body of thought focused on the changing economy and its social relations and as a practical discourse of popular radicalism—crystalized from the material circumstances and aspirations of skilled workers themselves.

As an alternative set of impulses to the ones that cohered into the centralist social democratic model—that is, as a vision of socialism stressing various kinds of locally grounded mutualism and cooperation and "an economy run not by a collectivist state but by autonomous units of producers"[9]—this popular oppositional culture achieved its greatest historical staying power in Spanish anarcho-syndicalism from the 1860s to the Spanish Civil War. Mutualist ideals also showed great resilience in countries with strong movements of producer co-operation up to 1914, such as the Low Countries and Switzerland.[10] They also provided vital rallying points for the local clusters of working-class associational activity in the 1860s and 1870s that formed the basic building blocks of the earliest phase of socialist party-building in Germany and the Habsburg Empire. Moreover, as socialist ideas sank roots further to the East in the last third of the nineteenth century, notions of consumer cooperation invariably gave people their first encounter with this new tradition.[11] But the most striking case appears not on the Iberian or Slavic peripheries, but in the metropolitan center of nineteenth-century European political culture, France. Bernard Moss argues that for the whole period before 1914 the French labor movement remained basically wedded to an ideal of "federalist trade socialism," in which collective ownership in the means of production was to be organized through a democratic federation of self-governing skilled trades and communes. William Sewell goes further to argue that "the socialism of skilled workers" was inscribed in a larger "idiom of association" through which older meanings of mutual aid were appropriated and reshaped during the radicalizing moments of 1830–34 and 1848–51. Similarly, we know from Agulhon that the idiom of association also articulated social circumstances beyond the economic processes of proletarianization, distinct patterns of popular sociability through which workers fashioned their own public sphere for social, cultural, and political exchange, grounded not just in the formal fabric of the trade and mutual aid associations but in the cultural world of the choral societies and social clubs and in the everyday life of the workshops, lodging houses, taverns, and cafes.[12]

What these regionally specific alternatives had in common was a stronger emphasis on the local sovereignty of popular democratic action, whether based on the communal organization of the Russian peasant village, on the local syndication of trade union and cultural activity through the workers' *centro* and *bourse du travail*, or on one version or another of the more general cooperative ideals mentioned previously. In this sense, there was a larger heritage of popular radicalism that was only partially captured by the formal traditions of the Left. One form of this was the practical or "home-grown" socialism so attractive to artisans and skilled workers under pressure of proletarianization, and of which the theories of Proudhon, Cabet, and the rest should be seen as only a particularly elaborate formulation. Beyond this, we should also note the salience of certain popular democratic experiences of the mid-nineteenth century that registered quite unusual degrees of politicization across a wide spectrum of social and cultural issues and carried the Left's momentum beyond the normal boundaries of political and economic agitation. In local settings ordinary militants contested with the dominant culture on matters of schooling, recreation, religion, and much else besides (although stopping short at the family and the established patterns of sex-gender relations). British Chartism was the most impressive fund of experience in this regard, closely followed by the popular radicalism of 1848 to 1851 in France, where the political clubs and workers' corporations achieved an impressive peak of associational activism in Paris and other towns and the democratic-socialists ("democ-socs") managed a remarkable penetration of the villages. Smaller-scale equivalents of these experiences could be found elsewhere, too, between the 1840s and 1860s.[13]

Thus the model of socialist politics consolidated in the parties of the Second International did not exhaust the range of socialist practice and belief available in the nineteenth century. Past discussion has been thickly encrusted with teleological and normative assumptions that see the dichotomous contest of socialist parliamentarianism and proto-Bolshevik revolutionary purism as the logical form of the search for an effective left-wing strategy. Other options (like populism or anarcho-syndicalism) can then be dismissed as symptoms of backwardness or national peculiarity. Out of phase with the main logic of political development, they would soon disappear, condemned to marginality by their own contradictions. Likewise, the various precursors—utopians, communitarians, mutualists, and cooperators—could be safely disregarded as confused but interesting eccentrics, transitory symptoms of an immaturity already being overcome (as in the "socialism—utopian and scientific" framework bequeathed by Engels). In most accounts they form an exotic preamble to the main story, before the serious work of building the party gets under way. This hegemony of the classic social democratic model in most perceptions of the Left before 1914 was hardened by the splits after 1917, because most social democrats and communists proceeded to dig themselves in behind variants of centralism, the one focused on parliament, the other on the extra-parliamentary apparatus of the party, which renewed their indifference to local participatory forms. After the first flush of enthusiasm for the soviets and workers' councils from 1917 to 1920, for instance, the 1920s saw a continuous displacement of priority in communist thinking away from these public arenas of popular decision making toward the private arena of the party. Workers' councils became increasingly demoted into secondary media for mobilizations initiated elsewhere. Social democrats, of course, had always treated them with suspicion.

How, then, are we to conceptualize the alternative tradition of locally based participatory forms, given this long-term hegemony of the centralist mode? At one level, there'll always be a tension in activist movements between the assertion of sovereignty by the rank and file and the leadership's desire for careful or "responsible" direction. In particular situations of intense mobilization, ranging from strikes and community struggles to general revolutionary crises such as the one between 1917 and 1921, we would usually expect to see the popular creativity breaking through, outgrowing the institutionalized framework of established politics and outpacing the directive capacity of leaders. Depending on the strength of the popular challenge, the imagination of the leadership, and the resilience of the existing sociopolitical order, some new institutional framework will eventually be negotiated. The range of outcomes can be very great—for example, incremental advances of popular sovereignty, reactionary blockages of the latter, and occasionally a revolutionary opening toward more fundamental change. In other words, the tension between participatory and centralist modes is partly inherent and structural, built into the very process of popular mobilization. Even during the long hegemony of centralist organizational forms, forms of local self-management remained an important dimension of left-wing politics. Although latent for long periods, any raising of the political temperature was likely to reactivate such aspirations. The most impressive movements combine both impulses, lending the stability of centrally directed permanent organization to the maximum scope for rank-and-file resurgence.[14]

With this in mind, and allowing for regional unevenness in Europe as a whole, I would suggest the following periodization.

1. An initial period of flux and indeterminacy was mainly characterized by locally based associational initiatives for various kinds of self-governing cooperative living and working arrangements as the cellular bases for a new type of federated democratic state. Such activity coalesced only occasionally into a national movement (e.g., Chartism, or democratic socialism between 1849 and 1851 in France) and produced little in the way of durable political structures.

2. From the 1860s this amorphous activity became steadily sup-

planted by the new idea of the socialist party, usually oriented toward a parliamentary arena, accompanied by a corresponding form of trade unionism and stressing the value of a centrally organized permanent presence at the heart of the national policy. As noted, a version of the earlier associational socialism persisted in southern Europe as anarcho-syndicalism, while the politically backward societies to the East followed a pattern of their own. But by 1900 even these other movements were striving for stronger forms of national federation.

3. Next, the conjuncture of war and revolution from 1914 to 1923 amounted to a massive interruption of this continuity, which fractured the existing party structures and produced a huge explosion of locally based direct-democratic mobilization. However, this resurgence of grass-roots participatory forms, this time articulated around the soviets and workers' councils, proved transitory, and by 1923 the political stabilizations were bringing a restoration of centralist norms, whether in the Soviet Union or elsewhere. In this particular respect (although not, obviously, in general), the great watershed of 1917 made no lasting difference.

4. Consequently, the centralist model basically persisted until the mid-1950s, and the intervening moment of general European radicalization, the antifascist high point of the mid-1940s, had brought no equivalent resurgence of direct democracy. In fact, the postliberation circumstances had brought a remarkably speedy dispossession of such local initiatives as promised to materialize into a potential of that kind. There had been many smaller cases of such direct-democratic resurgence in particular countries after 1923 (e.g., Britain in 1926, France in 1936, Spain from 1931 to 1937, Italy from 1943 to 1945, and so on). But as a general alternative to the national-centralist mode, direct democracy was kept off the agenda. The challenge raised by the experience of the workers' councils from 1917 to 1923 was left hanging by the general counterrevolutionary outcome, as other more defensive priorities moved in to occupy the Left's attention.

5. It is only really since 1956, as first communist and then the latterday social democratic traditions entered a period of long-term decay, that this challenge has been properly resumed. A series of dramatic political moments—precisely the type of breakthrough mentioned previously, when popular creativity breaks the mould of existing politics—helped reawaken interest in alternative political forms. The Hungarian Revolution of 1956, the Czechoslovak reform communism of 1968, the French events of 1968, and those in Italy in 1969 provided

the principal occasions of renewal, galvanizing a long-term reorientation. The Campaign for Nuclear Disarmament and the first New Left in Britain (1956–64), the student movements in Europe as a whole (ca. 1967–70), feminism in western Europe (ca. 1970 to the present), the various movements for workers' control and industrial democracy since the late 1960s, the various forms of community politics since the same time, the broader-based sexual politics since the mid-1970s, and the peace movements of the 1980s—these have been the vehicles of renewal. The German Greens and Solidarity in Poland have been the major cases of national movements incorporating the new perspectives. In fact, the contemporary Left problematic of democracy has involved a full-scale confrontation with the continuous centralist tradition, so that certain themes of earlier periods (1917 to 1923, before the 1860s) have been recognizably reappropriated—direct democracy, industrial self-management, community politics, and local forms of democracy, together with new ones like the politics of sexuality and subjectivity. It is no accident that these shifts have been accompanied by a conscious revival of historical interest in the utopian socialists and other earlier movements.[15]

Socialism and Democracy

The most powerful ideological motif in the East European revolutions of 1989 has been the claim that liberalism and democracy are an inseparable politicoeconomic unity—not just that the breakthrough to democracy is simultaneously the freeing of the market and the recognition by the small size of socialist movements until closer to 1914. By any strict definition of democracy—for example, popular representation on the basis of free, universal, secret, adult, and equal suffrage backed by legal freedoms of speech, assembly, association, and press— the coupling of "liberalism" and "democracy" makes no sense for most of the nineteenth century because liberals showed themselves consistently wedded to highly restricted and exclusionary systems of political representation. When democratic reforms were introduced, they came through broad popular mobilizations outside the framework of normal liberal politics, even though the more flexible liberal leaderships may sometimes have taken them up.

Indeed, it was the agency of the nationally organized labor movements of the later nineteenth century that properly introduced what we now recognize as "liberal democracy" (a combination of parliamentary government, welfare statism, and national economic management) into European political discourse, and if there is a historical lineage to the democratizations currently under way in eastern Europe, then this can be just as appropriately located in the democratic agendas of the pre-1914 socialist parties as in the classical heritage of nineteenth-century liberalism. But what of the other features of that older socialist tradition, such as the centralized state, the planned economy, or the primacy of an economistic notion of class, which are also the features of the post-1947–48 East European regimes against which the democratic movements are in full-scale revolt? Again, the record and structure of the overall socialist tradition are much more complicated than the simple equation of the latter with statist socialism *tout court* would suggest. We can see this, perhaps, if we look at the form of politics with which the Stalinist forms of communism are most easily associated, that is, a "vanguardist" concept of their relationship to the working class and the corresponding centralism of such parties' internal organization. I'll do this by beginning again in the nineteenth century, this time with the conspiratorial tradition of insurrectionary politics usually associated with the indefatigable revolutionism of Auguste Blanqui.

Abstracting from the most dramatic feature of the French Revolution in its most radical phase—the dynamic but unstable relationship between the Jacobin dictatorship and the mass acts of popular insurrection—Blanquism stressed the necessity of a secret revolutionary brotherhood, the character of the revolution as an exemplary act triggering a general uprising of the people, and the need for a centralized form of popular dictatorship. It originated with Gracchus Babeuf and the "Conspiracy of the Equals" in 1796, and was transmitted through the career of Babeuf's surviving comrade, Filipo Buonarroti. It worked best during the most overbearing phase of the post-1815 reactionary restoration in Europe, which produced a climate of censorship and repression especially conducive to conspiratorial styles on the Left. Blanqui learned the "art of insurrection" from Buonarroti in this period and came to personify an ideal of selfless revolutionary heroism (or egocentric, subversive fanaticism, depending on one's point of view) that formed the commonest popular image of the revolutionary in the nineteenth century. His politics were a form of optimistic adventurism—the masses were always available for revolution, if only the right moment could be seized—which seemed vindicated in the great revolutionary crises of 1830 and 1848 that exploded so unexpectedly and owed so little to formal organizational preparation by the Left. The last act of the Blanquist drama was the 1871 Paris Commune in this respect, although the fiasco of the 1839 uprising was its most fitting scene.

The point about Blanquism was its profoundly undemocratic character. The conspiratorial ideal of a small, secretive elite acting on behalf of a popular mass whose consent was to be organized essentially after the revolution by a program of systematic reeducation, but whom in the meantime could not be trusted, is powerful evidence to this effect. Logically enough, Blanqui was opposed to universal suffrage until after the revolution and showed little interest in the popular democratic politics that actually emerged in Britain and France between the 1830s and 1870s, when the conditions of extreme repression that originally justified the conspiratorial mode no longer applied. As well as being a departure from liberal and associational political forms, therefore, the social democratic tradition inaugurated in the 1860s was also a decisive repudiation of the Blanquist insurrectionary temptation. This was true above all of Marx.[16] The possible need for an armed mobilization to defend the revolution against the counterrevolutionary violence of the ruling class was left open, but between 1871 and 1917 the dominant model of revolutionary politics for the parties of the Second International became one that hinged on the achievement of an irresistible parliamentary majority. The Paris Commune, which displayed both the heroism and the tragic limitations of the pure insurrectionary tradition—and the need for forms of popular democratic action beyond the Blanquist horizon—was the crucial watershed in this respect.

Henceforth, the pure insurrectionary mode became the property of the anarchists, for whom Mikhail Bakunin was in this respect the major spokesman. But after the decisive debates in the First International (1868–72), which secured the general hegemony of a party-political and parliamentarist approach within the Left (with the regional exceptions noted previously), the earlier unity of the Blanquist tradition divided into a series of discrete orientations, one of which was conspiratorial forms of organization. But they now became theoretically separable from insurrectionism as such on the grounds that a genuine rising of the people had no need of any directive leadership (as in the "strong-men-need-no-leaders" strain of anarchism). This applied to a large part of Spanish anarchism between the 1900s and 1930s, in both industrial Catalonia and rural Andalusia. On the other hand, it was hard to stop conspiratorial tendencies emerging within the anarchist movement as a whole. Thus in Spain the libertarian anarcho-syndicalist federation formed in 1919, the Confederación Nacional del Trabajo (CNT), which was the very opposite of a centrally managed trade-union bureaucracy or party-political machine, was matched by the clandestine Federación Anarquista Ibérica (FAI) formed in 1927, the quintessence of élitist and conspiratorial revolutioneering. The same contradiction had been present at the very center of the career of Bakunin himself. Moreover, such activity easily spilled over into simple terrorism. The conspiratorial and terrorist temptations were strongest in conditions of repression or defeat, when the chances for public activity were narrowly reduced: in tsarist Russia in the later 1870s and early 1880s, and then again in the early 1900s; and in Spain, France, and Italy in the 1890s. (The terrorism and "armed-struggle" scenarios of sections of the West European ultra-left in the 1970s were a different phenomenon.)

But the most troubling of the Blanquist legacies was vanguardism—the idea that small minorities of disciplined revolutionaries, equipped with sophisticated theories and superior virtue, can anticipate the direction of popular aspirations, act decisively in their name, and in the process radicalize the popular consciousness. At one level, that of the imperfections of democracy in practice and the complex reciprocities of leaders and led, this is an inescapable problem of political organization in general because even in the most perfect of procedural democracies a certain latitude and initiative necessarily fall to the leadership's discretion, beyond the sovereign people's practical reach. But in the Blanquist tradition this practical condition was elaborated into a positive theory of action. Moreover, it has been commonly suggested that this is also a basic feature of the Marxist tradition, and in particular of Lenin's politics in the Bolshevik party, which as such became transmitted both to the Soviet state and to the communist political tradition after 1917, including to the official cultures of most postrevolutionary socialist states since World War II. Given the forthright critiques developed by Marx and Engels in the 1860s and 1870s of both Blanqui and Bakunin in this respect, and the frequently stated support of the Second International parties for democratic principles—indeed, the constitutive importance for the social democratic tradition of a bitter political struggle against precisely that kind of vanguardism—this accusation seems manifestly misplaced. As a sufficient description of Lenin's politics, it also seems too crude.[17] But at the same time, vanguardism is too salient a feature of "Leninism" as the official ideology of communist political practice since the mid-1920s for this aspect of the charge to be easily dismissed.

Here it is worth considering the forms of restriction socialists and communists have admitted on the exercise of democracy. Earlier I referred to the antidemocratic dispositions of nineteenth-century liberalism, but of course left-wing theory and practice have also not been free of such restrictiveness. On the contrary, sometimes whole categories of the population have been excluded from the moral-political community of "the people" in the popular democratic sense. After all, the first means of cementing the popular legitimacy of revolutionary governments tends to be the focusing of hostility against the ancien régime—the monarch or despotic head of state, the agents of repression under the old system, the ruling class, or simply "the oppressors." This may range from the spontaneous wreaking of popular revenge—against priests (classically in Spain from 1931 to 1936 and earlier in 1909 and 1868), against army officers (e.g., the events of March 18, 1871 that precipitated the Paris Commune), against landlords (Russia in 1905 and 1917), or against the secret police (Hungary in 1956, Portugal in 1974, Iran in 1979, Romania in 1989)—to the more systematic campaigns of the revolutionary authorities themselves against the "enemies of the revolution." The more fragile the revolution's survival, due to international isolation or civil war, the more violent such campaigns may be. Consolidating the revolution's social base may produce a similar effect. The great Soviet purges of the 1930s and the Stalinist repression from 1949 to 1957 in eastern Europe may be seen in this light.

In each case, definite categories of people were not only excluded from participating in the revolution, but also were specifically targeted as its foes, becoming legitimate objects of legal and police attack. Both principles were institutionalized during the Russian Revolution in the Constitution adopted in July 1918 by the All-Russian Congress of Soviets in the name of "the Toiling and Exploited People." The franchise for soviet elections was both restricted and unequal, but, by contrast with the liberal constitutional practice of the nineteenth century, the restrictions were turned against inequalities of property rather than in their favor. On the one hand, the franchise was limited to those who "earn their living by production or socially useful labor," together with soldiers and the disabled, while the dominant classes in industry and agriculture, together with their agents—the employers of hired labor, rentiers, private traders, monks and priests, and agents and officials of the former police, but not the professions, who were functionally too crucial to the new order—were specifically excluded. In addition, the towns (and therefore the working class) were given more representation relative to population than the countryside and the peasantry. On the other hand, the Constitution also made it clear that the power of the new state was to be turned directly at the disenfranchised class enemy, hardly surprising at a time when the dominant classes were mobilizing for a counterrevolutionary civil war against the Bolshevik government. It spoke of the transitional need for a strong state power if "the exploitation of man by man" [sic] was to be ended, socialist construction put in train, and the state ultimately abolished. Consequently, it temporarily instituted a popular dictatorship of workers and peasants, internally democratic but externally combative and if necessary repressive, "for the purpose of the complete crushing of the bourgeoisie."[18]

This discriminatory franchise remained in force under the amended Constitution of 1923, before being dropped in the new Constitution of 1936. Moreover, it was supplemented by a battery of related restrictions in other areas of civil freedom, as the Soviet state gradually criminalized forms of oppositional activity in the context and aftermath of the Civil War. Furthermore, a debilitating logic of international, social, and domestic political isolation drove the Bolshevik leadership into growing disrespect even for the internal democracy of the soviet structure itself, so that the latter became inexorably transformed into a narrowing command apparatus, substituting for popular democratic initiatives rather than responding to them.[19] This situation became radicalized under the industrialization and collectivization drives of the 1930s, so that the paper democracy of Stalin's 1936 Constitution masked an apparatus of discrimination and terror that practically negated any operative democratic category of the sovereign people.

This is not the place for a detailed discussion of the Russian Revolution and its degeneration. The point I want to make is that the revolutionary Left's preferred formula for the seizure of power and the building of a new society between the French Revolution and the 1970s—the idea, that is, of a temporary democratic dictatorship of the insurgent people, empowered to act decisively in the interests of securing the revolution and its programmatic objectives, if necessary over the resistance of the former dominant classes by means of coercion—explicitly delimits the category of "the people." Moreover, this limitation is a necessary function of the class-based analysis of the revolutionary process: if the realistic prospect of genuine democratic advance is socially and politically stymied by class inequalities of access to power, and if in addition the logic of capitalist accumulation and crisis is bound to make those inequalities ever-more obstructive, then some form of class confrontation, organized through the medium of a popular revolutionary challenge to the status quo, becomes unavoidable. And if that is the case, then the boundaries of popular sovereignty have to be drawn reluctantly but securely against the counterrevolutionary vested interests. "The people" then become less a descriptive term for the whole population and more a kind of moral-political category that can be either more or less sociologically specific.

This model of the democratic vanguard placed into power by massed insurrection, which then proceeds to enact a program of revolutionary transformation, was pioneered by the extreme Left in the Jacobin dictatorship, before being transmitted through Babeuf and Buonarroti to Blanqui. It was taken up by Marx and Engels, who attached it to the class analysis of the historically determined revolutionary confrontation of proletariat and bourgeoisie. It was vital to the thought of Lenin and the Bolsheviks in the Russian Revolution, whence it became transmitted to the orthodox communist tradition. On the other hand, it has been specifically rejected by the other main tradition of the Left since 1917, that of noncommunist and reformist social democracy. Indeed, pinned to the arresting formula of the "dictatorship of the proletariat," with its implications of coercion, police powers, and the ruthless suppression of the proletariat's enemies (positively fueled, one might add, by many statements and actions of the Bolsheviks in the revolution), it has been one of the principal dividing lines between the revolutionary and reformist Left in the twentieth century, already inscribed in some major debates of the pre-1914 Second International, whose theorists gave little attention to matters of immediate revolutionary transition. But the prevailing parliamentary perspectives disposed them to be suspicious of the Bolsheviks' anti-parliamentary soviet route. Kautsky, for one, roundly denounced the latter as the undemocratic dictatorship of an unrepresentative political minority.

Since 1917, often quite radical socialists have been reluctant to embrace a revolutionary course from fear lest a confrontationist strategy necessarily lead to an authoritarian dictatorship of this kind. If the Left were to find themselves in control of the state, the advantages to the working class of more aggressively implementing a socialist transition would be heavily outweighed by the costs to democracy of having to suppress other social interests and coerce the opposition. On that basis, most noncommunist socialists (aside from the smaller Trotskyist and other revolutionary sects and the anarchists) have opted for gradualist routes through the existing parliamentary and related institutional frameworks. This does not have to spell the abandonment of socialism. But it does mean reducing socialism to a series of intermediate and essentially socialist objectives attainable within the given parameters of capitalist society, it has been argued, or else hoping that the cumulative effect of such reforms will eventually facilitate a democratically managed transition to socialism on a broadly constructed foundation of popular legitimacy and without having to abandon the continuing parliamentary representation of plural viewpoints and social interests.

The interesting thing is that since the mid-1970s at the latest many communist parties have been pursuing this kind of strategy too. In some cases, such as the PCI, this shift goes back to the mid-1940s and more ambivalently to the Popular Front campaigns after 1935. In others, such as the left-socialist formations in Scandinavia, it grew from the ferment after 1956; as a general phenomenon, it accompanied the emergence of Eurocommunism between 1968 and 1974. From the mid-1970s a number of communist parties increasingly abandoned terms like *dictatorship of the proletariat* and other essential phraseology of the Leninist tradition. In so doing, they opted unambiguously for a noninsurrectionary and nonvanguardist mode of politics predicated on the realistic possibility of a parliamentary road to socialism. While such parties retained an interest in complementary forms of democratic mobilization outside the immediate parliamentary arena, this has brought them recognizably onto the ground of left-wing social democracy, as represented by Kautsky's thinking earlier in the century and the Left-socialist discourse of 1919–21, or (for example) certain aspects of Austrian and German social democratic politics in the 1920s, or the strategy of Swedish social democrats since 1945, or certain tendencies of the British Labour party between 1970 and the mid-1980s. The incipient passage of the PCI into the socialist camp is a formal ratification of this change, as in a smaller way is the politics of the British communist party and *Marxism Today* since the mid-1970s.

This shift is the result of long-term processes of de-Stalinization—

of continuing disillusionment with the Soviet model of socialist construction under Brezhnev provoked by the tragic suppression of successive reform movements in eastern Europe (1956, 1968, 1981), and since 1968 aided by the infusion into some parties of new social and political forces. Such processes have gradually encouraged a more critical attitude toward the legacy of the Russian Revolution itself, so that the more independent parties have come to share much of the social democratic critique of Leninism. There are many sides to that critique, but what interests me here is the withdrawal from a politics of class confrontation based on the unqualified primacy of the working class. As soon as the concept of the dictatorship of the proletariat (in this sense as well as in the coercive one) is given up—that is, the idea of the insurgent working class moving coercively through its party to destroy the power of the bourgeoisie and erect the scaffolding of socialism in its place through a pitched and violent confrontation—it becomes necessary to think more creatively and less schematically about winning the cooperation and consent of other social forces to the process of socialist construction.

For social democrats before 1914, this tended not to be a problem: eventually the working class was to become an overwhelming majority of society, as capitalist development ran its course and other popular groups became proletarianized, in which case the question of democratic alliances didn't need to be posed, and the working class could come to power by the forces of its own numbers alone. Communists inherited much of this thinking after 1917—that is, the working class as the subject of world history, borne necessarily toward the socialist future by the objective circumstances of capitalist accumulation, contradiction, and crisis and concentrating in its consciousness and agency the progressive potentialities of humankind. They conceived a far more active role, however, for the working-class party as the interpreter of working-class consciousness and the executor of working-class interests. But what socialists and communists shared in common, perhaps, was a belief in the proletariat as a new "general" or "universal" class, whose progressive dynamism represented the general interest of society as a whole, just as the liberal bourgeoisie had represented the general interest of society in the earlier transition from feudalism to capitalism. The teleology of this idea, implying as it did such confidence in the direction and outcome of history, desensitized its exponents to the importance of "nonclass" identities such as gender and nationality and the legitimate rights and interests of nonproletarian classes (like the peasantry, small-business and white-collar strata, the professions, and the intelligentsia), which were doomed in any case to disappear with industrialization into the ranks of the working class, either before the revolution or after. "The people" were identified uncritically with the actual or anticipated working-class majority. Marxists have not been alone in this tendency. Liberal celebration of the "middle class" is another example, as is Russian and East European idealization of the peasantry earlier in the century. In each case a particular social category is made the repository of society's general interest—the *authentic* people, the real source of virtue, the true bearer of social progress. Privileged in this way, its interests easily override the legitimacy of other social and political claims.

On the other hand, once the automatic primacy of the working class becomes questioned as a basis for socialist politics, the category of "the people" has to be filled with a more complex democratic content. In their different ways, both social democrats and communists have made efforts in this direction without exactly abandoning the historic attachment to their core working-class support. Since 1945, social democrats have increasingly opted for the "classless" ideal of the electoral "people's party," in the sense of a general appeal across social categories, involving deemphasis of the party's working-class and specifically socialist history, and a conscious play for the votes of the "middle class" in particular. More recently, some parties have also developed a broader "popular democratic" strategy on a similar basis of constructive unity between working-class and other interests. In the more sophisticated versions, this amounts to something more than the mere aggregation of social interests or a mechanical grouping of the latter around the central value of the working class. Rather, the "popular democratic" becomes a dimension of political strategy in its own right, upholding the importance of democratic values for themselves and making possible the integration of a range of issues into left-wing politics that were previously devalued due to their seeming remoteness from the primary materialist concerns of the working class: so-called "nonclass" issues concerning gender and sexuality, race and nationality, youth, peace, ecology, and so forth.

At one level, this willingness to step back from the traditional socialist stress on the primacy of the working class reflects the entry into left-wing consciousness of certain long-term tendencies in the composition of capital and the sociology of the working class. In the discursive order of the socialist tradition "working class" has a definite connotation—essentially manual workers in classic extractive, trans-portation, and manufacturing industry, from the miner, steelworker, and skilled machinist to the lineworker, unskilled or semiskilled ma-chine-minder, and general factory laborer. Yet in the process of work-ing-class formation, the simple category of the worker (someone selling labor power for a wage) encompasses a far more complex sociology than this and includes people working in a much wider variety of so-cial and physical settings than the archetype of the (male) proletarian usually implies. Moreover, contrary to the predictions of Marx and En-gels and the assumptions of most socialists and communists of the Second and Third Internationals, the working class in the traditional sense has not become the overwhelming majority of the population. Almost without exception in the developed capitalist economies, manual workers in manufacturing industry have accounted for an ever-diminishing proportion of the employed population, a trend that was already discernible early in the twentieth century.

Now, if that is true, the old vision of the conquering proletariat makes no practical sense, quite apart from the larger questions of dem-ocratic principle. In fact, it imposes a double priority on left-wing strategy, partly sociological, partly political. The Left needs both to think again about how else the working class is to be constituted, so that neglected categories of workers can be brought more clearly into focus, and to work for the kind of alliances that would allow working-class interests in this stricter sense to be effectively pursued. It is im-portant to appreciate just how restrictive a notion of working-class interests most socialist and communist politics have tended to reflect. Particular parties have launched quite imaginative campaigns to or-ganize various categories of more "marginal" workers at different times. In particular localities and under the pressure of particular is-sues and events, such parties have also stumbled willy-nilly into a "nonclass" politics. But on the whole, working-class parties have re-mained strongly oriented toward only a specific section of the working class in the strict sociological sense—namely, skilled, manual, male workers of respectable culture, majority religion, and dominant na-tionality. Historically speaking, the disregarding of women workers has been the most egregious of these possible neglects. But more gen-erally, the culture of the working class has been finely structured by sectional divisions among workers in different grades and occupa-tions, and by complex hierarchies of race, nationality, age, skill, and so on. Reevaluating traditional notions of the primacy of the working class has begun to make the Left more sensitive to these matters as well.

Thus in left-wing discussion a number of revisions hang together: deep skepticism about forms of confrontationist revolutionary strategy based on the unqualified primacy of working-class interests, usually deriving from the Bolshevik experience of 1917; associated doubts about the traditional slogan of the dictatorship of the proletariat, with its hard-faced intimations of coercion, command centralism, and suspensions of democracy, however temporary and transitional these are claimed to be; a new interest in parliamentary routes to socialism based on broad strategies of democratic alliance; a critical awareness of changes in the composition of the working class, combined with a greater sensitivity to issues and interests that can't be subsumed in a notion of working-class politics as traditionally defined; and the reappropriation of participatory and direct-democratic forms. Together, these add up to an important range of discussion about the meaning of "the popular" in popular sovereignty. Clearly, "the people" can never be a totally inclusive category for any movement stressing the limitation of democracy by class inequalities of access to power and ownership and control in the economy. Such disparities of access to effective power in state and society will always render significant democratic advance problematic. Democratic advance can only proceed through dynamic processes of political conflict that are necessarily highly divisive, ranging some coalitions of interest against others. There will always be some exclusions from "the people" because there will always be powerful interests ranged against democracy. But a genuine politics of popular democracy will try to isolate such interests— the reigning form of the "power bloc"—by the broadest possible coalition of society.

Conclusion

I've tried to suggest that the socialist tradition encompasses a richer set of histories and a wider repertoire of possibilities than the "crisis of socialism" formula easily allows. This is true whether we look at the actual gains registered by the Left in the revolutionary conjuncture of 1917–23, as opposed to the political model which became abstracted from the Bolshevik experience into the main measure of what a successful revolutionary outcome would have been, or whether we look at the earlier nineteenth-century history of the socialist tradition as it emerged from the constitutive debates of the 1860s, with its primary focus on questions of national democracy conceptualized in parliamentary terms. On the one hand, these two contexts of formation (1860s–1914 and 1914–23) reveal the salience of such themes as parliamentary democracy, civil liberties, the importance of a democratic public sphere, and the rights of peoples to national self-determination within an overall framework of peace and international cooperation. On the other hand, they involved the suppression or marginalization of a valuable countertradition of participatory direct-democratic forms, which flourished explosively from 1917 to 1923 before returning sporadically in particular national crises since. In both cases these histories speak eloquently to the concerns of the present—that is, the 1980s and 1990s in East and West—where questions of parliamentary democracy, local accountability, decentralization of control in state and economy, human rights and personal freedoms, civil society and the opening of the public sphere, and national self-determination are (among other things) powerfully structuring the Left's agenda.

Socialism is certainly in "crisis," if by "socialism" we mean the unimaginative statist traditions consolidated on either side of the Iron Curtain since the late-1940s and the economistically derived teleology centered on the progressive political agency of the working class. However, the critique of Stalinism, the crisis of the Keynesian-welfare-state synthesis, and the late-twentieth-century processes of transnational capitalist restructuring have all forced sections of the Left to think hard about how else socialism might be understood, whether through the "Forward March of Labour Halted"-"Farewell to the Working Class" type of analysis, the challenge of feminism, the rise of the new social movements, the success of popular conservatisms such as Thatcherism, or emergent "post-Fordist" analyses of the structural setting.[20] My point is that the rethinking is as important as the crisis, and that the deeper history of the tradition contains rich resources for this purpose. Finally, I have concentrated exclusively on the history of the tradition itself, and this focus necessarily reproduces some of the limitations I haven't discussed, whereas in the present the strongest impetus toward renewal has come from the outside—from the new social movements and especially from feminism. The final part of my discussion, on the difficulties with the received notion of the working class and the importance of "nonclass" issues, gestured in this direction. But the disastrous neglects of the post-1860s' tradition in this respect (rather than its positive resources), the feminist reappropriating of the earlier utopian moment of the 1820s and 1830s, and the external pressure of the post-1960s' women's movement would have to be central to a discussion of the current rethinking as such. However, that was not my specific purpose here. Had I been directly addressing the present, gender would have been at the center of the account, but by now the critique of socialism's past omissions should be so familiar as to become axiomatic. On this front it is the socialist tradition as such, and not simply its post-1923 statist manifestations, that has been insufficient, and the impact of contemporary feminism on the Left has been finally to make this clear.

Notes

1. Stuart Hall, "Coming Up for Air," *Marxism Today*, March 1990, p. 25.
2. Hall, "Coming Up for Air," p. 25.
3. Enrico Berlinguer, *After Poland: Towards a New Internationalism* (Nottingham, 1982), p. 16.
4. Fora stimulating exploration of this issue, see Fernando Claudin, "Democracy and Dictatorship in Lenin and Kautsky," *New Left Review*, 106 (Nov.–Dec. 1977): 59–76; and for a pertinent critique of Lenin in this context, see A. J. Polan, *Lenin and the End of Politics* (Berkeley, 1984).
5. This point was originally made by Arno J. Mayer, *Wilson vs Lenin: Political Origins of the New Diplomacy, 1917–1918* (New York, 1984), pp. 293–312.
6. Lenin, quoted in Mayer, *Wilson vs Lenin*, p. 298; see also D. Boersner, *The Bolsheviks and the National and Colonial Question, 1917–1928* (Geneva, 1957; Westport, 1981).
7. Nikolai Bukharin, "The Communist International and the Colonies," *Pravda*, March 6, 1919, in *Founding the Communist International: Proceedings and Documents of the First Congress, March 1919*, ed. John Riddell (New York, 1987), p. 308.
8. Britain is an odd case in this respect, because until the 1890s and the formation of the Labour Representation Committee (LRC) in 1900, the relative effectiveness of channeling labor representation through the popular Liberal party tended to inhibit moves for the independent representation of working-class interests through a separate socialist party. But allowing for this, and for the weakness of specifically socialist beliefs among British trade unionists until after the socialist revival of the 1880s and the post-1889 rise of the New Unionism, the main European pattern of post-1860s socialist activity basically holds. France is also an ambiguous case. On the one hand, the strength of the radical republican tradition encouraged one tendency of French socialists to direct their energies either through the left wing of the republican coalitions after 1871 or through a separate socialist party of the classic parliamentarian

kind. But on the other hand, cooperative and mutualist traditions dating from the 1830s and 1840s remained very strong among French labor, and in some opinions amounted to the paramount strain of French socialism until after 1914.

9. Eric J. Hobsbawm, "The 1970s: Syndicalism without Syndicalists?" in *Workers: Worlds of Labor* (New York, 1984), p. 277.

10. See Jürg K. Siegenthaler, "Producers' Cooperatives in Switzerland," *International Labor and Working-Class History* 11 (May 1977): 21. Siegenthaler summarizes the bases for the strength of producer cooperation in Switzerland: "a comparatively small scale of enterprise in all sectors of industry; considerable influence of Latin socialist programs in the labor movement; and the long-term, pre-industrial agrarian-cooperative and political-cooperative tradition of the country."

11. See, for example, the excellent analysis in John-Paul Himka, *Socialism in Galicia: The Emergence of Polish Social Democracy and Ukrainian Radicalism (1860–1890)* (Cambridge, Mass., 1983).

12. See Bernard H. Moss, *The Origins of the French Labor Movement 1830–1914: The Socialism of Skilled Workers* (Berkeley, 1976); William H. Sewell, Jr., *Work and Revolution in France: The Language of Labor from the Old Regime to 1848* (Cambridge, 1980), esp. 210ff., 275ff.; and Maurice Agulhon, *The Republic of the Village: The People of the Var from the French Revolution to the Second Republic* (Cambridge, 1982).

13. The democratic-socialists were the broad grouping of the republican Left that had coalesced from the various Left factions by the first anniversary of the revolution in February 1849. See Edward Berenson, *Populist Religion and Left-Wing Politics in France, 1830–1852* (Princeton, 1984). For Chartism, see especially Eileen Yeo, "Some Practices and Problems of Chartist Democracy," and James Epstein, "Some Organizational and Cultural Aspects of the Chartist Movement in Nottingham," in *The Chartist Experience: Studies in Working-Class Radicalism and Culture, 1830–1860*, ed. James Epstein and Dorothy Thompson (London, 1982), pp. 345–80, 221–68. See also Eileen Yeo, "Culture and Constraint in Working-Class Movements, 1830–1855," in *Popular Culture and Class Conflict 1590–1914: Explorations in the History of Labour and Leisure*, ed. Eileen Yeo and Stephen Yeo (Brighton, 1981), pp. 155–86.

14. Of course, this is easier said than done and rarely achieved for more than brief moments. As possible examples of such a creative unity of centralist and participatory impulses I would suggest the Bolsheviks in 1917; the Yugoslav and other antifascist partisan movements during 1943–45; some anticolonial national liberation movements from the mid-1940s to the present; the PCI in many dimensions of its history since 1943; Polish Solidarity in 1980–82. The ideal is more easily achieved within local communities. See, for example, Stuart Macintyre, *Little Moscows: Communism and Working-Class Militancy in Inter-War Britain* (London, 1980).

15. A sense of the new developments can be gained from Sheila Rowbotham, Lynne Segal, and Hilary Wainwright, *Beyond the Fragments: Feminism and the Making of Socialism* (London, 1979); and John Minnion and Philip Bolsover, eds., *The CND Story: The First Twenty-Five Years of CND in the Words of* *the People Involved* (London, 1983). In my view the contribution of the post-1968 women's movement has been crucial to the transformed problematic of Left politics at the end of the twentieth century, just as the gender front has been the most persistent and debilitating weakness of the late-nineteenth and twentieth-century socialist tradition before that time. This dimension is not dealt with directly in this chapter because my purpose was specifically to reaffirm certain submerged strengths.

16. This seems agreed by most serious historians of Marx's politics. See especially, Richard N. Hunt, *The Political Ideas of Marx and Engels*, vol. 1: *Marxism and Totalitarian Democracy, 1818–1850*, and vol. 2: *Classical Marxism, 1850–1895* (Pittsburgh, 1974, 1984); Monty Johnstone, "Marx, Blanqui and Majority Rule," in *The Socialist Register 1983*, ed. Ralph Miliband and John Saville (London, 1983), pp. 296–318; and, authoritatively, Eric J. Hobsbawm, "Marx, Engels and Politics," in *The History of Marxism*, vol. 1: *Marxism in Marx's Day*, ed. Eric J. Hobsbawm (Brighton, 1982), pp. 227–64. George Lichtheim, *Marxism: An Historical and Critical Study* (London, 1961), esp. pp. 65–129, is still excellent in making clear the watershed character of the 1860s. These interpretations are advanced in opposition to an older and less sympathetic one that crudely assimilated Marx in this respect to a Jacobin insurrectionary tradition of "totalitarian democracy." See J. L. Talmon, *The Origins of Totalitarian Democracy* (London, 1970).

17. The most careful exegesis of Lenin's thinking in this respect is Neil Harding, *Lenin's Political Thought* (London, 1981). The most compelling case for Lenin's relative insensitivity to detailed matters of democratic participation and accountability is made by Polan, *Lenin and the End of Politics*.

18. This description of the 1918 Constitution of the Russian Socialist Federal Soviet Republic (RSFSR) is based on the excellent account in E. H. Carr, *The Bolshevik Revolution 1917–1923*, vol. 1 (Harmondsworth, 1966), pp. 134–59. The 1918 Constitution was superseded by the 1923 Constitution of the Union of Soviet Socialist Republics (USSR), which stayed in force until the introduction of the famous Stalin Constitution of 1936.

19. Concurrent with the impoverishment of popular democracy in the Soviets was the overriding of the rights of the non-Russian nationalities to self-determination, which had also been guaranteed by the 1918 Constitution. The transforming of the popular dictatorship into a dictatorship of the party was replicated in the emergence of a greater Russian centralism, as opposed to the federalism of self-governing peoples originally envisaged.

20. See Eric J. Hobsbawm et al., *The Forward March of Labour Halted?* (London, 1981); André Gorz, *Farewell to the Working Class* (London, 1982); and Rolf Ebbighausen and Friedrich Tiemann, eds., *Das Ende der Arbeiterbewegung in Deutschland? Ein Diskussionsband zum sechzigsten Geburtstag von Theo Pirker* (Opladen, 1984). For the readiest access to the new thinking see Stuart Hall and Martin Jacques, eds., *New Times* (London, 1989).

Revolution and

Counterrevolution

in Eastern Europe

Norman M. Naimark

For a while the memory of my Soviet officer's uniform provided me with
a measure of protection, but by now the very pillars of my conscience were
giving away. If the people in that meeting room were Communists, then I
wasn't one. Or was I the real Communist and they the fakes.
—George Konrád, *The Loser*

Comrade Stalin writes to us from Russia,
Oh Partisans, be afraid no more!
But we send him an open letter
We were never afraid at all.
—Sreten Zujovic, Crni (1941)

They bore us and bore us, bore us to tears, they torment us, drive us crazy
with endless talk, piss boring boredom all over us.
—Tadeusz Konwicki, *The Polish Complex*[1]

The recent upheavals in the communist world have prompted in the
Soviet Union a flourish of intense, introspective examinations of the
origins of the Soviet experience. What happened to the promise of the
Revolution of 1917? How did the Russian Revolution degenerate into
one of the cruelest dictatorships of the twentieth century? Why was
the Soviet administrative system, even in the post-Stalin period, unable to adjust to the demands of a changing society and the needs of
a modern economy? Some Soviet historians even go so far as to ask

whether the revolution itself constituted a form of original sin because it was led by the Bolsheviks, a minority party on the political spectrum. Others think that Lenin understood the dangers of the seizure of power by socialists in a backward country and tried to provide mechanisms—the Workers' and Peasants' Inspectorate among them —that would protect the revolution from bureaucratic fossilism and administrative chicanery. Did he fail because he did not sufficiently recognize the dangers or because the new state structure could not emancipate itself from its autocratic forerunner? Was Leninism itself the problem in that it took Russian social democracy down the unnatural road of chiliastic exclusionism? More often than not, Soviet scholars point to Stalin as the problem and not to Lenin, to Stalinism as the perversion of Marxism in power, not to Leninism. Brezhnevist *zastoi* (stagnation) is under attack, as are the excesses of the Stalin period. Lenin's extremist policies under War Communism are under scrutiny, as are the Bolshevik maneuvers to exclude from power other parties on the Left—Mensheviks, Socialist Revolutionaries, Left Socialist Revolutionaries, and anarchists. The NEP is being reexamined for its positive models, as is the period between the February and October revolutions. But it is significant how quickly Soviet historians have returned to the revolution itself to understand the widely recognized "deformities" of the Soviet socialist system.[2]

The Soviet Union's creative and intellectually stimulating confrontation with its revolutionary past is clearly part and parcel of the ongoing struggle for power and of the competition among political platforms in the Soviet leadership. In east central Europe, on the other hand, the debates about the nature of the revolutions that brought communists to power have been buried in the whirlwind of democratic upheavals. The compelling symbols of capitalist development and free parliamentary elections dominate political (and historical) discourse. East German historians tried briefly—and too late—to reexamine their postwar history in search of legitimacy for their fragile socialist republic.[3] But like their colleagues in Poland, Czechoslovakia, Hungary, Bulgaria, and Romania, history quickly became the property of a blend of public imagination and popular memory. The rock of reformed historical consciousness that they had been assiduously pushing up the hill against dogmatic resistance was halted by the crowds on the street—and began rolling back down the hill over the protests of both the dogmatists and reformers. Paradoxically, then, Soviet scholars have been able to be more forthcoming about the history of their revolution than scholars in the more open societies of eastern Europe.

This does not mean that interesting and important work is not being done in eastern Europe on the history of the immediate postwar period, but rather that the stunning defeat of communist parties by their rivals in the center and on the Right has made it nearly impossible to ask fundamental questions about the East European revolution.[4] Now the focus of historical inquiry is almost exclusively on the Soviet occupation, Stalinist manipulation of national politics, and the culpability of the West for allowing the Yalta "solution" in the first place. The historical model is transparent; a few Soviet puppets in each of the countries—encouraged by the NKVD and backed by the power and influence of the Red Army—successfully employed "salami tactics" (after the politics of Hungary's Matyas Rakosi) to capture free societies, halt the growth of democracy, and stunt the development of economic prosperity throughout eastern Europe. Western-style Cold War historiography, suppressed for so long in the countries of east central Europe, has come to dominate perceptions of the past.

The power of this Cold War model of recent East European history derives in good measure from its verisimilitude. Indeed, from one of the first western analyses of postwar East European history, Hugh Seton-Watson's brilliant *The East European Revolution*, to one of the most recent, Joseph Rothchild's *Return to Diversity*, the communist takeover of eastern Europe is seen as the inevitable result of the Soviet occupation of eastern Europe and the development of the Cold War.[5] Milovan Djilas's *Conversations with Stalin* serves as textual proof of the hypothesis that no other result in eastern Europe was possible. In a famous and often-cited passage, Djilas quotes Stalin: "This war is not as in the past; whoever occupies a territory also imposes on it his own social system. Everyone imposes his own system as far as his army can reach. It cannot be otherwise."[6]

The problem with this paradigm is that it obscures the origins of the socialist regimes of eastern Europe by reducing them—intentionally or not—to byproducts of Soviet power. It also implicitly understands the contemporary breakup of communist parties in eastern Europe as a return to the pristine, mythological "democratic" eastern Europe that would have emerged from the war if the Soviets had not moved in. Both Vaclav Havel in Czechoslovakia and Tadeusz Mazowiecki in Poland are marvellous symbols of this "return to the future,"

Havel as an ironic reincarnation of the philosopher-president Tomas Garrigue Masaryk and Mazowiecki as the classic nonparty Catholic conservative of the Sanacja era. The commonly told joke in eastern Europe and in the West that "socialism is the stage of development between capitalism and capitalism" reveals the same kind of thinking, that the past forty-five years has seen eastern Europe drawn down a false path by the Soviets. Now these ex-socialist countries, aided by the Americans and the European Community, can start afresh down their natural roads to capitalism and parliamentary democracy.

The fallacies of this kind of thinking are abundant. But in this chapter I will concentrate on the historical problem of the revolutions in eastern Europe in an attempt to understand better the origins of the regimes now being dismantled in the region. Part of my intention here is to redefine the chronology of the revolutionary experience. If one begins in 1944 and 1945 with the invasion and occupation of Soviet forces, then it is only natural to ignore the indigenous roots of the East European revolution. The social history of the revolutionary experience becomes overwhelmed by the sheer magnitude of Soviet power; the discontinuities between interwar and postwar eastern Europe— Soviets aside—are less apparent. This chapter argues that eastern Europe emerged from World War I in a revolutionary situation, to use the Leninist terminology if not the Leninist definition. Socialism and democracy were the watchwords of the day in 1945, not because of the presence of the Red Army and what came afterward, but because of what came before. Certainly the Soviet Union deeply influenced the evolution of the East European Left and with it the party and state structures that emerged from the chaos of the war. There is also no reason to ignore the important role the Soviets played in crushing democratic movements aimed at the partial restoration of prewar regimes, especially in Poland and Romania. But our understanding of the revolution that shakes eastern Europe today depends on an accurate analysis of the postwar period, one that includes the indigenous sources of socialism as well as the role of the Soviet occupiers.

In my view, the use of a particular set of terms to identify eastern Europe—southeastern Europe, east central Europe, and central Europe—is less important than keeping in mind the principle of great diversity within the region, especially during the immediate postwar period. In contradistinction to Stalinism, revolution is not a homogenizing experience. Moreover, the countries of eastern Europe had vastly different problems at the onset of the war. Some were allies of the Germans, some were enemies. As a result, they looked at Allied victory and Axis defeat through different eyes. Their social structures varied markedly, as did their levels of economic development. Their attitudes toward the Russians and toward the West related to the variety of cultures from country to country, indeed from people to people within the same countries. Their revolutions developed in the Soviet hothouse; their governments were later forced to mimic Soviet models. But these models quickly broke down, and the "return to diversity" in some senses brought eastern Europe full circle to the end of the war, despite the enormous social and economic changes fostered by communist rule.

The Old Regimes

On the eve of World War II, the countries of eastern Europe were dominated by dictators and semifeudal monarchies. Tsar Boris in Bulgaria, King Carol in Romania, Prince-Regent Paul in Yugoslavia, King Zog in Albania, and Admiral Horthy in Hungary controlled government activities, some more some less parliamentary, in a spirit of conservatism and nationalism. In Poland, the government of colonels and the decrepit remnants of *sanacja* looked on indifferently as Hitler took apart the only moderately "democratic" country in the region, Czechoslovakia. Vulturelike, the Poles moved in on the kill, annexing the Cieszyn territory. The conservative governments in eastern Europe were pressured by the forces of fascism, domestic and external, to curtail the already restricted rights of the Jews and to expand those of the Germans. Anti-Semitism was rife in the area; chauvinistic slogans increasingly dominated the language of politics. Freedom of expression was severely limited, and the political Left was forced into hiding, exile, or—at best—isolation and fragmentation. Government parties dominated politics, prearranged election results, and shared power with only the narrowest of bureaucratic and technocratic elites. Financial and industrial leaders joined government conservatives in an attempt to isolate (or co-opt) the radical Right, which showed signs, especially in Romania and Hungary, of leading a popular movement against the contemporary policies.

If the political life of eastern Europe had degenerated badly since the great hopes of parliamentary democracy in the immediate post-Versailles period, economic development had proceeded in fits and starts. The worldwide depression certainly inflicted severe wounds in eastern Europe. Some countries, like Poland and Hungary, took six or seven years to recover; others, like Bulgaria, were less severely affected.[7] Land reform had been delayed in countries like Hungary; where it was undertaken, in countries like Romania, it was often ineffective.[8] At least a third, if not more, of rural eastern Europe lived in desperate poverty caused in good measure by severe rural overpopulation. By the end of the 1930s, however, the countries of eastern Europe experienced an economic recovery, the result primarily of state investment in armaments and armaments-related industries. In some cases—Poland, Yugoslavia, and Hungary are the best examples—the managerial and technical elites had done their work well. New industries emerged on the outskirts of the capitals and in other large cities, drawing peasants to the urban work force. The percentage of industrial workers in the countries of eastern Europe grew rapidly at the end of the 1930s, accompanying the growth of GNP in many areas that continued until the German reversal at Stalingrad.[9]

Consequently, it would be inaccurate to conclude from the weaknesses of East European governments and societies that they were on the brink of revolution when the war broke out. If anything, the apparent triumphal march of fascism in the 1930s and the growing influence of German capital indicated the possibility of fascist-style takeovers rather than revolutions of the Left. At the same time, it is important to register the fact that these governments were thoroughly discredited in the eyes of a significant part of their populations even before the war broke out and before they were occupied by or allied to German military power. The process of capitulation to German pressure (or worse, of being subjected to German occupation) discredited the prewar governments even more. By the end of the war, large segments of the politically active elites now looked to socialism as a way to overcome the weaknesses of parliamentary democracy. The susceptibility of liberal democracy to coups d'etat and fascist influence was seen by the intelligentsia in particular as proof of the need for a new socialist system. Similarly, bourgeois capitalism had been thoroughly discredited among many members of these elites by its subservience to German military needs. As Eduard Benes put it, the wartime experience had made clear that even in Czechoslovakia the prewar system must be transformed "into something substantially changed," into "social and economic democracy."[10] The Hungarian radical democrat and historian Oscar Jaszi expressed much the same sentiment: "In

Hungary the road is open to really constructive experiments in so-cialization, since there are very few people there who would shed tears for that hybrid form of capitalism which amassed enormous profits by the ruthless exploitation of monopolistic positions."[11]

Social Upheaval

Socialist revolution was on the minds of workers and peasants as well as politicians and intellectuals. The harshness of peasants' lives dur-ing the war made radical land reform the center of their political am-bitions. Large landowners were perceived as having been the mainstay of conservative and fascist regimes. Indeed, sometimes they fled with the retreating German armies. Periodically, they were driven off their land by peasant committees or armed socialist activists. There were spontaneous land seizures, not to mention land grabs, like those in Silesia and Pomerania by Poles resettled from the eastern provinces, or in the Sudetenland, where Czechs seized German property. The re-maining owners of junker estates and of normal German farms spread out between Brandenburg and East Prussia were brutally handled by invading Soviet troops, who classified them as kulaks and *pomesh-chiki* (rural capitalists and gentry), by definition supporters of Hitler and the war.[12] The burgeoning political weight of the agrarian reform parties, like Ferenc Nagy's Smallholders party in Hungary, Stanislaw Mikolajczyk's Peasant party in Poland, or Nikola Petkov's Agrarian Union in Bulgaria, reflected the long-suppressed needs of peasants for land and political power. The cooperative movement—already well-established in many East European countries before the outbreak of the war—gained strong support in the countryside. "Collectivism" in a segment of the peasantry was so widespread that several Polish com-munists, for example, were worried that peasants might take unwar-ranted steps toward actual collectivization.[13]

The situation of workers in many ways paralleled that of the peas-ants. In some areas, especially in Moravia and Bohemia but also in the north of Hungary and in the Polish mines and textile centers like Lodz, workers had emerged from the war more powerful and better organ-ized than before.[14] The demands of the German war industry primed the growth of the economies of these and other similar regions of east-ern Europe. Often influenced by underground communists, social democrats, and syndicalist leaders, workers took their own fate increasingly in their own hands as the Germans retreated and Soviet troops advanced. They took over the factories, kept them going, and founded factory committees to run administration. In some cases, the workers chased off factory managers; in others, the owners and managers fled on their own. In short, in the factories as well as on the land, a popular revolution was taking place before and simultaneous to the Soviet invasion.[15] It is important to draw a balanced picture of these and other "revolutionary" activities. There were also many cases where local peasants defended their landlords against charges of "counterrevolutionary" activity or connivance with the Nazis. Even after some landowners were dispossessed, peasants tried to provide housing and upkeep for their former landlords. In the factories, too, workers sometimes protected their factories' owners from political persecution, coming to their defense for having treated them decently during the war.

Despite the highly differentiated treatment of factory proprietors and landowners by workers and peasants, the war deprived the former political classes of the countries of eastern Europe of much of their claims to legitimacy. Equally important, the war redefined the social bases of politics by its savage restructuring of the demographic structure of East European societies.[16] The small middle classes that did exist in these countries were completely rearranged by the Nazis' attack on and elimination of the vast majority of European Jewry. Equally important for the future of the East European middle class was the fact that Germans ceased to be welcome in eastern Europe with the retreat and then collapse of the forces of the Third Reich. Based on an ambiguous clause in the Potsdam agreement, Germans were hounded out of the Sudetenland, what was to become western Poland, Hungary, and the Yugoslav Voivodina. Wladyslaw Gomulka made it clear to his party comrades that the Germans must be forced to leave Polish-administered territory; otherwise, Polish claims would never be secure.[17] With the elimination of the Jews and the forced deportation of the Germans, eastern Europe was deprived of a good measure of its entrepreneurial, banking, and merchant activity outside the government sphere. Little wonder, write John Lampe and Marvin Jackson, that state planning seemed the only road to economic development in the postwar world, socialist ideology and Soviet influence aside.[18]

The situation of the native intelligentsia was not much better than the middle classes. Poland serves as the most shocking example of the fate of the intelligentsia, both under the Nazis and the Soviets. During the "fourth partition" of Poland from 1939 to 1941, the Nazis rounded up tens of thousands of teachers, doctors, and professors, shooting most and placing the rest in labor camps. During the same period, the Soviets deported some 1.25 million Polish citizens from "Poland's Western Belorussia and Western Ukraine" to Siberia and Central Asia.[19] In addition to the 4,500 Polish officers who were murdered in Katyn, and the ten thousand officers whose fate is still unknown (reports circulated that they were drowned in barges in the White Sea), at least half of the deportees perished by the end of the war. The destruction of the Polish intelligentsia culminated in the crushing of the Warsaw Uprising (June 1944), in which 20,000 Polish fighters were killed, not to mention more than 130,000 civilians. As if these terrible losses were not sufficient, the Soviets arrested and sometimes exiled or executed soldiers and especially officers of the underground Home Army (AK), some of whom continued to resist, others of whom were forced to "surrender" to the Red Army despite years of fighting the Nazis.[20]

Twenty percent of all Polish citizens were killed during the war—roughly three million Polish Jews and three million ethnic Poles. In Yugoslavia, fratricidal warfare took a tragic toll on the intelligentsia, especially, but also on the population as a whole. One out of ten Yugoslavs were killed in the war. Even in those countries like Hungary, where the numbers of deaths were not so dramatic, the traumatic human suffering caused by hunger and pillage cannot be underestimated.[21] Equally important for the development of the social bases of politics was the fact that the war uprooted tens of millions of East Europeans from their native towns and villages and propelled them across the European continent from Buzuluk, headquarters of the Anders Army in Central Asia, to London. They were sometimes called away as army recruits or driven away as forced labor in Germany or elsewhere in the Reich's vast economic system. They left as refugees from war zones or victims of the redrawing of borders. With some exceptions—the Bulgarians and Czechs come to mind as the most obvious—East Europeans belonged to nations in movement, under way for most of the war. If one out of every five Polish citizens died during the war, one out of four who remained alive ended up in a different place from where they started.[22] After the war, Edward Shils wrote that this displacement had a particularly negative impact on the morals and political judgment of youth.[23] Not dissimilarly, Gabriel Almond, writing from Berlin, noted the negative effects on the morality of young women in particular of the occupation by victorious Allied armies, and also—one might add—of the defeated German army.

The East European Revolution

Two political forces on the Marxist Left dominated socialist thinking during the war, both of which found considerable resonance among the local populations, but neither of which survived the Stalinization of East European communism. First, there were the so-called "sectarians," a term of opprobrium attached to communist revolutionaries by their more evolutionary opponents domestically and by their Soviet "betters" who treated them with skepticism, if not scorn. Sectarians were most prominent in those areas of eastern Europe—Yugoslavia, Albania, and Greece prominent among them—where revolutionary groups had fought the Nazis on their own and looked to begin a socialist transformation of the societies under their rule, duplicating the experience of the Soviet Union. Other sectarians could be found in areas of German-occupied eastern Europe where communications with comrades in Moscow were difficult and ideas about the postwar transformation could take place in isolation from Stalin's concerns about the maintenance of the Grand Alliance. Sectarianism was widespread, for example, in a number of surviving communist cells in Germany, in isolated pockets of Polish communist resistance—Krakow being the most prominent—as well as in Hungarian communist circles made up of the old fighters from the Bela Kun revolution. East of the Tisza River, revolutionary councils that formed in some towns were able to seize power. Party activists in Szeged called for the immediate establishment of the dictatorship of the proletariat.[24] East German communists asked their Soviet army comrades for guns and ammunition to start a revolutionary upheaval, like those they much admired in Greece and Yugoslavia.[25] The Polish sectarian Wlodzimierz Zawadzki (Jasny) took half-Polonized Jews into the Krakow town government and opposed cooperation with any noncommunist party. Polish and Hungarian sectarians called for the incorporation of their countries into the Soviet Union.[26]

The second important political trend on the Left was eventually labeled "revisionist" and "nationalist" by the Soviets and included communists and left-wing social democrats who looked to put an end to the fratricidal warfare on the Left that had so badly weakened resistance to the Nazis in Germany and to the various dictatorships in eastern Europe. In some cases, like that of the German socialists, common experiences in prison or concentration camps had forged a unified approach to problems of political organization and resistance. A large Buchenwald "League of Democratic Socialists"—made up both of communists and social democrats—called for the immediate disbanding of the two former parties, the SPD and KPD, in the name of a new German socialist party that would create a new socialist republic of Germany.[27] In the underground in Poland, Polish Workers' party leaders, like Wladyslaw Gomułka, looked to intensify cooperation with the PPS, especially its left wing, in order to pursue a "Polish road to socialism." It is important to point out that the communist programs at the end of the war were—for the most part—less radical than those of their social democratic counterparts, who often called for the immediate nationalization of land and industry.[28] On the other hand, communists were called by Moscow to much more modest programs of completing the democratic revolution and doing away with the remnants of fascism and feudalism. It seemed perfectly natural for social democrats and communists, then, to throw away the old banners of struggle on the Left, to new ones of a united front, even of unity.

It is also interesting to note that in both the cases of Poland and the Soviet Zone of Germany, the national-oriented communist parties—led temporarily by Gomułka in Poland and Anton Ackermann in Germany (Ulbricht stayed very much in the background until 1947)—attacked the "sectarians" and removed them from positions of power and influence. Competent administration, social solidarity, and good East-West relations demanded, they argued, the suspension of the class struggle and the crushing of revolutionary utopianism, that persistent "infantile disease" of the Left.[29] Once the sectarians had been completely removed from the scene, usually by being unwillingly absorbed into the growing administrative apparatus (like the German ultra-left) or excluded from power altogether (like the Bela Kun fighters), the national roads to socialism could be pursued without interference from the revolutionaries. For the immediate postwar period, this meant that the communist revolution would not be pursued at all. Rather, socialists, working carefully with the Soviets, would carry out the "bourgeois revolution" while insuring that potential opposition to Soviet power in eastern Europe would have little social or economic bases for a political future. Certainly the hope was widespread among national communists in east central Europe (here, the cases of southeastern Europe were somewhat different) that the Popular Front could be revived. Left and left liberal parties could merge in a coalition bloc and move slowly and progressively through the "new democracy" toward socialism.[30]

The Yugoslav, Albanian, and Greek cases were very different. In these countries, out of the reach of the Red Army, communist parties absorbed the sectarian spirit during the war and isolated revisionist opponents from power. The Yugoslav communists in particular chafed under the orders from Moscow to abandon their intention and practical steps to carry through the communist revolution to its completion. Instead, the Soviets insisted that they negotiate with the exile government in London, even to the point of bringing the king back to Yugoslavia. In fact, Tito, Djilas, Rankovic, and Kardelj kept to their goal of setting up a socialist government in Yugoslavia while conceding on a number of symbolic issues to the Soviets. In the Yugoslav leadership, Andrija Hebrang, who was committed to a revisionist-style alliance among Croat communists, Peasant party members, and social democrats, resisted the quickening internal measures of revolutionary transformation: summary tribunals, forced collectivization, nationalization, and the banning of opposition parties. During the Soviet-Yugoslav split, Hebrang and many of his supporters were imprisoned as "Cominformists"—Soviet agents in the Yugoslav party—when in fact their only "crime" was to support a popular front political alignment.[31]

The Counterrevolution

The first act of the Soviet-led counterrevolution in eastern Europe was to crush the sectarian Left and subsume the interests of revolution to those of administration, coalition, and the maintenance of alliance. The Soviets abandoned the Greek insurgents, refused to support Yugoslav claims to Trieste, and insisted on coalitions with peasant parties in Poland, Bulgaria, Hungary, and Romania. The powerful Czech Communist party, which received 38 percent of the votes in the free election of 1946, making it the largest single party in the country, was encouraged to follow parliamentary tactics and to shed revolutionary slogans. To be sure, in Czechoslovakia, as in other countries of east central Europe, critical ministries of the Interior and Defense were to be led by communists, or at least communists were to be close to the mechanisms of control. But outwardly, in any case, one could argue, as did Oscar Jaszi immediately after the war and Charles Gati more recently, that Hungary and Czechoslovakia especially could be seen as evolving in a "third way," allied neither with the Soviet nor the Western camps.[32]

But this possibility ended with the second act of the counterrevolution, in which the national communist parties, good coalition builders and purveyors of the idea of a gradual and peaceful path to socialism, were attacked by a new and powerful combination of sectarian rhetoric and an administrative hierarchy tied closely to the Soviets. In some ways, the situation resembled Stalin's seizure of power in the Soviet Union, where Stalin's opponents on the "Left" (Zinoviev, Kamenev, and Radek) were eliminated by his coalition with the "Right" (Bukharin, Rykov, and Tomsky), at which point Stalin used the bureaucracy to isolate and remove the Right. Stalinist bureaucrats in eastern Europe (Ulbricht in the Soviet Zone, Beirut in Poland, Rákosi in Hungary, Gheorgiu-Dej in Romania, and Chervenkov in Bulgaria) turned on the national communists (Ackerman in the Soviet Zone, Gomułka in Poland, Nagy in Hungary, and Kostov in Bulgaria) once the challenge on the Left had been eliminated.

The attack was launched, significantly enough, by the original sectarians, the Yugoslavs, who took up the cudgel against "national communism" at the first meeting of the Cominform held at Szklarska Poreba in September 1947. What was to have been a celebration of the strength of the Left in the coalitions of postwar Europe, East and West, turned into a denunciation of national roads to communism, cooperation with bourgeois parties, and a lack of vigilance in face of the imperialist enemy. The message to the revisionists was unambiguous; they stood in the way of revolutionary progress by not sufficiently following the model of the Soviet Union. There is considerable evidence that the attack by the Yugoslavs was coordinated by Andrei Zhdanov and his allies within the Soviet leadership. Power struggles among Stalin's leading lieutenants were endemic to the Soviet Union in the years after the war. In this case, Zhdanov's "two-camp" theory neatly fit the needs of the Yugoslavs and other "radicals" within the Soviet leadership, while the more moderate and evolutionary policies of Zhdanov's principle rival, Georgii Malenkov and his allies including the economic theorist Evgenii Varga, did not.[33] Moreover, by the summer of 1947, the growing anticommunist militancy of the Truman administration, manifested in part by the Marshall Plan, the Truman Doctrine, "containment," and the attack on communist participation in the French and Italian governments, only increased the appeal of the hard-line criticism of the "third way." Colonel Sergei Tiul'panov, political officer of the Soviet Military Administration in Germany and a radical ally of Zhdanov's, expressed the group's admiration for the Yugoslavs in the following terms: "Yugoslavia has already reached the other bank [the socialist revolution]; Bulgaria is taking the last few strokes to reach it; Poland and Czechoslovakia are about in the middle of the river, followed by Romania and Hungary, who have gone about a third of the way, while the Soviet Occupied Zone has just taken the first few strokes away from the bourgeois bank."[34]

Once the meeting at Szklarska Poreba was concluded, the attacks in the East European parties commenced. Gomułka was forced to engage in self-criticism and removed himself from party life because of "illness." The PPR in which he was so prominent was merged with elements of the PPS Left to form a new party, the Polish United Workers party (PZPR), which was to serve as the basis for the Stalinization of the Polish Left. Gomułka was fortunate, in the end, to have to spend only a few years in prison for his deviations. Moscow clearly indicated that he and other Polish national communists should be purged and perhaps even executed.[35] A barrier was put up as well on the "German road to socialism." Anton Ackermann was forced to recant, and Ulbricht pressured former SPD members of the SED to conform completely to the new "Moscow" line. Many fled to the West, fearing imprisonment or deportation to the USSR. In Hungary, Rakosi's famous "salami tactics" were applied deftly to the Smallholders party and the Hungarian social democrats, while in Bulgaria and Romania, the process of eliminating independent noncommunist political elements was completed. In Czechoslovakia, by February 1948, the communists fell in line with the new politics by carrying out a coup, seizing power, and methodically forcing the former democratic parties into a communist-led bloc.

The irony of the Yugoslav's position is ably analyzed in Ivo Banac's study *With Stalin against Tito*.[36] The same dogmatics who drove the national communists out of the international socialist movement for their revisionism now faced the wrath of the master because of their haughty claims to revolutionary parity. Tito—the arch-Stalinist—crossed his master because he had learned his lessons too well. Indeed, Tito had learned so well that all of Stalin's "finger-shaking," as Khrushchev put it, could not budge the Yugoslavs from the feeling that they had been unjustly maligned and once their true contribution to socialism was known, the merciless attacks from the Cominform and the Soviets would cease. While they pleaded their cause, the Yugoslavs continued to push forward their revolutionary transformation, in the process aiding the Greek sectarians in their war against the British and crushing domestic opposition under the slogan of the struggle against Cominformism.

Therefore, except in Yugoslavia, the counterrevolution succeeded. A new Stalinist uniformity was imposed over eastern Europe—brutal, mindless, and repressive. Stalin's "Short Course," *The History of the Communist Party of the Soviet Union (B)*, became the Bible for the counterrevolution; the chant became the same throughout eastern Europe:

> —The study of the heroic history of the Bolshevik Party arms us with a knowledge of the laws of social development and of the political struggle, with a knowledge of the motive forces of revolution.
> —Study of the history of the C.P.S.U. (B.) strengthens our certainty of the ultimate victory of the great cause of the Party of Lenin-Stalin, the victory of Communism throughout the world.[37]

Stalinism

In his superb study of the Soviet occupation of Poland from 1939 to 1941, *Revolution from Abroad*, Jan Gross discusses the ways in which Soviet power is able to break the back of society by its inherently destructive powers.[38] Stalinism appealed to society's ability to turn one institution against another, leaving neither standing. The atomization of the citizenry and the remarkably efficient demolition of civil society that Stalinism accomplished came from a brutal manipulation, inherent in the system, of the legal and illegal, moral and immoral, progressive and reactionary, turning peoples' values on their head and making day into night. This Stalinist system was turned loose on eastern Europe at the end of 1947 and the beginning of 1948 with disastrous results. Political parties that had been under pressure and forced to dodge and feint to keep their influence in society were now pulverized. Election campaigns, which already contained elements of civil war, now lost any resemblance to political contests.[39] Cultural diversity was eliminated—both within and to some extent among countries. Politics was reduced to pure administration. Opponents were severely treated. Everywhere, except in part in Yugoslavia, the Soviet model was copied in education, art, and theater, in architecture and science (especially Lysenkoism), in film and literature, in styles of work and even of family life. Each country of eastern Europe had its own Stakhanov, its own workers' emulation movement that harkened back to the ostensibly magnificent accomplishments of the first Soviet five-year plan and collectivization. Huge industrial projects were built across the landscape of eastern Europe; the enormous cakelike Stalinist architecture marked the skylines of the capitals.

It is important to point out that the Stalinization of eastern Europe differed in some measure from its Sovietization. In other words, the sources of Stalinization were sometimes domestic rather than Soviet. Each Communist party sought to acquire Stalin-like powers and used Stalinist principles to run their own countries. The call for great sacrifices was direct and personal within each country, justified by a Manichean view of the world that brought the enemy to the very doorstep, if not the hearth, of each household. But reconstruction did demand sacrifices, and most citizens of eastern Europe understood their necessity. Stalinism was also fed in eastern Europe by the huge social transformations that had occurred at the end of the war and the beginning of the peace. Great numbers of rough-hewn peasants had moved to the cities and were ready to work in the ranks of the bureaucracy and police without asking too many questions. Communist and socialist workers were willing and able to staff the new governments' ministries and agencies, raising themselves to new and unexpected social heights.[40] There were also the minorities, who hated the old regimes, suffered terribly at the hands of the Nazis, and were ready to join the "army of the future—the Communist party."

Jews in particular showed up in notably large numbers in communist parties. In Hungary, Charles Gati writes, 70 to 80 percent of the political police were Jewish, and "most of the reliable [communist] cadres available after 1944–45 were of Jewish background," including Rákosi, Gerő, Farkas, Vas, Gábor Péter, Márton Horváth, and others.[41] In their determination to shed a past tainted with anti-Semitism and discrimination, Jewish communists threw themselves with abandon into the new Stalinist faith. Like Trotsky, who once replied "I am a Social Democrat" to the question of whether he was a Jew, these Jewish communists felt very little attraction to their heritage and religion. Also like Trotsky, they aroused intense resentment among both noncommunist victims of the new regimes and communist rank-and-file members, who saw the Jews as servants of Stalin and betrayers of national communism. The widespread perception in Poland, for example, that Polish Jews sympathized with the Soviets and welcomed them to Poland in 1939–41 as well as in 1944–45, gave rise to the image of *Zydo-kommuna* (the Jew-communist), who served willingly in the secret police as agents and torturers.[42] Popular anti-Semitism was inflamed by these perceptions, and pogroms broke out in 1946 in Hungary (Kunmadaras and Miskolc), in Romania (Jassy), and in Poland (Krakow, Rzeszow, Tarnow, Sosnowiec, and Kielce). In the case of the Kielce pogrom, the most notorious of several dozen that occurred in Poland, an accusation of kidnapping and blood libel set off a crowd of several thousand Poles who attacked a building full of recently returned Jewish refugees and internees, killing forty-seven and wounding many more.[43] Considerable evidence exists that in Kielce as well as the pogroms in Hungary at least some members of the party and police hierarchy were not unsympathetic to the expressions of popular resentment against the Jews.[44] In any case, the postwar pogroms only further convinced the Jews in the party of the need for an iron hand, for Stalinism.

Perhaps the greatest social ally of Stalinism in eastern Europe was apathy and indifference, born of upheaval, rootlessness, and the general poverty of politics that the war and its aftermath seemed to reaffirm. There was also intense physical misery and hunger in eastern Europe after the war. The population had been turned into masses of often homeless beggars; politics were not foremost on their minds. What the Germans didn't take away, the Soviets did. It was little consolation to the Poles, Hungarians, and Romanians that the herds being driven off to the East were intended to feed the Soviet population, which was even more destitute than their new East European "friends." Certainly, the plundering Soviet soldiers increased the resentment of the local populations against the Soviet Union. The widespread incidence of violence and rape would not easily be forgotten by the victims in Budapest, Berlin, or the Voivodina. But the violence and anarchy at the end of the war and beginning of the peace also created a desperate need for order among the population. Many displaced people were uninterested in the work of reconstruction. Stalinism was seen as a way to force them to participate. The very helplessness of society made Stalinism all the more appealing.

With the leadership of the far Left crushed and the more plausible programs of the national communists in disgrace and retreat, Stalinism filled the gaping void with a ready-made political structure and organization. In other words, like the onset of socialism in eastern Europe, the domination of East European Stalinism should not be attributed solely to Soviet insistence. Still, the argument should not be overstated. In the main, Stalinism came to eastern Europe because the representatives of Soviet power in the region, the Red Army, the political and police organs (NKVD/MVD), and the political authorities found it the most conducive method of creating friendly allies and passive populations.

Afterword

From the widespread and nearly total defeat of "mature socialism" throughout eastern Europe, it is hard to imagine that the socialist impulse after the war could ever have led to positive results. The argument I have made here is that for better or worse it never had a chance. This derived primarily from two factors. First, the Soviets crushed the sectarians and the national communists because of their own immediate needs, showing little interest—one has to conclude—in the spread of forms of the socialist system that might in any way differ from, or more importantly rival, their own. Second, Stalinism within the native parties exerted an appeal to the demoralized, displaced, and often apolitical populations of eastern Europe. These populations were deprived by the war of their natural leaders; they were remade socially and demographically by border changes, forced migrations, and the displacement of large segments of their co-nationals. The prewar system had failed; the Soviet Union under the "Great Helmsman" had won the war. Stalinism was not just an alien phenomenon imposed by the hegemon of the East on the countries of eastern Europe. It responded to the social and political needs of these societies as they emerged from the war and the upheaval it fostered.

Imposed from the outside and part of the internal political struggle among communists, the product of Soviet overlordship and of the social ambitions and lack of ambitions of diverse segments of East European society, Stalinism dominated East European socialism from 1949 until 1955–56, with remnants lasting until only a short time ago. Stalinism completed the counterrevolution, wiping out any initiatives on the part of groups in society looking to improve the organization of labor and production. Destructive forced collectivization was introduced. Small businesses were expropriated; the service sector disappeared into state-run conglomerates. "Socialist emulation" ruined the rational division of labor and organization of work. The art of politics was reduced to sloganeering. East Europeans were force-fed indigestible Soviet cultural and social norms, and the Cold War cut off eastern Europe from economic and cultural developments in the West.

Like the beginnings of Stalinization, the breakup of East European Stalinism derived primarily from circumstances in the Soviet Union, in this case from the death of Stalin in March 1953 and the subsequent confusion and political struggles among his lieutenants over the appropriate course of de-Stalinization. But specific East European conditions tested the limits of de-Stalinization more forcefully than in the Soviet Union, where the Communist party remained firmly in control and the habits of almost a half-century of communism were harder to break. While sectarianism in eastern Europe seems to have suffered a permanent defeat in 1944–45, revisionist ideas lived long enough to inspire a spirited revival in 1956 of national communism and "socialism with a human face." Unfortunately, the replacement of Stalinist politicians by national communists of the traditional sort, like Wladyslaw Gomułka in Poland or János Kádár in Hungary, proved to be a bitter disappointment for intellectuals and workers who had gone into the streets in 1956. Government-sponsored national communism seemed to be transparently tactical, cynically using national symbols and idioms to keep communist parties in power. The one exception might have been the 1968 Prague Spring, which seemed capable of re-creating the social and political democracy Beneš called for in 1945. But the Soviet invasion and the enunciation of the Brezhnev Doctrine saw to it that the autocratic manipulation of political and military power would crush any resurgence of democratic socialism in eastern Europe. Equally important, the communist parties themselves seemed to return almost naturally to an equilibrium of administration and control, the kind of equilibrium that destroyed socialism in eastern Europe in the first place.

Stalinism had destroyed the ability of the communist parties in eastern Europe to move beyond the immediate concerns of administration and control. However, despite its enormously destructive power, Stalinism, in the end, had worked imperfectly. East European intellectuals could swallow one frog and maybe a second, Czeslaw Milosz wrote, but not the third.[45] In some cases, like that of Poland, East European peasants had resisted collectivization; in others, like Hungary and Czechoslovakia, they turned the collective farms to their own benefit. The Church withstood splitting tactics of the communist governments, especially in Poland and Czechoslovakia, and soon would create the institutional bases for social resistance, in the Protestant GDR, as well as in predominantly Catholic countries. Perhaps most interesting in this connection is the extent to which East European workers—whether in Berlin in 1953, in Poznan and Budapest in 1956, or on the Baltic Coast in 1970—turned their ostensible "leading role" in society into a rationalization for strike action. The culmination of this process, the formation of Solidarity in 1976, and its remarkable revolution of 1980 demonstrated that Stalinism had created the conditions for its own demise, a large and active industrial working class that took the promises of socialism and "peoples democracy" at face value. Although, in the end, the rebellion of the workers turned against the communist government and all the symbols and trappings of "socialism," many of Solidarity's articles of faith, and those of workers' groups throughout eastern Europe, have socialist underpinnings that derive in part from forty-five years of a communist system.

Still, if socialization was on everyone's mind in 1945, privatization is the watchword of 1990. Capitalism and parliamentary democracy have captured the imagination of the revolutionary leaders of 1989, just as socialism and the needs of rebuilding dominated the East European consciousness of the immediate postwar period. Stalinism dealt the postwar experiment a death blow. One can hope that the social concerns of 1945 will not be forgotten by the new revolutionaries; otherwise, their experiment, too, will be doomed to failure.

Notes

1. George Konrád, *The Loser*, translated from Hungarian by Ivan Sanders (San Diego: Harcourt Brace Jovanovich, 1982); Sreten Zujovic, Crni (1941), cited in (and translated by) Ivo Banac, *With Stalin against Tito: Cominformist Splits in Yugoslav Communism* (Ithaca: Cornell University Press, 1988), p. 3; Tadeusz Konwicki, *The Polish Complex*, translated from Polish by Richard Lourie (New York: Farrar Straus Giroux, 1981).

2. Many of these kinds of questions have been asked by Iurii Nikolaevich Afanas'ev, rector of the Moscow State Historical Archive Institute, specialist on the October Revolution, and member of the Congress of People's Deputies. See, for example, his "The Agony of the Stalinist System," in *Voices of Glasnost: Interviews with Gorbachev's Reformers*, ed. Stephen F. Cohen and Katrina Vanden Heuvel (New York: W. W. Norton, 1989), pp. 97–115.

3. See, for example, the long-awaited (and much disputed) volume 9 of

German History, published by the Academy of Sciences of the GDR: *Deutsche Geschichte*, vol. 9: *Die antifaschistischdemokratische Umwaelzung, der Kampf gegen die Spaltung Deutschlands und die Entstehung der DDR von 1945 bis 1949*, ed. Ralf Badstuebner et al. (Berlin: VEB Deutscher Verlag der Wissenschaften, 1989).

4. Among the most interesting historians at work on the East European revolutions are Krystyna Kersten in Poland and Guenter Benser in the GDR. See, for example, Kersten, *Narodziny systemu wladzy 1943–1948* (Paris: Libella, 1986), and Benser, *Die KPD im Jahre der Befreiung* (Berlin: Dietz, 1985).

5. Hugh Seton-Watson, *The East European Revolution* (New York: F. A. Praeger, 1965); Joseph Rothschild, *Return to Diversity: A Political History of East Central Europe since World War II* (New York: Oxford University Press, 1989).

6. Milovan Djilas, *Conversations with Stalin*, trans. Michael B. Petrovich (New York: Harcourt Brace Jovanovich, 1962), p. 114.

7. Ivan T. Berend and Gyorgy Ranki, *Economic Development in East Central Europe in the Nineteenth and Twentieth Centuries* (New York: Columbia University Press, 1974), pp. 251–52.

8. John R. Lampe and Marvin R. Jackson, *Balkan Economic History, 1550–1950: From Imperial Borderlands to Developing Nations* (Bloomington: Indiana University Press, 1982), pp. 352–56.

9. See Joseph Rothschild, *East Central Europe between the Two World Wars* (Seattle: University of Washington Press, 1974), pp. 68–69, 188–90, 276; see also E. A. Radice, "Economic Developments in Eastern Europe under German Hegemony," in *Communist Power in Europe 1944–1949*, ed. Martin McCauley (Savage, Md.: Barnes and Noble Books, 1977), pp. 16–20.

10. Eduard Beneš, "Postwar Czechoslovakia," *Foreign Affairs*, no. 24 (April 1946): 407.

11. Oscar Jaszi, "The Choices in Hungary," *Foreign Affairs*, no. 24 (April 1946): 465.

12. See *Weissbuch ueber die "Demokratische Bodenreform" in der Sowjetischen Besatzungszone Deutschlands: Dokumente und Berichte*, new and expanded ed. (Berlin: E. Vogel, 1988); see also M. K. Dziewanowski, ed., *Poland Today as Seen by Foreign Observers* (London: Polish Freedom Movement, 1946), p. 15, and Norman Davies, "Poland," in *Communist Power in Europe*, ed. McCauley, p. 44.

13. Antony Polonsky and Boleslaw Drukier, eds., *The Beginnings of Communist Rule in Poland* (London: Routledge and Kegan Paul, 1980), p. 432.

14. See Kersten, *Narodziny systemu wladzy*, pp. 134–35.

15. For the East German case, see Gregory W. Sandford, *From Hitler to Ulbricht: The Communist Reconstruction of East Germany 1945–46* (Princeton: Princeton University Press, 1983), p. 73; on Yugoslavia, see N. I. Kasatkin, "Rabochii kontrol' v iugoslavii v pervye gody narodno-demokraticheskoi vlasti," *Slavianskoe slavianovedenie*, no. 1 (1986): 21–23.

16. See Ernest Gellner, "Ethnicity and Faith in Eastern Europe," *Daedalus* 119 (Winter 1990): 291; see also Jan T. Gross's suggestive "Social Consequences of War: Preliminaries to the Study of the Imposition of Communist Regimes

in East Central Europe," *East European Politics and Societies* 3 (Spring 1989): 198–214.

17. For example, in a speech to the plenum of the PPR Central Committee, May 20–21, 1945, Gomułka said, "We must expel all the Germans because countries are built on national lines and not on multi-national ones," in *The Beginnings of Communist Rule in Poland*, ed. Polonsky and Drukier, p. 425.

18. Lampe and Jackson, *Balkan Economic History*, pp. 573–74; see also Gross, "Social Consequences of the War," pp. 201–2.

19. See Jan T. Gross, *Revolution from Abroad: The Soviet Conquest of Poland's Western Ukraine and Western Belorussia* (Princeton: Princeton University Press, 1988).

20. On the Polish losses in this period, see Norman Davies, *God's Playground: A History of Poland*, vol. 2: *1795 to the Present* (New York: Columbia University Press, 1984), pp. 439, 451–52.

21. Ferenc Nagy, *The Struggle Behind the Iron Curtain* (New York: Macmillan, 1948), p. 80.

22. Kersten, *Narodziny systemu wladzy*, p. 132; see also Stefan Banasiak, "Settlement of the Polish Western Territories in 1945–1947," *Polish Western Affairs* 1, no. 6 (1965): 149.

23. Friedrich Ebert Stiftung, Gniffke Nachlass, 7/3 (22), October 11, 1945.

24. Sagvani, "Popular Organs," p. 243; Charles Gati, *Hungary and the Soviet Bloc* (Durham: Duke University Press, 1986), p. 84.

25. Benser, *Die KPD im Jahre der Befreiung*, pp. 189–90, 363 n. 432.

26. Polonsky and Drukier, eds., *The Beginnings of Communist Rule in Poland*, pp. 97, 441, 450–51. These party documents indicate that in the spring of 1945 the rank and file of the PPR was "very prone to 'left-wing extremism.'"

27. Benser, *Die KPD im Jahre der Befreiung*, pp. 80–81.

28. See, for example, Polonsky and Drukier, eds., *The Beginnings of Communist Rule in Poland*, p. 25; *Za antifashistskuiu demokraticheskuiu Germaniiu: Sbornik dokumentov 1945–1949 gg.* (Moscow: Politizdat, 1969), p. 67; Norman Davies, "Poland," in *Communist Power in Europe 1944–1949*, ed. McCauley, p. 48; and Karel Kaplan, *The Short March: The Communist Takeover in Czechoslovakia, 1945–1948* (London: C. Hurst, 1987), p. 34. Here, Kaplan cites the October 1945 platform of the Czech social democrats, typical of SD platforms in eastern Europe: "Our mission was not and is not to reform the capitalist order, but to abolish this order, as the main cause of all the poverty that the population suffers."

29. Gomułka was later criticized by the party for his excessive attacks against sectarianism. Jakub Andrezejewski, ed., *Gomułka i inni: Dokumenty z archiwum KC 1948–1982* (London: Aneks, 1986), pp. 10–11. For the Germans, see Siegfried Thomas, "Der Wiederbeginn des politischen Lebens in Berlin und die Aktionseinheit der Arbeiterparteien (Mai-Juli 1945)," *Zeitschrift fuer Geschichtswissenschaft* 8, no. 6 (1960): 320, 323–24.

30. See, for example, Anton Ackermann, "Gibt es einen besonderen deutschen Weg zum Sozialismus?" *Einheit*, no. 1 (1946): 23–32.

31. Banac, *With Stalin against Tito*, pp. 14–17, 86–89. On Greek militancy and Soviet gradualism, see Peter J. Stavrakis, *Moscow and Greek Communism 1944–1949* (Ithaca: Cornell University Press, 1989), pp. 125–28.

32. Jaszi, "The Choices in Hungary," p. 454; Gati, *Hungary and the Soviet Bloc*, pp. 4–6.

33. See Werner Hahn, *Postwar Soviet Politics: The Fall of Zhdanov and the Defeat of Moderation 1946–1953* (Ithaca: Cornell University Press, 1982); Jerry F. Hough, "Debates about the Postwar World," in *The Impact of World War II on the Soviet Union*, ed. Susan J. Linz (London: Roman and Allenheld, 1985); William O. McCagg, Jr., *Stalin Embattled* (Detroit: Wayne State Press, 1978); and especially Gavriel D. Ra'anan, *International Policy Formation in the USSR* (Hamden, Conn.: Shoe String Press, 1983).

34. Wolfgang Leonhard, *Child of the Revolution* (Washington, D.C.: H. Regnery, 1958), pp. 495–96, as cited in Ra'anan, *International Policy Formation*, p. 97.

35. M. K. Dziewanowski, *The Communist Party of Poland: An Outline of History*, 2d ed. (Cambridge: Harvard University Press, 1976), pp. 208–14.

36. Banac, *With Stalin against Tito*, pp. 117–42.

37. A Commission of the CC of the CPSU (B), ed., *The History of the Communist Party of the Soviet Union (Bolsheviks): Short Course* (London: Cobbett Publishers Unlimited, 1938), p. xiv.

38. Gross, *Revolution from Abroad*, pp. 125–26, 231–39.

39. M. K. Dziewanowski, *Poland in the Twentieth Century* (New York: Columbia University Press, 1977), p. 251.

40. Kersten, *Narodziny systemu wladzy*, p. 137.

41. Gati, *Hungary and the Soviet Bloc*, p. 100.

42. Yisrael Gutman and Shmuel Krakowski, *Unequal Victims: Poles and Jews During World War Two* (New York: Holocaust Publications, 1986), pp. 367–69.

43. Gutman and Krakowski, *Unequal Victims*, p. 370.

44. Gati, *Hungary and the Soviet Bloc*, pp. 102–3; also on Hungary, see Nagy, *The Struggle Behind the Iron Curtain*, pp. 246–47. On the communists and the Kielce pogrom, see Stefan Korbonski, *Warsaw in Chains*, trans. Norbert Guterman (Winchester, Mass.: Allen and Unwin, 1959), p. 122.

45. Czeslaw Milosz, *The Captive Mind*, 3d ed. (New York: Random House, 1981), pp. xii–iii.

The Crisis of Socialism in Central and Eastern Europe and Socialism's Future

Sharon L. Wolchik

Given the dramatic developments that have occurred throughout central and eastern Europe since 1989, the question of the crisis of socialism in the region has outgrown the terms in which it was defined at the outset of this project. The task of accounting for the crisis, however, still retains its importance. To this task one must now add explanation of the sudden collapse of communist rule itself throughout much of the region. This collapse and the results of multiparty elections held in 1989 and 1990 suggest that the future of socialism in the region as a system of government, a political movement, or a body of ideas is far dimmer than could have been anticipated prior to 1989.

The pages to follow, then, will explore two primary issues. The first of these is the question of why socialism, in its communist variant, failed so miserably in central and eastern Europe. The second is the future of socialism in the region. In the current circumstances, this question is very closely related to another, the future of democracy.

The Origins of the Crisis of Socialism in Central and Eastern Europe

The crisis of socialism in central and eastern Europe was illustrated most graphically by the events of 1989. Beginning with the January agreement in principle of the Hungarian party leadership and opposition to negotiate and ending with the Christmas Day executions of Nicolae and Elena Ceauşescu in Romania, elite negotiations, elections, and mass popular protests brought about the collapse of communist governments throughout much of the region. By the end of 1989, communist-dominated governments retained a firm hold on power only in Albania and Yugoslavia, and in the latter country, the party's monopoly on power had been challenged successfully in Slovenia. The impact of these developments, whose details are by now well known, in turn changed the entire shape of the international order that prevailed since the end of World War II.

Although the crisis came to a head in 1989, its roots stretch far back into the history of communist rule in central and eastern Europe. The dramatic events of 1989 resulted from both international and national factors. Of these, international influences have received the most attention from Western observers. Thus, changes in such countries as Poland and Hungary that were at the forefront and, ultimately, changes in the Soviet Union's domestic policies and its policies in regard to central and eastern Europe served as critical catalysts for change in those countries that had lagged behind. The increased importance of mass communications and the greater accessibility of information across international boundaries also played a key role in keeping Central and East Europeans informed of developments elsewhere, and thus contributed to the impact of the demonstration effect.[1]

As I have argued in other contexts,[2] the nature of the crisis, as well as the unfolding of events in 1989, were also influenced in important ways by factors particular to individual countries. First, the influence of domestic factors is evident in the different ways in which communist regimes fell. The ability of the opposition to bring about the end of the Communist party's monopoly of power by negotiation in Hungary and by the ballot box in Poland, for example, reflected the greater freedom of organization and action for independent activists in Hungary and Poland as well as the decade-long existence of Solidarity in Poland. The lack of a strong reformist faction in the East German and Czechoslovak parties and the failure of those regimes to take any but the most halting steps toward reform before late 1989 were factors that encouraged opponents of those regimes to take to the streets in massive numbers in 1989. Similarly, the extremely brutal nature of the repressive, personalized dictatorship of Nicolae Ceauşescu had its parallel in the violent nature of its overthrow.

The many ways in which the communist systems of central and eastern Europe differed from each other were also evident in the extent and shape of the opposition to the government before the fall of the old regimes and in the forces working for change within particular countries. These differences, as well as other important differences in levels of development, cultural orientations, and values and attitudes toward politics derived from the precommunist legacies of these countries, continue to be reflected in the pattern of party organization and in the political movements that have emerged in the region. They also condition the prospects for a successful transition to democracy.

Although national differences in these respects are extremely important and significant variations exist in the causes and nature of the crisis in particular countries, a number of common elements run through the region. One of the major problems of the Stalinist model of economic development, social transformation, and political change imposed in the name of communist elites in central and eastern Europe after 1948 was the lack of attention to the many underlying differences between Soviet and Central and East European reality; however, many of its elements proved problematic wherever they were implemented.

The major weaknesses of this model have been appreciated by Western analysts, as well as by Central and East European critics, since Stalin's death, if not earlier. In fact, discussion of the problematic aspects of this form of social, economic, and political organization comprised the dominant part of Western scholarship on the region. The most glaring failings of the communist system as it existed in central and eastern Europe, then, were well recognized and cataloged.

From their leaders perspectives, the Stalinist model initially appeared to have a number of important advantages over competing methods of promoting political and economic change and social transformation. Thus, it allowed the leaders of the communist parties to take ruthless but seemingly effective action to destroy the old political, social, and economic order. Measures designed to limit the political power of actual or potential opponents of the new order were supplemented by policies that, either by design or in actuality, eliminated the economic base of the opposition and prevented representatives of the old ruling groups from passing their advantages on to their offspring. As Kenneth Jowitt argues in his study of these policies in Romania, communist elites appeared to have achieved a "revolutionary breakthrough," that is, to have made the return to the old order impossible.[3]

The model's emphasis on harnessing all aspects of life to political ends—reflected in the effort to politicize all areas of life from the workplace, to culture, to leisure—also allowed the mobilization and concentration of the nation's resources to achieve articulated goals.

In certain cases, communist leaders also achieved a certain degree of national integration. In the Balkans, for example, which were largely agrarian societies with high levels of illiteracy before the institution of communist systems, large numbers of citizens did not become aware of being part of a larger, national community and polity until the communist period. Finally, particularly before the death of Stalin and subsequent de-Stalinization measures, the terror and police control associated with the model seemed for a time to provide a reliable, if costly, answer to the issue of political control.

In its early phases, the Stalinist model associated with communist rule in the region also seemed to have a number of economic advantages. The ambitious programs of industrialization and rapid growth targets of the early communist years initially yielded favorable results in many Eastern and Central European countries, particularly in those that were least developed before the institution of communist rule. These results were accompanied by an increase in social mobility and by social changes, both planned and unintended, that markedly increased the urbanization levels and complexity of many of these societies. Changes in the educational levels of the population and labor force were further positive results.[4]

However, the weaknesses of the model and the form of political and economic organization derived from it soon outweighed its advantages in the eyes of both those who lived under it and those who observed it from outside. From a political perspective, these problems were particularly great during the Stalinist period, when the high cost of terror in both human and political terms was most evident. Thus, although the model seemed to allow effective control of the population and the elimination of actual and potential threats to the power of the ruling elite, it achieved these goals only at the cost of alienating and atomizing the population. Similarly, the breakup of old social and political structures, as well as the disruption of many patterns of behavior and attitudes favorable to the old system that the model fostered, were accompanied by social disruption and the creation of new social problems. Further, the communist system was notoriously weak in reintegrating the population into new institutions and in fostering acceptance of new patterns of behavior. Its ability to promulgate new political and other values and attitudes was similarly limited.[5] the system's disregard for legal norms and capricious use of justice had certain advantages from the perspective of the elites, but, ultimately, these features undermined the morality of communist societies; they also led to widespread evasion of the law. A final cost of the model was its heavy reliance on terror and coercion. This aspect of the system was most noticeable during the Stalinist period, but it was also evident in later periods, as force, whether exercised by domestic actions or foreign armies, was the final guarantee of the party's monopoly of power.[6]

The economic costs of the model also soon became evident. These deficiencies, which have also been cataloged extensively, appeared first in the more developed economies. Eventually, they came to characterize the performance of economies that were initially at lower levels of development. Thus, sooner or later an imbalanced pattern of investment, disregard for the resource base of particular countries, and extensive strategy of economic growth led to declining economic performance. Other costs of central planning that soon became endemic in the region included the lack of appropriate incentives for managers or workers, which resulted in poor work morale and labor productivity, as well as in poor-quality goods that could not compete on the world market, an inability to gauge the true cost of products, and increasing disproportions between demand and supply of essential goods. The failures of the model became increasingly evident as the means of extensive economic growth were exhausted. The obstacles to innovation and accurate information built into the central planning mechanism in turn were reflected in the increasing technology gap between central and eastern Europe and the West European and many Far Eastern countries.[7] Other costs of the model included the growth of corruption and the practice of evading the official economy by working, selling, and buying in the second, black, or gray economies that burgeoned in all of these countries.[8] The slowing of social mobility and other results of declining economic performance in turn removed one of the main supports for the system and undermined the political formula used to ensure mass compliance with, if not acceptance of, the political system.[9]

The decrease in overt use of force that occurred after the death of Stalin was accompanied by an effort to make the institutions and policies of the ruling elites correspond more closely to the underlying conditions in individual Central and East European states. It was also accompanied by a shift in the formula of rule in many of these countries. In contrast to the heavy reliance on coercion to keep the population in line during the Stalinist period, most Central and East European communist leaders in the post-Stalin era came to rely on a combination of material improvements and the selective use of coercion. In certain cases, as in Romania after the mid-1960s, they attempted to gain greater legitimacy by attempting to link communism to national traditions and sentiments.[10] In others, they attempted to achieve this goal by fostering somewhat greater opportunities for participation and consultation of the population.[11]

These changes were also accompanied by a shift in the perceptions of many Western analysts concerning the nature of these systems, particularly their ability to change. Following changes in Central and East European, and also Soviet, reality, Western analysts elaborated new models of politics that recognized division and disunity within the ruling elite and eventually encompassed the numerous independent groups or groupings that became evident in many of these societies.[12] In the last decade of communist rule, efforts were also made to apply corporatist models and insights derived from political economy and the study of policymaking in other societies.[13]

Despite these changes, and below the increasing diversity in many of the policies of leaders in individual Central and East European countries, the essential characteristics of the system remained unchanged. In the political realm, these included the continued monopoly of effective political power by the Communist party, official prohibition of organized opposition or independent groups (although these grew in number in many of these countries and were tolerated on a de facto basis in several), censorship, and the subordination of governmental organs, the legal system, and the courts to the will and direction of the Communist party. In the economic realm, there was more variation in policies and also in the extent to which these systems remained centralized or decentralized. However, in all, the party controlled economic policies, and in all, with the exception of Yugoslavia, the central planning apparatus continued to exercise a good deal of control. Even in those countries such as Poland and Hungary, where some degree of economic decentralization was achieved before 1989, the central planning authorities continued to make many important economic decisions and the role of market forces remained circumscribed. The chronic and sometimes acute economic crises that ensued from these organizational principles in turn exacerbated the political difficulties of communist regimes in the region.

Yugoslavia was, of course, an early exception in some respects to both of these patterns. However, despite the many differences in the way the political system worked in Yugoslavia, the party, although itself fragmented along republic lines, maintained its monopoly of power until 1990. Although the limits of debate were much broader and the range of activities that authorities viewed as dissent was far smaller, the party retained in principle, and at times exercised in practice, the right to control information. Similarly, although the decentralization of the economy proceeded to the extent that any central decisions were difficult to make before the modest and evidently temporary increase in the powers of the federal government in the 1980s, private ownership remained extremely limited.[14]

The economic and political crises in many of these states increased throughout the 1970s and 1980s. As the bookshelves full of works on Poland in crisis and numerous studies of other countries written during this period illustrate, Western analysts and internal critics clearly perceived deep and fundamental problems in the organization of political life and in the economies.[15]

On the economic side, international factors, particularly the effects of the oil crisis in the West in the mid-1970s, had a delayed but real impact on economic performance in the region. The impact of these factors was greatest in countries such as Poland, Hungary, and Yugoslavia that were most integrated into the world economy. It was also felt most severely by the countries that had borrowed most heavily from the West. But international trends eventually had a negative effect even in those countries such as Czechoslovakia and Bulgaria, where external economic relations remained largely confined to the socialist world.[16]

The political repercussions of economic crises were most clearly reflected in Poland, where the political instability evident throughout the 1970s and early 1980s gave way to an uneasy standoff between the regime and the population during much of the 1980s. But deepening economic crises and the evident inability of communist leaderships and their experts to stem them also eroded public acceptance of the communist system elsewhere in the region. These factors were instrumental, for example, in the unraveling of the celebrated Kadar compromise between the regime and the population in Hungary in the late 1980s.[17] They also undermined the tenuous support for the regime that existed in Czechoslovakia after 1968.[18]

The deepening economic and political crises also led to the emergence of forces working for change in many Central and East European countries. In some cases reformist forces arose within the ruling parties themselves. The difficulties arising from the party's monopoly of power, the *nomenklatura* system, and the primacy of political criteria in many areas of life were recognized by some of the more reformist political leaders. Coupled with economic failure, and in some cases popular discontent, this recognition led to attempts at reform in Poland and Hungary. The risks of such attempts were illustrated clearly by earlier efforts at reform, including those in Hungary and Poland in 1956, Czechoslovakia in 1968, and Poland in the 1980s. The so-called "lessons" from these crises and, perhaps, the perception that even had they succeeded these efforts would have proved insufficient to stem the demands for change in their societies served to prevent more dramatic efforts at change in many of the other countries in the region. Nonetheless, by the mid-1980s, the extent of the economic and political crises in several countries was such that fear of the consequences of not attempting to reform eventually proved greater than fear of failing to control the process.[19]

Reform efforts that political elites initiated were given added impetus in some cases by mounting pressure from below. These pressures were particularly widespread in Poland and Hungary, where independent activities by intellectuals, including samizdat publishing, sessions of alternative ("flying") universities, unauthorized performances of plays in the form of apartment theater, the formation of unauthorized and technically illegal clubs and groups, and participation in unauthorized public protests, demonstrations, and commemorations were widespread.[20] In Yugoslavia, the political leadership tolerated such activities quite openly, particularly in the more progressive northern republics.

In the other countries in the region, independent activists and members of the opposition worked under much harsher conditions. In Czechoslovakia, for example, signatories and spokespersons of Charter 77, the primary dissident group, were routinely interrogated, and they and their families suffered serious penalties. The authorities also dealt harshly with other independent activists, including unorthodox or unofficial artists, performers, writers, and publishers. Conditions were similarly poor for the expression of dissent or nonconformity in Romania, East Germany, and Bulgaria, as well as in Albania.[21]

However, despite the high cost of dissent, dissident movements developed and continued to gain support throughout the 1980s. In

Czechoslovakia, older dissidents centered around Charter 77 and the Committee for the Defense of the Unjustly Persecuted (VONS), and they were joined in the late 1980s by younger activists, including students and young workers. Less cautious than their elders in certain respects, these young people founded many of the new independent groups that arose between 1987 and November 1989; they also took the lead in organizing the unauthorized protests and commemorations that occurred with increasing frequency during that period. Religious dissent, expressed by participation in pilgrimages and also religious observance, which the regime defined as dissent, also increased markedly.

As I have argued elsewhere, to some extent these activities represented a continuation of the trends evident in Czechoslovakia after the formation of the Charter in 1977. However, there were also a number of new elements.[22] In addition to the greater numbers of individuals involved, there were also other important changes, including the greater involvement of young people and the more openly political nature of the demands of protestors and new groups, which began calling not merely for the regime to observe existing guarantees of human rights or for a return to efforts to recreate socialism with a human face, but for "real democracy." In addition, in a process that had parallels elsewhere in the region, it became clear in 1988 and 1989 that dissent had begun to emerge from the intellectual ghetto to which it had been confined. Illustrated by the willingness of establishment intellectuals and artists to sign petitions calling for Václav Havel's release when he was imprisoned following his participation in the commemoration of the twentieth anniversary of the suicide of Jan Palach in January 1989, as well as a petition calling for fundamental political change circulated during the summer of 1989, disaffection with the existing system had spread far beyond the small group of dissidents by mid-1989. Similar developments occurred in East Germany in the 1980s. The growing support for the peace, ecology, and other independent movements there illustrated the extent to which the Honecker regime had lost support among those groups of the population that had benefited most from its policies and, in the past, had supported it.[23]

Even in Bulgaria and Romania, where conditions remained much worse for the expression of any sort of disagreement with official policies, the late 1980s saw the development of small dissident groups and the growing disaffection of many of Zhivkov's and Ceauşescu's former supporters within the communist parties. In Bulgaria, this development was most evident in the capital among intellectuals; in Romania, it involved primarily individuals who in the past had been associated with the regime.

An important aspect of this phenomenon was the growing alienation of formerly loyal intellectuals. As in the Soviet Union under Brezhnev, intellectuals throughout central and eastern Europe came increasingly to question the value of the policies, and, in some cases, eventually, the very basis of the communist system. In Hungary and Poland, reform-minded economists, sociologists, writers, and other intellectuals aided the party and the opposition in drawing up plans for change. Elsewhere there was far less room for influencing official policies, but intellectuals who remained in the good graces of the regime became increasingly critical in the late 1980s and increasingly willing to speak their minds openly. When mass protests began in East Germany, Czechoslovakia, and Romania, many of these people joined the demonstrators and some, particularly those who were not too implicated in the policies of the communist period, came to serve as leaders in the movements for change and eventually as members of the governments that replaced communist rule.

The events of 1989, which revealed the hollowness of the communist house of cards in this region, vindicated many of the analyses of the nature of the crisis in the region. However, the speed and extent of the changes caught most analysts of the region, as well as most participants, by surprise.

The dramatic collapse of communism also illustrated aspects of the crisis that were often overlooked. The first of these is the extent to which communist systems had in fact failed where many analysts thought they had succeeded, at least in a relative way. In contrast to the earlier views of certain analysts, there was clearly no revolutionary breakthrough. One of the main failures in this respect was the inability of communist elites to change popular values and attitudes. As the events of 1989 demonstrated, few citizens in most of these countries actually believed in the promises of communist elites by the late 1980s. Communist systems were able to achieve outward compliance and changes in behavior in many areas, as evident in the decline of religious observation and the suspension of overt ethnic conflict, for example. They also succeeded in promoting acceptance of certain official values, particularly those regarding the responsibility to the state to provide a high level of social security for citizens and, in some countries, a belief in the need for social justice.[24]

Certain values and attitudes of the populations also changed in unanticipated ways as the unintended consequences of elite policies. Unfortunately, these attitudes, including the belief that politics is not the business of ordinary people and that it is not the task of citizens, but of governments and public officials, to solve all public problems, may have negative repercussions as these countries attempt to create democratic political systems. The alienation and apathy toward public issues fostered by the focus on individual gain since the late 1940s will pose further obstacles to the creation of democratic values.[25] Central and East Europeans often discuss this issue in terms of moral decay and the corruption of moral values and argue that the discrepancy between public and private values and between behavior and values led to the degradation of human relations in all areas.

A second, related, aspect of the crisis illuminated by the events of 1989 is the extent to which communist systems remained alien phenomena in much of the region. Even in Czechoslovakia, where the Communist party had a fair degree of indigenous support before the establishment of a communist system, communism came to be seen as an alien import, imposed and kept in power from without. The situation was somewhat different in Bulgaria, Albania, and Yugoslavia, where in one case friendly attitudes toward Russia appear to have moderated this view, and in the others, the role of domestic leaders in setting up communist systems provided a certain degree of legitimacy, at least among certain segments of the population. But elsewhere, popular support, which appears to have been based largely on the ability of the system to provide material rewards by the late 1980s as well as on fear, was lower than expected. Thus, in some of these countries, such as Poland, the communist system never put down strong roots. In others, such as the former GDR, Hungary, and also to some extent Czechoslovakia, the compromise forged between the population and the leadership was eventually eroded by economic failure. In all but Yugoslavia and Albania, the final guarantor proved to be Soviet force. When it became clear that the Soviet Union would no longer back them up with armed force, these systems fell.

One of the fatal weaknesses of the communist systems, then, was their formula of rule. As noted, the political formula, or elite strategy of rule, in these societies relied on a combination of incentives to encourage citizens to comply. The emphasis on normative, material, and coercive incentives varied from country to country and over time. But, whether the ruling elites chose to emphasize material incentives or link the fate of the communist system to the fate of the nation, as in Romania, all had come to base their legitimacy to some degree on economic performance. As events in 1989 and 1990 illustrated, however, efforts to create true legitimacy were unsuccessful, in even those cases in which there was originally some support for communism.

Still another aspect of the crisis that became evident in the 1980s and was highlighted by the events of 1989 and 1990 was the failure of these systems to deal with generational change. This failure was in part due to the inability of leaders to elaborate a convincing vision of the future that could retain the allegiance of the population, especially young people. Nor could leaders explain why problems were proliferating in the economic, environmental, and social spheres; why these countries had fallen so far behind the West in material goods; or why cultural isolation from the West was necessary. The latter, in particular, became an especially difficult policy to justify once Gorbachev came to power.

Throughout the region, then, the late 1980s saw the progressive alienation of many segments of the population, including those groups who had previously supported the communist regimes. As in earlier periods of the region's history, the inability of the leaderships to either solve the pressing problems facing their nations, or, in the end, maintain sufficient force to repress opponents, led to the downfall of these systems. Although external factors in many cases provided the catalyst for this fall, the failure of communist systems reflected a number of common weaknesses in the underlying pattern of social, economic, and political organization and the growing economic and political crises that resulted from these features. In many cases, the fall of communist regimes also reflected the fundamental incompatibility between the values and orientations of the regimes and the Western orientations of the populations as well as the inability of the structures of a command economy to meet the needs of relatively advanced industrialized economies.

The Future of Socialism in Central and Eastern Europe

Unfortunately for the prospects of socialism in the region, the future of socialism as a body of ideas or as a political movement in central and eastern Europe appears to be linked inextricably to the failure of the communist system. Although many of the values of socialism are compatible with democracy and other elements of Western culture, in the eyes of many Central and East Europeans, the term itself has acquired a significant number of negative connotations given its association with the experiences of the last forty-odd years of political history. Many East and Central European intellectuals as well as ordinary citizens feel that they have already experienced "real socialism" in one form or another. Although they may admit that socialism cannot or should not be identified solely with Marxism in its Leninist form or the experiences of the communist period, most are not eager to give the ideals associated with socialism another try. This reluctance is evident in the fate of the communist parties in the region since the changes of late 1989. It is also evident in the difficulties that leaders and activists of democratic socialist parties are encountering in these countries.

Communist parties, or their renamed successors, continue to exist in all of these states with the exception of Romania, where the party has been outlawed. Although the number of Communist party members has decreased dramatically in all of these countries since late 1989, the party apparatus continues to control substantial financial and other resources. New leaders view efforts to deal with the party's remaining sources of power as an important political task; this issue is particularly important in the economic realm, where there is a need to prevent members of the party and security apparatus from translating their former privileges into legitimate power in the new system.[26] The parties also had resources that gave them certain advantages in the election campaigns of 1990, including long-established, well-equipped organizations that extended to the local levels; hierarchical organizational principles that could ensure unity of effort; and more money than most of their opponents to purchase needed supplies and equipment.[27]

At the same time, there is little indication that these resources will matter, at least in the near term. Despite such advantages, there is little support for the communist parties or their successors in any of the countries, with the exception of Bulgaria and Albania, that have undergone significant change since 1989. Reformist reincarnations of the communist parties have far fewer members than their predecessors; they also did very poorly in the free elections held in 1989 and 1990. In Poland, the thorough trouncing of the party's candidates in the June 1989 elections, which were held in circumstances that still gave the party's representatives certain advantages, was in fact one of the factors that led to the eventual formation of a Solidarity-dominated government. Representatives of the successor to the Communist party won 0.65 percent of seats in the May 1990 local council elections. In Hungary, the Hungarian Socialist party, successor to the Hungarian Socialist Workers' party, led by Imre Poszgay and other reformist communist leaders responsible for negotiating away the party's monopoly of power in roundtable negotiations with the opposition, received a far smaller proportion of the vote (approximately 9 percent) than anticipated in the Hungarian legislative elections in March 1990.[28] The remnant of the old Communist party, the Hungarian Socialist Workers' party, received 3.7 percent of the vote, less than the 4 percent required to seat deputies and thus is not represented in the new parliament. In the former GDR, the Party of Democratic Socialism, the renamed Communist party, also did poorly, with approximately 16 percent of the vote.[29]

These results were not surprising given the way in which the communist regimes were set up in these societies and popular attitudes toward the parties during much of the communist period. In Poland and Hungary historic antagonism toward Russia and, in the Hungarian case, an earlier abortive experience with socialism in 1919, further complicated attitudes toward the party. In the GDR, where the party could draw on the strong socialist tradition that existed in earlier periods of German history, the legitimacy of the party was undermined from the beginning by the fact that the East German state was a creation imposed on a defeated nation.

The situation of the Communist party is somewhat different in Czechoslovakia, Bulgaria, Romania, Yugoslavia, and Albania. In Czechoslovakia, the party had indigenous roots that stretched back to the interwar period, when it was legal and had a fair degree of support, especially in the Czech Lands. As I have argued more fully in other contexts, the luster of this heritage has undoubtedly been tarnished by experiences since the late 1940s.[30] Efforts to reform the party and regain public support since the end of the party's monopoly of power were also hampered by the defection of more than one-half of the 1.7 million members of the party by mid-1990, as well as by the fact that those who remained were predominantly older or so involved in the old system as to have no other political option. Short of a reversal of the process of democratization, which does not appear probable, the party is not likely to play a major role in politics in Czechoslovakia.

However, in contrast to the situation in Poland the party will in all likelihood continue to have a place in the multiparty system in Czechoslovakia, where it received 13 percent of the vote in the June 1990 elections and approximately 17 percent of the vote in the local elections in November 1990. Although a far cry from the dominant position of the party during the communist period, this proportion is similar to the levels of electoral support (10–13 percent) that the party received in the precommunist period. In contrast to the situation in the interwar period, support for the party was equal in the Czech Lands and in Slovakia.[31]

The outlook for the Communist party is also somewhat more positive in Bulgaria than in most countries in the region. Leaders of the party initiated and controlled the pace of reform to a far greater extent than elsewhere through the first six months of 1990, although they faced increasing challenges from the opposition that emerged after November 1989. As in Czechoslovakia, the Bulgarian Communist party had a certain degree of indigenous support during the communist period. Although the party was outlawed in 1925 after a terrorist attack on the Bulgarian king, the party carried on its activities to some extent through front organizations during the interwar period. It benefited during this period, as after World War II, from the high degree of egalitarianism evident in Bulgarian society and from the radical peasant tradition, which it attempted to appropriate. It also benefited from the generally favorable attitudes toward Russia and later the Soviet Union that existed in Bulgaria. The party also gained a certain degree of support during the communist period from the social mobility and improved living standards that the Stalinist model created in its early phases.

Opposition to the party materialized quickly in Bulgaria once the hardline leader Todor Zhivkov was removed in late 1989, but the opposition was fragmented, with little experience in practical politics and few links to voters in the countryside at the time of the elections. Thus, although many Bulgarians left the party and still larger numbers expressed their deep disagreement with many of its policies once conditions permitted, the Communist party retained control of the government after the elections of 1990. The renamed Communist party, now the Bulgarian Socialist party, won 211 of 400 parliamentary seats in the June 1990 elections, a significantly higher proportion than its main opponents; the Union of Democratic Forces, a coalition of twelve organizations, won 144 seats, the Agrarians won 16 seats, and the

Movement for Rights and Freedoms, an organization representing the interests of the Turkish minority, won 23 seats.[32]

Support for the successor to the Communist party, the Bulgarian Socialist party, declined throughout 1990. Popular protests, fueled by increasing dissatisfaction with the government and evidence that then President Peter Mladenov had suggested that tanks be used against demonstrators in late 1989, resulted in his resignation in July 1990. His replacement in August 1990 by Zhelyu Zhelev, a longtime dissident and leader of the opposition Union of Democratic Forces, reflected the growth of support for the opposition. The fall of the government of Prime Minister Lukanov after popular protests in November 1990 and the creation of a government headed by a noncommunist prime minister, in which nine of seventeen members are not communist, provided further evidence of the erosion of support for the Communist party. Public opinion polls conducted in the first months of 1991 suggest that the party is likely to receive fewer votes in the upcoming parliamentary elections than the Union of Democratic Forces.[33] Nonetheless, as in Czechoslovakia, the successor to the Communist party and other left-wing parties are likely to continue to receive more support in Bulgaria than similar groups in Poland and Hungary.

The Communist party also continues to have a considerable degree of support in Albania, which, not unexpectedly, was the last country in the region to begin the process of change. In multiparty elections held in March 1991, the Albanian Workers' party won two-thirds, or 168, of the 250 seats in Parliament, compared to the 75 seats won by the main opposition party, the Albanian Democratic party. However, attitudes toward the party are clearly bifurcated in Albania. The party's strong showing in rural areas, as well as the difficulties the opposition faced in organizing support after the harsh conditions that prevailed in Albania until very recently, ensured its victory. However, the party lost decisively in urban areas, and Ramiz Alia, the party's leader, who ran in an urban district, was also defeated.[34]

The Romanian situation is something of an anomaly in this respect as in others. Due in large part to the harshness and personalized quality of Ceauşescu's rule, the Romanian Communist party itself was totally discredited and outlawed soon after Ceauşescu was executed. However, given the high level of surveillance and the impossibility of organizing opposition groups outside of the party, many of the individuals who opposed Ceauşescu and many of those in the government of the Front of National Salvation were former Communist party members. Most of the seventeen newly formed political parties that competed in the May 1990 elections were poorly organized and had few resources. Ion Iliescu, leader of the National Salvation Front, won 85 percent of the vote for president. Front candidates won 67 percent of votes to the senate and 66.3 percent for the chamber of deputies in the May 20, 1990 elections. Of the remaining parties and movements, only the Hungarian Democratic Union of Romania and the National Liberal party gained more than 5 percent of the vote for the legislature.[35] The Romanian Socialist Labor party formed in November 1990 is widely regarded as a new incarnation of the outlawed Communist party; however, there is little evidence concerning the extent of its support.

The role of the Communist party in Yugoslavia is still an open question, as is the future of the Yugoslav state. Judging from the results of elections held in Slovenia and Croatia in May 1990 and in other republics in late 1990, the party may reap certain benefits from Yugoslavia's history as the communist world's earliest rebel as well as from efforts of certain republican party leaderships to promote liberalization. At the same time, the outcome of the elections of 1990 and 1991 also illustrate the limits of popular willingness to remain under communist rule, however it is defined. The renamed, reformist successors of the republic Leagues of Communists were defeated by opposition forces in the multiparty elections held in both Croatia and Slovenia in April and May 1990. However, the League of Communists of Slovenia–Party of Democratic Renewal, led by reformist communist leaders who had come to be seen as supporters of liberalization in the late 1980s, received the single highest proportion of votes in the most numerous chamber of the legislature, the Socio-Political Chamber (17.3 percent), and also elected deputies to the other chambers of the legislature. Although the communists' main opponents, a coalition of several parties known as DEMOS, captured a total of 55 percent of the vote for the legislature, Milan Kucan, former head of the League of Communists of Slovenia, was elected president of the Republic of Slovenia with 58.6 percent of the vote. In Croatia, where the party leadership was less consistently identified with the cause of reform, a nationalist party, the Christian Democratic Union, won a majority of approximately 59 percent of the vote to the legislature on a platform of separatism. The League of Communists of Croatia–Party of Democratic Changes nonetheless received 20.8 percent of the vote for parliament. Similarly, although Franco Tudjman, a former communist general purged from the party for nationalist views in the 1970s, was selected as president of Croatia by the newly elected parliament, a reform communist was chosen to fill one of the seats on the republic's collective presidency.[36]

As in Slovenia and Croatia, the fate of the communist parties in the rest of Yugoslavia has been influenced to some degree by their previous efforts at reform and, most importantly, by the extent to which party leaders have been able to link the party to nationalist sentiments. Representatives of the successors to the communist parties fared best in elections held in Serbia and Montenegro in late 1990. Thus, the Socialist Party of Serbia, formerly the League of Communists of Serbia, emerged as the strongest force in the Serbian legislature, winning 194 of the 250 seats, compared to the 19 won by the second-place Serbian Renewal Movement.[37] Slobodan Milosevic, the leader of the Socialist Party who successfully linked the party's fortunes to Serbian nationalism, was reelected as president of Serbia by a wide margin 65 percent). The League of Communists of Montenegro also did well in the December 1990 elections. The party won a majority (58 percent) of the vote, and a reform communist leader was elected president of the republic.[38]

In Bosnia-Hercegovina and Macedonia, the successors to the Leagues of Communists have run second to nationally oriented parties and groupings. In Bosnia-Hercegovina, nationalist forces prevailed in the November 1990 elections, as three ethnically based parties each won more seats in the republic legislature than the reform communists. Thus, the Moslem Party for Democratic Action won 41 seats, the Serbian Democratic party 34 seats, and the Croatian Democratic Community 20 seats. The League of Communists of Bosnia-Hercegovina– Socialist Democratic party won 13 seats alone and 5 as part of a coalition with the Democratic Socialist party. Representatives from ethnic parties won all 7 seats on Bosnia-Hercegovina's collective presidency.[39]

In Macedonia, the League of Communists of Macedonia–Party for Democratic Transformation was defeated by the nationalist Internal Macedonian Revolutionary Organization (IMRO), which won 37 of the 120 seats in the republic's legislature in the December 1990 elections. With 31 seats, the League of Communists nonetheless fared better than the Albanian Party for Democratic Prosperity (25 seats) and the Alliance of Reform Forces of Macedonia (19 seats), both of which won some seats in coalition with other political forces. The president chosen after the elections was a member of the Communist party. However, the League was not represented among the members of the nonparty government of experts formed after extended negotiations in March 1991.[40]

Socialist Parties

The prospects of noncommunist, socialist parties are also dim at present throughout much of the region. To a larger extent than is the case for the communist parties or their successors, which will continue to suffer in the near future from their responsibility for the old system, the fate of the newly organized or reorganized socialist parties will depend on their ability to compete in the newly pluralized political systems. Socialist parties separate from the communist parties have been established or gained new independence since the fall of communism throughout the region. As is the case with most other parties in these countries, their organizations are weak, their leaders inexperienced with the demands of electoral politics, and their resources limited. In addition to these handicaps, which exist to one degree or another in all of the newly organized parties and nonpartisan groupings, leaders of the various socialist parties that have developed are also hindered in some cases by guilt by association with the old regime, and in all cases by the popular tendency to equate socialism in all of its variants with the experience of the communist period. The former problem exists primarily in those countries, such as Czechoslovakia, where small socialist parties were allowed to mobilize segments of the population unlikely to join the Communist party during the communist period, but were permitted little independence. The latter problem exists throughout the region.

The impact of these factors has been documented by the growing number of surveys of public opinion and political orientations being carried out in these countries, which indicate a general lack of support for socialist parties of whatever form in central and eastern Europe at present, although there are important variations within the region. It is also evident in the results of the elections held in the first half of 1990.

As the results of the East German elections held in March 1990 illustrated, the results of public opinion polls may not be very revealing of how people will actually vote. The high degree of volatility of partisan preferences evident in studies of other new or newly recreated electorates has its parallel in this part of the world.[41] The fate of the German Social Democratic party is illustrative. Thought to be the most likely victor in the March 1990 elections in East Germany, the SDP emerged second with 22.9 percent of the vote, behind the coalition of three Christian-democratic parties that received 49 percent of the vote. The party received a similar portion of the vote (21.3 percent) in the local elections held in May 1990.[42] However, in contrast to the situation of socialist parties elsewhere in the region, the level of support for the SDP was considerably higher than that of socialist parties in the rest of the region due in part to the influence of West German politicians and resources on politics in the GDR in the period between the fall of the Berlin Wall and the unification of Germany in 1990. In the rest of the region, social democratic parties did very poorly. In Hungary and Czechoslovakia, the social democratic parties did not receive enough votes to seat a single deputy.[43] In Bulgaria, one deputy in the new legislature represents a non-Marxist social democratic party.[44] Two small socialist parties in Romania, the Romanian Socialist Democratic party and the Social Democratic party of Romania, won approximately 1 percent and 0.5 percent of votes to the legislature; together they occupy a total of seven seats.[45] Perhaps as a reflection of the greater credibility of the reformist successors to the communist parties' claims to be social democratic parties of the West European variety, socialist parties also did relatively badly in the multiparty elections in Yugoslavia in 1990. Candidates of the Socialist Alliance won only 0.9 percent of the vote running alone and 4.8 percent running with the Communist party in Croatia in the May 1990 elections. In Macedonia, the Socialist party won 4 of the 120 seats in the legislature and an additional 8 seats in coalition with other political forces in the December 1990 elections.[46] In Slovenia, the Alliance of Socialists captured 3–5 percent of the votes to the various chambers of the legislature. However, the Social Democrats of Slovenia, who won 6 percent of the vote to the Socio-Political Chamber, are part of the winning DEMOS coalition and hold two of the positions in the Slovenian government.[47]

As the experience of the Slovenian social democrats illustrates, social democratic candidates and groups that ran as part of broader coalitions were somewhat more successful in several of these countries than parties that ran independently. Several candidates of the Civic Forum in Czechoslovakia were socialists, for example. The Union of Democratic Forces in Bulgaria also included members of a social democratic group that won twenty-three seats in the new legislature.[48]

The defeat of many of the socialist parties can be traced in part to factors peculiar to individual countries. In Czechoslovakia, for example, the social democrats were hurt by poor organization and by the fact that a bitter fight over the party's leadership was resolved by choosing a man who had spent much of the past forty years in the United States as head of the party. Poor organization and lack of resources also hurt the campaigns of socialist parties elsewhere. However, the uniformly poor showing of socialist parties everywhere but in the former GDR suggests that organized socialist parties suffered from the general rejection of the experiences of the last forty years evident in the fortunes of the communist parties in the region.

In Lieu of a Conclusion

Given the fact that the elections of 1990 and early 1991 were held in highly unusual political circumstances in electoral systems that were themselves still in the process of being created, their results may not be predictive of future political alignments. However, although the political preferences of Central and East European citizens undoubtedly remain fluid to some degree, the results of recent elections in central and eastern Europe indicate that a considerable backlash against socialism in all its forms exists in many of these countries. These sentiments led to the victory of new, nonpartisan groupings or coalitions dominated by forces such as Solidarity in Poland, the Hungarian Democratic Forum in Hungary, and the Civic Forum–Public Against Violence coalition in Czechoslovakia that are hard to classify on a traditional left-right continuum in certain cases. In others, parties or coalitions with centrist or right to center views were the victors.

The situation thus may tempt one to write off the chances of socialism in all forms in central and eastern Europe. However, such a conclusion would be premature. For, although the short-term prospects for either a restoration of communist rule or primacy or a significant role for noncommunist socialist parties are dim, the longer-term prospects for noncommunist socialist parties in particular are not quite as dismal.

Evaluation of these prospects, as well as of the likelihood of a future restoration of the pre-1989 status quo in the region, must include several factors referred to only in passing to this point. Two of the most important, in addition to the role of outside actors in the region, are the success of the transition to democracy in the region and the likely outcome of efforts to introduce radical economic changes.

The transition to democratic rule, which, as the transitions from authoritarian to democratic systems in other contexts have demonstrated, is an extremely complicated process, is at the beginning stages throughout the region.[49] Although some countries have moved further toward establishing or reestablishing pluralistic, multiparty democratic systems, all face a number of political tasks that are in fact daunting in their scope and complexity. As I have argued in greater detail elsewhere, these include the need to create new institutions, constitutions, and legal structures and refashion old institutions in such a way that they will be conducive to the establishment and maintenance of democracy.[50] The new leaders of these states must also find a way to channel the massive desire for change evident in late 1989 into coherent political orientations and policy alternatives, and methods to create and foster political attitudes and values supportive of democracy. They must identify and groom new politicians from populations that have had, with few exceptions, very restricted opportunities for meaningful participation in public life for several generations. They must also, as noted earlier, find a way to deal with the legacy of the communist past in terms of both the remaining sources of power of the communist parties or their successors and the impact of that past on the political values and attitudes of the population.

In addition to these tasks, leaders of the new governments in the region must also deal with the threats to democratic rule that may arise from a number of sources including aspects of their political structures that may, as they did in the interwar period, contribute to political instability; antidemocratic political values and traditions that date, in many cases, to the interwar or earlier periods in the history of these nations; potential extremist forces that may arise from unresolved ethnic or other cleavages; and possible threats that may emerge from outside the borders of individual countries. And they must do all of this while attending to the important issues that face governments of all kinds such as maintaining adequate levels of social services and social welfare, dealing with social and ethnic conflicts, and insuring public order and the external security of their states.

The success of these efforts, and the future of socialism as well as of democracy, will depend in large part on the extent to which the new governments in the region are able to deal with the severe economic crises that helped to precipitate the downfall of communist systems in the area. The tasks facing leaders in this respect are also formidable and include the need to introduce elements of the market and create greater scope for private ownership and enterprise, make important structural changes, reorient external economic relationships, and deal with levels of ecological degradation that in many cases are near catastrophic in terms of their impact on human health. In certain countries, notably Romania, new leaders also face the task of ensuring a bare minimum of life's necessities to all sectors of the population.

As in the political realm, the approaches the new governments in central and eastern Europe have taken to deal with these issues to date differ considerably. However, whatever the speed or extent of economic change attempted, in all countries there will be certain unavoidable, negative results for the population in the short run. The degree to which the new leaders are able to minimize these, distribute them equitably, or, failing either of these possibilities, have enough legitimacy and popular support to convince the population of the need for sacrifice for better futures will have a major impact on the success of the fledgling democratic political systems that are emerging in many of these countries. The prospects for a successful transition to democracy are not uniform throughout the area.[51] Briefly put, due to differences in factors ranging from levels of development to political traditions in the precommunist period to the current constellation of political forces, these prospects appear brightest in the case of Czechoslovakia. They are also fairly bright in Hungary and Poland but are far less so in Romania, Bulgaria, or Albania at present. In Yugoslavia, the survival of the country as a united state is itself in question.

The success or failure of democracy, in turn, is likely to have a different impact on the fortunes of socialist parties and communist parties in the region. There is little hope that the latter will regain their predominant role through the ballot box in the near future. Even should economic performance and a drastic deterioration in standards of living during the transition to market economies lead to an upsurge of support for the communist parties or their successors, the experience of communist rule will prevent that outcome in all likelihood. Popular dissatisfaction may also serve to increase support for nationalist rather than leftist parties. On the other hand, it is not clear that the failure of democracy would lead to a restoration of communist power short of massive intervention by the Soviet Union, if then. The more likely outcome in many of these states would be rightist, authoritarian governments that might outlaw the communist parties entirely as similar governments did in the interwar period.

Conditions for socialist parties of other stripes would also be unfavorable under such governments. The maintenance of democracy is therefore essential to the fortunes of democratic socialism in the region as well. A deterioration in the standard of living may also increase electoral support for the democratic socialist parties, particularly if it persists for some time. Such parties may also gain support in the future from two additional sources. First, they may well be the beneficiaries of the disillusionment with capitalism and conservatism that is bound to occur to some extent once Central and East Europeans begin to experience some of the less convenient and appealing features of market economies. Less closely associated with the past than the successors of the former communist parties, democratic socialist parties may be better positioned to benefit from these effects.

Democratic socialist parties may also benefit, in the future, from support arising from concern over new values and issues such as the ecological crisis and from the umbrella organizations that formed from the old opposition in many of these countries. Interest in these issues, as in the case of ecology, for example, now serves largely to increase support for new nonpartisan groupings devoted solely or primarily to these issues. But the socialist parties may at some point benefit from electoral alliances with such groups. They may also gain directly from the sorting-out process that is occurring in many of the nonpartisan umbrella groupings composed of groups and individuals with widely differing perspectives and policy orientations. Generational change must also be figured into the equation, although it is extremely difficult to predict the political attitudes of generations not yet involved in politics. The processes that might lead to a renaissance of interest in socialist ideals and support for socialist parties thus are largely outside the control of the current leaders of these parties. However, the fortunes of these parties will also depend to some extent on the skill with which their leaders take advantage of opportunities to change popular perceptions and increase their support through coalitions.

The political climate and recent experiences of the countries of central and eastern Europe give little reason to be optimistic concerning the short-term future of socialism in any form in the region. However, as numerous analysts have observed, in democratic political systems the processes of government are certain, but the outcomes are uncertain.[52] Despite the backlash against the concept of socialism evident in the results of the elections of 1990 and early 1991, there is evidence that significant elements of the population in many of these countries support certain values generally associated with socialism, including a set of expectations concerning the obligations of the state toward citizens and a certain degree of egalitarianism. Thus, although leaders of the nonpartisan groupings, center-right coalitions, and nationalist parties that dominate most of the new governments in the region eschew the very term itself, and despite the poor showing of leftist parties in the elections held since 1989, the rejection of socialism is not necessarily as complete as it would seem. Certain socialist values and ideals, shorn of their association with the Left and the experiences of forty-odd years of communism, will continue to be reflected in the public policies of the new governments. In the near future, support for these values is unlikely to be linked to support for organized parties of the Left. Given the strength of the noncommunist socialist tradition in several of these countries in the past and the factors noted previously, however, it is not farfetched to imagine that democratic socialist parties will emerge as important political actors in many of the countries in the region in the future if democratic governments can indeed be established and maintained.

As in western Europe in recent decades, policies based on socialist ideals may also reemerge as legitimate subjects of national political debate through the activities of nonideological social movements devoted to feminism, ecology, or other issues.[53] With the exception of Solidarity in Poland, the Hungarian Democratic Forum, and Civic Forum–Public Against Violence in Czechoslovakia, these coalitions did not fare well in electoral contests in 1990 and 1991. However, many will continue their activities from the sidelines of the political arena. Although not directly involved in government, such groups can play important roles in shaping the political agenda and public debate. Support for certain groups of this type may also increase once the region has accomplished some of the difficult tasks associated with the transition now under way. In the meantime, however, the legacy of forty-odd years of communist rule in regard to socialism is likely to retain certain socialist values that are not acknowledged as part of the patrimony of socialism and not linked to the organized Left.

Notes

1. This emphasis has been particularly prevalent in media accounts, but it also informs many of the emerging scholarly analyses. See, for example, A. James McAdams, "An Obituary for the Berlin Wall," paper presented at Institute for Sino-Soviet Studies conference on Changing Patterns in East-West Relations, Washington, D.C., April 2, 1990.

2. Sharon L. Wolchik, "The Roots of Change and the Transition to Democracy in Czechoslovakia," paper presented at the U.S. Army War College, Carlisle, Pa., March 9, 1990, and "Domestic Developments in Selected East European Countries," paper presented at Institute for Sino-Soviet Studies conference on Changing Patterns in East-West Relations, Washington, D.C., April 2, 1990.

3. Kenneth Jowitt, *Revolutionary Breakthroughs and National Development: The Case of Romania, 1944–1965* (Berkeley: University of California Press, 1971).

4. For brief summaries of these results, see Zbigniew K. Brzezinski, *The Soviet Bloc: Unity and Conflict*, rev. ed. (Cambridge: Harvard University Press, 1967), ch. 6, especially pp. 112–29; and Richard Lowenthal, "Development vs. Utopia in Communist Policy" in *Change in Communist Systems*, ed. Chalmers Johnson (Stanford: Stanford University Press, 1970), pp. 33–116.

5. See Zvi Y. Gitelman, "Power and Authority in Eastern Europe," in *Change in Communist Systems*, ed. Johnson; Kenneth Jowitt, "An Organizational Approach to the Study of Political Culture in Marxist-Leninist Systems," *American Political Science Review* 68 (September 1974): 1171–91; and the discussions of political culture in Jack Gray and Archie Brown, eds., *Political Culture and Political Change in Communist States* (New York: Holmes and Meier, 1979).

6. Alexander Dallin and George Breslauer, "Political Terror in the Post-Mobilization Stage," in *Change in Communist Systems*, ed. Johnson.

7. The literature on the difficulties of centrally planned economies is legion. See, for example, William F. Robinson, *The Patterns of Reform in Hungary: A Political, Economic and Cultural Analysis* (New York: Praeger Publishers, 1973); Paul Marer, "The Economies and Trade of Eastern Europe," in *Central and Eastern Europe: The Opening Curtain?* ed. William E. Griffith (Boulder: Westview Press, 1989); Joint Economic Committee, *Pressures for Reform in the East European Economies*, 2 vols. (Washington: U.S. Government Printing Office, 1989); and Martin R. Myant, *The Czechoslovak Economy, 1948–1988* (Cambridge: Harvard University Press, 1989). See R. V. Burks, "Technology and Political Change in Eastern Europe," in *Change in Communist Systems*, ed. Johnson for an early discussion of the difficulties central planning posed to innovation and technological advancement. See Karel Dyba and Karel Kouba, "Czechoslovak Attempts at Systematic Changes," *Communist Economies* 1, no. 3 (1989): 313–25, for recent Czech analyses.

8. A remarkable report on the extent of the second economy in Czechoslovakia is Martin Fassmann, "The Shadow Economy's Funds: From Where Are Drawn the Grey Billions on the Market and in Services?" *Hospodarske*

noviny, December 9, 1988, p. 3, as reported in Foreign Broadcast Information Service, *East Europe Report,* JPRS-EER-89-035, March 31, 1989, pp. 40–43. See Elemér Hankiss, "East European Elites: Why Have They Failed?" conference paper, Washington Institute for Values in Public Policy, 1988, for an analysis that links the extensive corruption that permeated all levels of society to the normal operation of a system that tries to regulate all areas of life and also to subvert and prevent the development of stable expectations concerning the behavior of bureaucrats and officials.

9. See Walter D. Connor, *Socialism, Politics, and Equality* (New York: Columbia University Press, 1979) for an anlysis of the impact of decreased social mobility in these countries.

10. Jowitt, *Revolutionary Breakthroughs.*

11. Zvi Gitelman, "Power and Authority in Eastern Europe," and "The Politics of Socialist Restoration in Hungary and Czechoslovakia," *Comparative Politics* 13 (January 1981): 187–210.

12. See H. Gordon Skilling and Franklyn Griffiths, eds., *Interest Groups in Soviet Politics* (Princeton: Princeton University Press, 1971); Vladimir Kusin, *The Intellectual Origins of the Prague Spring: The Development of Reformist Ideas in Czechoslovakia, 1956–1967* (Cambridge: Cambridge University Press, 1971) and *Political Groupings in the Czechoslovak Reform Movement* (New York: Columbia University Press, 1972); Jaroslav Krejci, *Social Change and Stratification in Postwar Czechoslovakia* (New York: Columbia University Press, 1972); and Jan Szczepanski, *Polish Society* (New York: Random House, 1970).

13. See Valerie Bunce and John M. Echols III, "Soviet Politics in the Brezhnev Era: Pluralism or Corporatism," in *Soviet Politics in the Brezhnev Era,* ed. Donald M. Kelley (New York: Praeger Publishers, 1980); Susan Woodward, "The Rights of Women: Ideology, Policy, and Social Change in Yugoslavia," in *Women, State and Party in Eastern Europe,* ed. Sharon L. Wolchik and Alfred G. Meyer (Durham: Duke University Press, 1985); Jane L. Curry, *Poland's Journalists: Professionalism and Politics* (Cambridge: Cambridge University Press, 1989); and Sharon L. Wolchik, "The Scientific-Technological Revolution and the Participation of Specialists in the Making of Public Policy," in *Domestic and Foreign Policy in Eastern Europe in the 1980s,* ed. Michael J. Sodaro and Sharon L. Wolchik (London: Macmillan, 1983).

14. See Steven L. Burg, *Conflict and Cohesion in Socialist Yugoslavia: Political Decision Making since 1966* (Princeton: Princeton University Press, 1983); William Zimmermann, *Open Borders, Nonalignment and the Political Evolution of Yugoslavia* (Princeton: Princeton University Press, 1987); Ivo Banac, *The National Question in Yugoslavia: Origins, History, Politics* (Ithaca: Cornell University Press, 1984); and Pedro Ramet, *Yugoslavia in the 1980s* (Boulder: Westview Press, 1985) for further discussion.

15. See, for example, Maurice Simon and Roger Kanet, eds., *Background to Crisis: Policy and Politics in Gierek's Poland* (Boulder: Westview Press, 1981); Jack Bielasiak and Maurice Simon, eds., *Polish Politics: Edge of the Abyss* (New York: Praeger Publishers, 1984); Martin R. Myant, *Poland, a Crisis for Socialism* (London: Lawrence and Wishart, 1982); and Bronislaw Misztal, ed., *Poland after Solidarity: Social Movement versus the State* (New Brunswick: Transaction

Books, 1985). See also Hankiss, "East European Elites"; and Sarah Meiklejohn Terry, "The Future of Poland: Perestroika or Perpetual Crisis?" Charles Gati, "Reforming Communist Systems: Lessons from the Hungarian Experience," and Viktor Meier, "Yugoslavia: Worsening Economic and Natonalist Crisis," all in *Central and Eastern Europe*, ed. Griffith.

16. See Morris Bornstein, Zvi Gitelman, and William Zimmerman, eds., *East-West Relations and the Future of Eastern Europe* (London: Allen and Unwin, 1981); and Sharon L. Wolchik, "Economic Performance and Political Change in Czechoslovakia," in *Prospects for Change in Socialist Systems*, ed. Charles Bukowski and Mark A. Cichock (New York: Praeger Publishers, 1987).

17. Gati, "Reforming Communist Systems"; and George Schopflin, Rudolf Tokes, and Ivan Volgyes, "Leadership Change and Crisis in Hungary," *Problems of Communism* 37 (September–October 1988): 23–46.

18. Sharon L. Wolchik, "Prospects for Political Change in Czechoslovakia," paper presented at Midwest Slavic Conference, Chicago, April 19, 1989.

19. Gati, "Reforming Communist Systems"; Terry, "The Future of Poland"; Valerie Bunce, "The Transition from State Socialism to Liberal Democracy," unpublished manuscript, 1989; Elemér Hankiss, "In Search of a New Paradigm," *Daedalus* 119 (Winter 1990): 183–214; and Bronislaw Geremek, "Between Hope and Despair," *Daedalus* 119 (Winter 1990): 91–110.

20. See the essays in Jane Curry, ed., *Dissent in Eastern Europe* (New York: Praeger Publishers, 1983); and Robert Sharlet, "Human Rights and Civil Society in Eastern Europe," in *Central and Eastern Europe*, ed. Griffith, pp. 156–77.

21. See Barbara W. Jancar, "Women in the Opposition in Poland and Czechoslovakia in the 1970s," in *Women, State, and Party*, ed. Wolchik and Meyer, for a brief overview. See also H. Gordon Skilling, *Charter 77 and Human Rights in Czechoslovakia* (London: George Allen and Unwin, 1981); and Vladimir Kusin, *From Dubcek to Charter 77* (New York: St. Martin's Press, 1978) for the Czechoslovak case.

22. See Wolchik, "Prospects for Political Change" and "The Roots of Change"; Sharon L. Wolchik, "Czechoslovakia in the Twentieth Century," paper presented at Rutgers University conference on the Troubled History of East Central Europe in the Twentieth Century, New Brunswick, N.J., February 24, 1990; and Sharon Wolchik, *Czechoslovakia in Transition: Politics, Economics, and Society* (London: Pinter Publishers, 1991).

23. See Peter C. Ludz, *The Changing Party Elite in East Germany* (Cambridge: MIT Press, 1972) for an analysis of these relationships at an earlier stage. For more recent developments, see William Griffith, "The German Democratic Republic," in *Central and Eastern Europe*, ed. Griffith; and Mike Dennis, *German Democratic Republic: Politics, Economics, and Society* (London: Pinter Publishers, 1988), chs. 1, 3, and 4.

24. This finding is best documented in the Soviet case but appears to hold true in central and eastern Europe as well. See Brian D. Silver, "Political Beliefs of the Soviet Citizen: Sources of Support for Regime Norms," in *Politics, Work and Daily Life in the USSR: A Survey of Former Soviet Citizens*, ed. James Millar (Cambridge: Cambridge University Press, 1987) for information on the

Soviet case. For evidence of similar attitudes in central and eastern Europe, see George Konrad and Ivan Szelényi, *Intellectuals and Class Power* (New York: Harcourt Brace Jovanovich, 1979); Rudolf Tokes, "Intellectuals and their Discontent in Hungary: Class Power or Marginality?" in *Domestic and Foreign Policy*, ed. Sodaro and Wolchik; and Connor, *Socialism, Politics, and Equality.*

25. See Hankiss, "In Search of a New Paradigm," pp. 206–9, for survey results in Hungary supporting this argument.

26. Jacek Tarkowski, "Endowment of the Nomenklatura: Or Apparatchiks Turned into Entrepreneurchiks: Or From Communist Ranks to Capitalist Riches," *Innovation* (March 1990); and "Enfranchisement of the Nomenklatura: From Feudalism to Capitalism?" Uncaptive Minds 2 (November–December 1989): 15–16; Jerzy Szperkowicz, "Enfranchise and Don't Worry About It," *Uncaptive Minds* 2 (November–December 1989): 16–17; Janos Lipinski, "Don't Franchise the Nomenklatura," *Uncaptive Minds* 2 (November–December 1989): 17–18; and Wolchik, "Domestic Developments."

27. Leaders of new parties and political groupings such as the Civic Forum in Prague, for example, had to worry about such simple elements of running an election campaign as finding adequate numbers of xeroxing and duplicating machines to make leaflets, as well as about larger issues of campaign strategy and finding appropriate candidates. The communist parties or their successors, on the other hand, had experienced activists and were well supplied. Interview with Ivan Havel, Prague, March 10, 1990; and interview with Jan Urban, executive director, Civic Forum, Prague, March 15, 1990.

28. "Free Democrats Take Lead in Elections in Hungary," *Washington Post*, March 26, 1990, pp. A1 and A16.

29. East Berlin ADN International Service, reported as "Provisional Overall Election Results Noted," in Foreign Broadcast Information Service, *Daily Report*, FBIS-EEU-90-053, March 19, 1990, p. 35.

30. See Wolchik, "Czechoslovakia in the Twentieth Century" and "Domestic Developments."

31. "Výsledky voleb do FS a CNR podle jednotlivých krajů," *Svobodné slovo*, June 12, 1990, p. 4; Marek Boguszak, Ivan Gabal, and Vladimír Rak, "Czechoslovakia Ready for Democracy," *Washington Post*, February 7, 1990, p. A23.

32. "Official Election Results," Foreign Broadcast Information Service, *Daily Report*, FBIS-EEU-90-119, June 20, 1990, pp. 2–3.

33. "Political Poll," *Report on Eastern Europe*, April 26, 1991, p. 26.

34. Louis Zanga, "The Multiparty Elections," *Report on Eastern Europe*, April 26, 1991, p. 4.

35. "Electoral Bureau Issues Final Vote Tally," Foreign Broadcast Information Service, *Daily Report*, FBIS-EEU90-103, May 29, 1990, pp. 39–40.

36. From information in U.S. Commission on Security and Cooperation in Europe, "Report on the April and May 1990 Elections in the Yugoslav Republics of Slovenia and Croatia," May 31, 1990.

37. "Serbian Election Results," *Report on Eastern Europe*, January 11, 1991, p. 45.

38. Milan Andrejevich, "The Election Scorecard for Serbia, Montenegro, and Macedonia," *Report on Eastern Europe*, December 21, 1990, pp. 37–39.

39. Milan Andrejevich, "Bosnia-Herzegovina: Yugoslavia's Linchpin," *Report on Eastern Europe*, December 7, 1991, p. 27.

40. Andrejevich, "The Election Scorecard for Serbia, Montenegro, and Macedonia," p. 39.

41. See Samuel H. Barnes, Peter McDonough, and Antonio Lopez Pina, "The Development of Partisanship in New Democracies: The Case of Spain," *American Journal of Political Science* 29 (November 1985): 695–720; Peter McDonough, Antonio Lopez Pina, and Samuel H. Barnes, "The Spanish Public in Political Transition," *British Journal of Political Science* 11 (January 1981): 49–79; and Laszlo Bruzst, "Without Us But For Us: Political Orientation in Hungary in the Period of Later Paternalism," *Social Research* 55 (Spring–Summer 1988): 43–76.

42. Barbara Donovan, "The Local Election in East Germany," *Report on Eastern Europe*, May 25, 1990, p. 24.

43. "Summary of Regional Election Results Nationwide," Foreign Broadcast Information Service, *Daily Report*, FBIS-EEU-90-060, March 28, 1990, p. 30; "Výsledky voleb do FS a CNR podle jednotlivých krajů," p. 4.

44. "Official Election Results," p. 3.

45. "Electoral Bureau Issues Final Vote Tally," pp. 39–40; "Final Count of Seats in Parliament," Foreign Broadcast Information Service, *Daily Report*, May 25, 1990, p. 39.

46. Andrejevich, "The Election Scorecard for Serbia, Montenegro, and Macedonia," p. 39.

47. From information in U.S. Commission on Security and Cooperation in Europe.

48. Vladimir Kusin, "The Elections Compared and Assessed," *Report on Eastern Europe*, July 13, 1990, p. 42.

49. Barnes, McDonough, and Pina, "The Development of Partisanship"; McDonough, Pina, and Barnes, "The Spanish Public"; Guillermo O'Donnell, Phillippe C. Schmitter, and Laurence Whitehead, eds., *Transitions from Authoritarian Rule: Prospects for Democracy* (Baltimore; Johns Hopkins University Press, 1986); Larry Diamond, Juan J. Linz, and Seymour Lipset, eds., *Democracy in Developing Countries*, vol. 4: *Latin America* (Boulder: Lynne Rienner, 1989); and James Malloy and Mitchell Selgson, eds., *Authoritarians and Democrats: Regime Transition in Latin America* (Pittsburgh: University of Pittsburgh Press, 1987). See Bunce, "The Transition from State Socialism," for an evaluation of what would be needed to transfer state socialist systems into liberal democracies.

50. Wolchik, "Domestic Developments" and "Czechoslovakia in the Twentieth Century."

51. See Wolchik, "Domestic Developments," for further elaborations of this argument.

52. Bunce, "The Transition from State Socialism."

53. See Geoff Ely, "Reviewing the Socialist Tradition," in this volume.

Classes and Parties in the Transition to Postcommunism

The Case of Hungary, 1989–1990

Iván Szelényi and

Szonja Szelény

In February 1989 the Hungarian Socialist Workers' party (Magyar Szocialista Munkáspárt [MSZMP]) formally accepted the principles of multiparty democracy. Within thirteen months of this decision, free elections were held and a complex political system emerged in which six parties came to represent distinct "political fields" in parliament. These thirteen months offer a fascinating study of political institution-building and sophisticated coalition politics.

The objective of this chapter is to describe the emergent political fields in Hungary. We will identify the principal issues around which these fields are organized, the political constituencies on which they draw, the way in which actors competing for these fields emerge, and the process by which their struggle unfolds. Our empirical observations are confined mainly to Hungary, but many of our conclusions might well be extended to the whole region in central Europe.

During the postcommunist transition in central Europe three different political fields are in the making: liberal, Christian nationalist (i.e., center-right), and social democratic. The Hungarian elections in March and April 1990 produced an impressive victory for Christian nationalist parties. With the slight exception of Czechoslovakia (where the victorious Civic Forum, on the liberal side of the political spectrum, opted rather than was forced to enter into a coalition with the Christian democrats), this seems to be the dominant trend in the entire non-Balkan region of central Europe. The dominant forces are Christian nationalist in East Germany, Poland, Croatia, and Slovenia.[1]

In the Hungarian case, the Christian nationalist field is made up of several political parties: the nationalist Hungarian Democratic Forum (Magyar Demokrata Fórum [MDF]), the petty bourgeois Independent Smallholders' party (Független Kisgazdapárt, [FKGP]), and the conservative Christian Democratic party (Kereszténydemokrata Néppárt [KDNP]). Despite some differences in their political programs, these parties have combined to form a coalition government. Together, they hold almost 60 percent of all seats in parliament. The liberals are represented by the Alliance of Free Democrats (Szabad Demokraták Szövetsége [SZDSZ]) and the Alliance of Young Democrats (Fiatal Demokraták Szövetsége [FIDESZ]). Between the two, they have acquired one-third of all votes and, for this reason alone, they constitute the main source of opposition. Finally, the political Left in Hungary is represented by the Hungarian Socialist party (Magyar Szocialista Párt [MSZP]). It is constituted by the reform wing of the old Communist party and, because of its relatively poor performance in the elections, holds less than 10 percent of all seats in the current parliament. Despite such variations in the political organizations, not a single organization has come forward to represent the social democratic field.

It might be tempting to argue that the outcome of the 1990 elections was not a surprise in that it reflected a return to the political traditions of the region. Such reasoning, in fact, has inspired at least one American commentator to label the current transformation of central Europe as a conservative revolution.[2] Arguments of this kind are not without historical evidence. In Hungary, for example, democratic elections prior to the establishment of the socialist regime have repeatedly produced center-right victories: in 1945 the Smallholders' party won 57 percent of the votes, in 1938 the Party of Hungarian Life (Magyar Élet Pártja) won 70 percent of the votes, and in 1906 the Independence party (Függetlenségi Párt) gained 62 percent of all seats in parliament.[3] A cursory glance at election results from the past might lead one to conclude that embedded in Hungarian political culture is a strong "taste" for Christian nationalist political rule.

As sociologist-commentators have tried to predict the outcome of events in Hungary, they have felt themselves seated in a theater with the curtains still drawn. They wondered what may be in preparation behind the curtains after forty years of communist rule. Astonishingly, as the curtains were raised, the audience was confronted with a still life: the "act" that was interrupted with the transition to socialism seems to have continued as if nothing has happened.

Given the success of the center-right in presocialist elections, one might have anticipated the historical pendulum to move in a "right-wing" direction after decades of the left-wing deviations. Such expectations notwithstanding, the restoration of prewar politics in Hungary requires an explanation. Since 1948, after all, Hungarian social structure has undergone fundamental changes. For example, the peasantry and the genteel middle class, the usual social base for center-right political forces in the past, were virtually eliminated under the socialist regime.[4] At the same time, the postwar industrialization of the Hungarian economy resulted in the creation of a massive industrial proletariat and, along with this, the emergence of a social democratic field. In light of these changes, one would have expected to see a general weakening of the traditional center-right and a strengthening of social democratic sentiments. Surprisingly, however, the outcome of the March–April elections produced the opposite result. How can one account for the exceptionally poor predictive power of structural factors and the apparent continuity of political culture in the Hungarian elections?

Class Structure and Political Fields

The class structure of postcommunist Hungary assumes a tripolar form. As indicated in Figure 1, the main distinctions are between professionals, proprietors, and workers. This mapping of the class structure has its origins in the old socialist regime. In the classical model of socialism, the state had complete monopoly over the organization of economic life. Class differences were characterized by a single hierarchy of positions in which the old communist (cadre) elite was at the top and the working class at the bottom.[5] With the gradual erosion of central management, this unimodal organization was complemented by a second hierarchy of occupations, a hierarchy based on market integration.[6] Here, ascent and descent were determined by ownership of wealth and entrepreneurial skills. Not surprisingly, therefore, owners and entrepreneurs were located at the apex of the hierarchy and wage workers at its bottom.

With the events of 1989, Central European societies began a swift but arduous journey toward market economy. At this stage in their de-

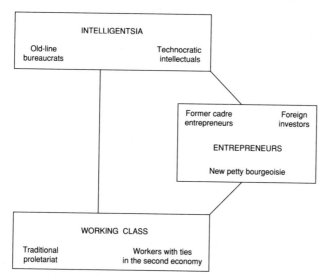

Figure 1. The class structure of postcommunist Hungary, 1990

velopment it would be premature still to designate them as fully fledged capitalist societies. They are best characterized as socialist mixed economies in which the state continues to dominate economic life, but the private sector plays a stronger and more complimentary role.

In spite of the continued hegemonic role of the state sector in Central European economies, the power relationships within the dominant elite have already begun to change. Fragments of the old elite are increasingly isolated from the new centers of power, while others are being forced out of elite positions altogether. Only those members of the old guard have managed to survive who were able to convert their political assets into cultural assets or economic capital. In the postcommunist regime, professionals in high-ranking positions (especially those without prior attachment to the MSZMP) are acquiring new powers of influence.

It follows from this that, in the transition to postcommunism, the ruling elite is highly fragmented. The old-line bureaucracy, in the Gouldnerian sense of the term, is shrinking in size, while a new class of intellectuals is becoming hegemonic.[7] Together they constitute 5–10 percent of the working population.

Not only professionals, but also the emergent entrepreneurial class is fragmented into at least three parts. Following Poulantzas, its first and largest section can be characterized as the new petty bourgeoisie.[8] This class fragment grew out of what used to be the second economy; its incumbents are small proprietors in agriculture, service industries, and, increasingly, manufacturing. This is potentially a large class fraction. According to an opinion poll, 25–30 percent of all Hungarians wish to start a business on their own, a figure that may be regarded as the percentage of aspiring, or potential, new petty bourgeoisie. Realistically, however, as of fall 1990, only about 10 percent of the working population could be regarded as being in this category.

The second fragment of the entrepreneurial class is made up of those members of the old communist elite who, through management buy-outs or joint ventures with Western firms, have successfully converted their political assets into economic capital.[9] They are what might be called a political bourgeoisie in central Europe. Although this class fragment is much smaller than the new petty bourgeoisie, it has attracted a great deal of political interest and, for this reason alone, it may end up playing a significant role in the shaping of Hungarian political culture.

Finally, the third segment of the entrepreneurial class grew directly out of foreign investments into the Hungarian economy. By fall 1990, foreign capital had begun to play a significant role in the economic life of Central European societies. Through joint ventures and by direct investments, foreign owners and their *comprador intelligentsia* (i.e., professionals hired by foreign capitalists to run their local affairs) began to have a significant impact on social and political life. The number of "players" in this group are still rather small, but their influence is considerable because they control many outlets in the mass media.[10]

The third class position (i.e., the working class) is also fragmented. In addition to the well-known cleavages (i.e., frictions between blue- and white-collar workers, skilled and unskilled manual jobs, and supervisors and supervisees), the presence of the second economy has produced another division among workers: those involved in the second economy and those left out. By the mid-1980s two-thirds of all Hungarian households made some of their living from the second economy. Most depended mainly on their wages from the state, but a growing proportion began to live a genuinely dual existence between the private and the state sectors.[11]

The three political fields among class cleavages are illustrated in

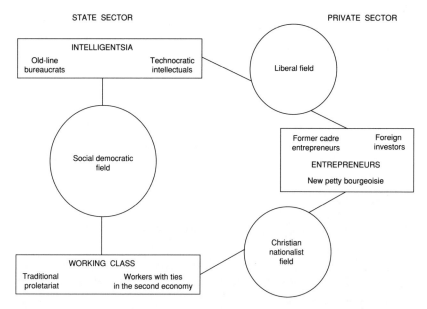

STATE SECTOR   PRIVATE SECTOR

INTELLIGENTSIA

Old-line   Technocratic
bureaucrats   intellectuals   Liberal field

                                                     Former cadre   Foreign
                                                     entrepreneurs   investors
                Social democratic
                     field   ENTREPRENEURS

                                                     New petty bourgeoisie

                                                     Christian
                                                     nationalist
            WORKING CLASS   field
Traditional   Workers with ties
proletariat   in the second economy

Figure 2. Political fields in postcommunist Hungary, 1990

Figure 2. The liberal field opens between the intellectual elite (especially its professional, or "technocratic" fraction) and the entrepreneurial class. SZDSZ and FIDESZ are the two parties that have thus far competed for this field. Bálint Magyar, one of the most articulate theorists of SZDSZ, has described the class character of his party by saying that "our social base is composed of three groups: the radical salaried workers, the small entrepreneurs, and a significant proportion of the intelligentsia."[12]

The Christian nationalist field is located between the entrepreneurial class and the working class. It is especially popular among those incumbents of the working class who participate in the second economy and is contested by the MDF, FKGP, and KDNP.

Finally, the social democratic field opens between the working class and the intellectual elite. With the transition to market economy, it is expected that a large fraction of the working class will suffer a great deal. Many will be thrown out of jobs and, without exception, all will experience a decrease in standard of living. In pushing for some protection from the state, this fraction of the working class may find allies not only in the old-line Stalinist bureaucracy, but also among those professionals who either have ideological reservations about full-scale

The Case of Hungary, 1989–1990   **119**

privatization or are existentially threatened themselves by the transformation.

Hungarian Election Results

The March–April elections produced the following distribution of parliamentary seats across the three political fields in Hungary.

1. The governing Christian nationalist (i.e., center-right) coalition was supported by 59.5 percent of all votes: 42.7 percent of these went to MDF, 11.4 percent to FKgP, and 5.4 percent to KDNP.

2. 29 percent of the population voted for the two liberal parties: 23.6 percent of these votes went to SZDSZ, and 5.4 percent to FIDESZ.

3. MSZP was supported by 8.5 percent of all voters.

4. The remaining 3 percent of all seats (of a total of 386 positions) were filled by members of other (primarily smaller) parties, as well as by independent candidates.

From the perspective of a class-analytic approach, the most surprising result of these elections was the poor showing of those parties nominally competing for the social democratic field. MSZP won only 8.5 percent of the seats in parliament, while the other two parties, MSZMP and the Hungarian Social Democratic party (Magyar Szociáldemokrata Párt [MSZDP]) just missed out on the 4 percent vote necessary to obtain a seat. On the whole, therefore, the political forces ready to use the "socialist" or the "social democratic" label in the elections received less than 16 percent of the popular vote, although the class-analytic approach predicted that at least 20–30 percent of the working population (that is, most of the working class and some segments of the professional class) could have voted for them. The discrepancy between the observed outcome of the elections and the prediction produced from analysis of the Hungarian class structure requires an explanation.

Along similar lines, it is important to account for the relatively unsuccessful performance of the liberal parties. To be sure, SZDSZ and FIDESZ both fared reasonably well given the extent of their potential social base. At the same time, when one considers how popular they were in the early stages of the election campaign, one must come to the inevitable conclusion that they fared much worse than expected. At the start of the election campaign (during the summer of 1989), SZDSZ trailed MDF in public opinion polls. By December, however, they obtained a draw, leading many observers to conclude that the March–April elections could well lead to a liberal victory. It is important to explain why szDSZ was able to get so close to victory and yet, in the end, still lose the elections.

The poor performance of political parties on the Left and weakening of szDSZ during the last few weeks of the electoral campaigns are both linked to the fact that the social democratic field remained unrepresented in the Hungarian contest. Neither the old Communist party (MSZMP) nor its reformed wing (MSZP) were able to transform themselves into genuine representatives of the working class. Consequently, the social democratic field was, at least in principle, wide open for szDSZ. The liberals, however, did not dare to grab the Left and, for this reason alone, they lost the elections.

The social characteristics of voters are accurately predicted by this class theory. Those who did not vote constituted an untapped reservoir of social democratic sentiments that szDSZ could have mobilized on its behalf. In fact, nonvoters in Hungary decided not to participate in the elections because none of the parties running articulated their interests.

The elections were conducted in two rounds; candidates who did not win absolute majority in the first series of votes were required to run again. During the first round, 35 percent of those eligible did not cast their vote, a percentage that rose to 55 in the second round. Which way this silent majority would have voted, who could have inspired them to participate, and what kind of political program would have mobilized them are decisive issues for the political future of central Europe.

Voters and Nonvoters

In May 1990, the Social Research Informatics Society (Társadalomku-tatási Informatikai Társulás [TÁRKI]) conducted a nationwide survey of public opinion in Hungary. Following the well-established format of Hungarian social stratification surveys, a sample of 981 individuals was questioned about their education, income, and occupation. In addition, they were also asked whether they participated in the March–April elections, which party they supported with their vote, and what their attitudes were on a range of social, economic, and political issues.[13]

Results from this survey indicate that the class-analytic approach predicts the outcome of elections reasonably. The two liberal parties, SZDSZ and FIDESZ, appealed primarily to professionals, whereas MDF enjoyed a more diverse class base. At the same time, results also show that class and class-based economic attitudes do not explain respondents' party choice fully. Social structural variables account for a much larger percentage of the total variation in voter turnout than they do in party choice.

Class and Party Preference

In examining class patterns in party preference, MDF was found the least class- or status-based of all the political parties in Hungary. In the March–April elections, its electoral base cut across class lines, and support for its policies came evenly from subpopulations with different age and educational profiles. By comparison, SZDSZ was favored primarily by white-collar workers (particularly by routine nonmanual workers and professionals), whereas FKGP and KDNP were popular primarily among peasants and blue-collar workers. The strength of the association between class background and party preference is not strong. It is important to note, however, that the patterning of the results conforms to expectations.

Results on the electoral performance of FIDESZ, FKGP, and KDNP lend further evidence to our claims. In line with expectations, FKGP was the most populist of all the parties: 73 percent of those who remember having voted for this party were farmers and blue-collar workers. KDNP followed closely with 70.2 percent of the populist vote, whereas only 44.1 percent of FIDESZ voters were farmers or blue-collar workers.

MSZP was the least popular among farmers and blue-collar workers; in addition, it received little support from less-educated respondents. Only 39.2 percent of MSZP voters were farmers or blue-collar workers, and only 32.7 percent of its constituency was composed by less-educated individuals.

As we expected, therefore, parties occupying the Christian nationalist field were most popular among peasants and blue-collar workers, whereas those occupying the liberal field appealed primarily to routine nonmanual workers and professionals. MSZP's performance with respect to the usual social democratic constituency was exceptionally poor.

The most significant finding that emerged from these analyses is that class is a more powerful predictor of voter turnout than it is of party choice. Specifically, we found that both blue-collar workers and less-educated respondents were vastly overrepresented among those who stayed away from the polling booths. In May 1990, for example, blue-collar workers constituted 52 percent of the Hungarian labor force, yet 63 percent of all "no-shows" came from this class category. Likewise, 38 percent of all Hungarians in May 1990 completed eight years of schooling or less, yet as much as 50 percent of those who did not vote in the elections came from this group of respondents.

In trying to account for the effects of class and education on voter turnout, two explanations are possible. On the one hand, it might be argued that the absence of blue-collar workers and less-educated individuals from the polling booths indicates their lack of interest in politics. This is by no means a new line of argument; in fact, it is frequently employed in explanations of the same general trend in Western democratic regimes.[14] In the case of Central European societies, however, a second argument could be made: the strength of the class effect on voter turnout indicates that none of the parties offered a political package attractive to blue-collar workers. Accordingly, one could entertain two alternative explanations of the nonvote in Hungary: one of these would tell a story about working-class "apathy," while the other would pay attention to characteristics of the "social democratic constituency" and, on the basis of this, consider the nonvote as a "protest vote"—that is, a vote against the absence of a viable social democratic alternative in the Hungarian elections.

Not surprisingly, perhaps, apathy as well as protest influenced nonvoter behavior in the March–April elections. However, lack of interest in political life seems to have played a surprisingly weak role. The question of apathy was tapped by a single item on the May 1990 survey; respondents were asked how interested they were in political issues.[15] Contrary to expectations on the basis of the apathy arguments, the overwhelming majority of nonvoters were either "considerably" or "very interested" in politics. What is more, the same pattern of responses was observed among voters as well. From this it follows that apathy, at best, provides a partial explanation for why people did not vote. Data from the May 1990 survey show a strong correlation between political attitudes and voting behavior. Specifically, we found that respondents who score high on social democratic values are significantly overrepresented among nonvoters.

Political Attitudes and Voting Behavior

It is not surprising that social, political, and economic values played an important role in the Hungarian elections, given the enormity of the social change that the electorate was being asked to make. In the course of their electoral campaigns, the two major opposition parties (MDF and SZDSZ) focused heavily on social and ethical issues. Candidates for SZDSZ were particularly outspoken on questions relating to civil liberties, and they were also quite critical of MDF for not being sufficiently committed to these issues. In its platform, MDF was indistinguishable from SZDSZ on human rights issues; however, its position on social issues (particularly with respect to abortion) was considerably more conservative.

The magnitude of the difference between the two parties became especially apparent in the closing speeches their leaders made on the night before the vital second round of the elections. In his final words to his television audience, the leader of MDF (József Antall) pledged that those who voted for his party would vote for a "quiet force," whereas the leader of SZDSZ (János Kis) promised the electorate a "radical change" and a "smashing of the party state."

While MDF and SZDSZ differed considerably on social issues, their stances on economic matters were similar. Both advocated the privatization of production units and the expansion of free markets, and neither paid much attention to questions of unemployment or growing inequalities. In other words, MDF and SZDSZ offered the electorate a clear choice between conservative and liberal values on social issues, but neither appealed to those voters who wanted to cast their ballot in favor of a welfare state, security of employment, and protected social benefits.

Results from the May 1990 survey indicate that the main difference between voters and nonvoters is much smaller on social issues and significantly more pronounced on attitudes toward economic reorganization. Thus, while nonvoters were, on average, more conservative than voters on social issues, it is also true that they held stronger social democratic opinions on economic matters.

This leads us to believe that there was a curious contradiction between popularly held attitudes and party platforms in the Hungarian elections. The major opposition parties all posited themselves on the political Right (in the Western sense of the term), but public opinion was overwhelmingly in favor of social democratic measures. Thus, for instance, when respondents in the May 1990 survey were asked whether it was the responsibility of the state to assure full employment, control prices, promote social justice, or monitor spending on health care, welfare, and education, 80–90 percent gave answers that favored a Scandinavian (i.e., social democratic) type of government.

Differences between voters and nonvoters were not restricted to issues relating to economic reform. At the time of the elections, nonvoters were particularly concerned with issues relating to jobs (i.e., unemployment and pensions, benefits), whereas voters were more interested in abstract social policy matters (i.e., government spending on culture, the environment, and education). In many ways, therefore, the main difference between these two groups of respondents is better described as the difference between left laborites and middle-of-the-road (or even right-wing) social democrats.

At any rate, it is clear from these results that there was a large social democratic constituency (both in terms of their class position and in the nature of their political attitudes) in Hungary and, moreover, the interests of this constituency were unrepresented during the last elections. For this reason, then, we believe that Hungarian political parties are skating on thin ice. What is emerging in political life may well be only the tip of the iceberg; dramatic changes could take place any day. The strong correlation between welfare statist attitudes (on economic matters) and conservative values (on social issues) makes the situation particularly explosive. It suggests that the silent majority in the last elections could be mobilized in the future, either around welfare issues (e.g., strong social democratic sentiments) or around issues of law and order (e.g., conservative social values). What follows is that the potential for Peronism is as much in the political future of central Europe as a Scandinavian-style welfare state government.[16] The direction that the political organization of these countries will take has less to do with the nature of their class structure, or the character of their political culture, than the dynamics of institution-building and the role of political leadership in the transition to postcommunism.

The social democratic constituency in Hungary is reasonably large, but it has also remained unmobilized in elections. By implication, therefore, the political culture of postcommunist societies is potentially less right-wing than it has demonstrated itself to be.

Given this argument, the obvious question is why none of the political parties in Hungary have tried to mobilize this social democratic constituency. In answering this question we hope to demonstrate that unique dynamics of political institution-building and questions of political leadership are probably just as important as the social composition of constituencies in the making of political fields.

During the summer of 1989, SZDSZ perceived MDF as a center-left party with close links to the communists (especially its populist wings represented by Imre Pozsgay). SZDSZ, therefore, focused its line of attack on the Left of MDF. In an interview during the summer of 1989, Bálint Magyar called MDF a "crypto-communist party" and suggested that it was designed by Pozsgay as a way to prepare himself for the collapse of communism while also trying to preserve his existing power base. Magyar argued that MDF was the postcommunist analogue of the Peasant party which, following 1945, was the gathering organization of a number of left-wing populist writers (i.e., the party of the "Third Way") who proved to be little more than communist fellow travelers.

During fall 1989, SZDSZ continued its line of attack on MDF by criticizing its link with the MSZP around the issue of the presidential elections. At this time, it appeared that MDF may have made a deal with MSZP. According to this deal, MDF was to have given the relatively strong presidency to MSZP (and, in particular, to Pozsgay) in return for majority rule in parliament. Suggestions were also made by SZDSZ ideologues that MDF may have even granted MSZP a "junior partner" role in government. Following the Polish pattern, the MDF-MSZP alliance had hoped to accomplish this by holding early presidential elections, an ingenious solution. If elections could have been held by the end of 1989 (or at the beginning of 1990), Pozsgay would have been guaranteed to win the presidency. After all, more than any other candidate, he was far ahead in public opinion polls. This is not surprising, of course, given that at this early date opposition candidates have not yet had a chance to make a name for themselves.

With good political insight, SZDSZ did not sign the agreement between MDF and MSZP, but called for a referendum to determine the timing of the presidential elections. According to Hungarian law, parliament is compelled to call for a referendum on an issue if more than a hundred thousand signatures demand it. SZDSZ had easily collected some two hundred thousand signatures toward this goal and, in November 1989, the referendum was held. MDF was in total disarray and unable to respond to the challenge SZDSZ posed. Members of MDF, however, began to sense that their ties to Pozsgay were becoming a handicap and that, in future, they would have to demonstrate greater distance from MSZP if they are to succeed in political life. During the referendum, MSZP advised its supporters to vote no on the question of whether presidential elections should be delayed. MDF, rather than following the MSZP suggestion, called for a boycott instead.

On the surface, this was not an unreasonable political strategy. According to Hungarian law, after all, 50 percent of the electorate has to vote in order for the referendum to be valid. Had the MDF strategy worked, SZDSZ could have lost the referendum. Unfortunately for MDF, however, the referendum produced good turnout (about 60 percent of those eligible voted) and, by a small margin, the yes vote was ratified. Against the wishes of MDF, therefore, the presidential elections were delayed.

The call for a referendum was a shrewd political move on the part of SZDSZ because it resulted in the breakup of the alliance between MSZP and MDF. In the process, it also succeeded in humiliating MDF, which, following the referendum, began to perform poorly in public opinion polls. In this manner, therefore, SZDSZ gained considerable popularity among Hungarian voters, although it did so by locating itself on the right of MDF. This initial success, however, was short-lived, and the dynamics of political institution-building began to take a new turn.

Soon after the referendum, József Antall took over the leadership of MDF. A historian whose father was a leading government official under Admiral Horthy, he had little to do with the left-wing populist writers of MDF that SZDSZ linked to the Communist party. Antall and the circle of friends around him had aristocratic connections; they were more center-right Christian democrats than the left-wing populists who were in charge of MDF before his leadership. In an effort to distance himself from MSZP, Antall gradually cut loose the Left populist wing of MDF and moved his party quite comfortably to the Right. He was very quick to realize that if the name of the Hungarian political game was anticommunism, he could play better than SZDSZ. After all, the leadership of SZDSZ included a large number of individuals who had relatively strong left-wing pasts: János Kis, for example, was a Lukács disciple and a prominent young Marxist during the early 1970s; Miklós Haraszti was a Maoist and a vocal opponent of the Kadárist re-privatization program during the late 1960s; even Gáspár Tamás (the most articulate supporter of nineteenth-century liberalism in SZDSZ) started his political career with anarcho-syndicalist aspirations. A large number of SZDSZ leaders also came from old (communist) cadre families. Beginning with January 1990, then, MDF politicians began to criticize the social and political origins of SZDSZ leadership and, in so doing, succeeded at beating SZDSZ at its own game. Antall and his circle of friends emerged from this battle as more authentically right-wing than members of SZDSZ.

Following this new line of attack from MDF, SZDSZ hesitated briefly over the nature of its political field. The leader of the party, János Kis, is thoroughly left-wing in his political values and would have been quite comfortable with a social democratic party platform. In an interview during one of his official visits to Paris, he characterized SZDSZ as a "center-left" party.[17] This statement was, quite simply, wishful thinking on his part. Given the nature of the attack from MDF, the leadership of SZDSZ considered it too risky to assume a left-wing stand, and Kis's Paris statement was swiftly shelved. Leadership of the party was taken over by a group of free-marketeers who continued the party's earlier policy of trying to position itself on the political right of MDF.

In light of the March–April election results, it is apparent that this move was a strategic error on the part of SZDSZ. By adhering to their initially winning tactic as a strategy in the long-run, SZDSZ lost the elections. Given the strength of the social democratic field in Hungary, SZDSZ could have performed much better if, following the MDF-MSZP split, it would have moved in the political field left open in the center-left.

After the elections, SZDSZ found itself in a difficult situation. Its representatives sit in a parliament dominated by fundamentally center-right political forces. Antall's confessed political model is Adenauer; no matter how one looks at it, there is no room to the right of this position. To demonstrate its difference from the ruling party, SZDSZ continues to display its liberalism on social issues. Thus, it fought bitterly against the reintroduction of religious training in schools, beyond doubt a noble cause, but one unlikely to produce further votes. According to a survey conducted by the Public Opinion Research Institute in Budapest, by end of May 1990, MDF and SZDSZ both began to lose public support, with SZDSZ being the bigger loser of the two parties.

Given its location across the three political fields, SZDSZ is probably destined to become little more than the free democrats in Germany or the Liberal party in England. From its current position it will never be able to take power away from MDF. Its success in the political arena is contingent on its ability to transform itself: it needs to move into the center-left position and construct a program that emphasizes welfare state policies and issues of social justice.

Despite its numerous strategic errors, SZDSZ continues to be the party best located to fill the social democratic field in Hungarian political culture. The predicaments of all other contenders appear to be considerably worse. First, the successor parties of the old communist elite (i.e., MSZMP and MSZP) do not appeal to the social democratic constituency. MSZP relies more heavily on the upper-middle class than any other party; its support among the working class is the weakest across all parties. This is not surprising, of course. The Communist party is seen as having betrayed fundamental working-class interests for forty years. In this context, it is unclear why workers should begin to trust it now.

The poor performance of MSZDP, the only party that announced its social democratic sentiments, is more surprising. Early commentators on the elections expected this party to do well in the campaigns. It received a great deal of support from Western social democratic parties and, given the strength of social democratic sentiments in Hungary, was located in the winning spot on the eve of the elections. These expectations notwithstanding, MSZDP failed to obtain even as much as 4 percent of the votes and, consequently, was not able to place any of its representatives inside the parliament. Reasons for this failure are complex but worthy of attention. Unlike the winning parties, MSZDP had considerable trouble with institution-building. In the initial stages of the election campaigns, an old guard of communists tried to rebuild the party from the inside, a strategy that had two problems. First, members of this old guard were all men in their seventies and eighties with little political future left. Second, they were unable to get along with each other. Their efforts to rebuild the party were delayed by constant disagreements, until they gave up and broke away from the party. At this point, a group of younger members tried to institute reforms, but their strategies did not work either. Young members of the party came into constant conflict with the old guard; due to their political inexperience and vulnerability, they ultimately lost out.

Following these internal fights, the party tried, once more, to restructure itself by rebuilding its public image. In so doing, however, it made further mistakes; it tried to return to the tradition of the 1920s and appeal to the worker with a hammer in his hand. This appeal seemed entirely unauthentic and cost the party a large number of votes. As a final strategy, MSZDP elected a woman, Anna Petrasovics, as chair. She possessed considerable charm and in the course of the campaigns demonstrated some political talent as well; however, she suffered from chronic lack of charisma and thus was unable to garner votes. Internal conflicts, lack of leadership, wrong policies, and an unauthentic image led to nothing for the party.

Postelection Political Life in Hungary

Events during the second half of 1990 gave further support for the argument that political institutions in postcommunist central Europe failed to represent the strength of social democratic sentiments in civil society. The municipal elections of October 14 are a case in point. Just as earlier, the rate of voter turnout in October was abysmally low: fewer than one-third of those eligible to vote did so. Low participation of this kind would normally be regarded as serious cause for concern. The October results, however, were particularly disturbing because political parties campaigned explicitly with the slogan that municipal elections, more so than any other attempt at restructuring the economy, represented the real change in the regime. It is apparent from the results that voters disagreed with this assessment and, to make matters worse, they actually reelected a significant percentage of mayors from the old government.

The municipal elections produced a humiliating defeat for MDF and its allies. Unlike in the March–April elections, SZDSZ and FIDESZ obtained almost equal proportion of the votes and, in so doing, gained absolute majority in most municipal governments. Above all, these results represented a major victory for FIDESZ, which increased its popular support significantly. SZDSZ did not receive more support from eligible voters than in the March–April elections. However, even with the same number of votes, it now had a larger share of the total number of votes cast in October. This is because a significant proportion of those who voted MDF earlier in the year either did not turn up at the polls or had cast their vote in favor of FIDESZ.

The municipal elections held in October also showed that the newly elected government suffered from a growing problem of legitimacy. During the early stages of the transition to postcommunism, forces of the opposition (among them, of course, MDF and its allies) argued that the power of the communists was illegitimate because it was not ordained by popular support. Ironically, the first freely elected government in Hungary also lacked popular support; it was chosen by a majority of that minority of voters who cast their ballot in the March–April elections. By October 1990, the democratic process deteriorated to such an extent that mayors were elected to their offices with as few as 15 percent of eligible voters supporting them.

Those who attributed low voter turnout to apathy were taught an important lesson during the last week of October, when cabdrivers staged a major blockade and brought the entire city of Budapest to a complete halt. The reasons behind this strike were straightforward. The Hungarian government—without consultation with the Chamber of Commerce, trade unions, or members of parliament—announced its intention to double gasoline prices from one day to the next. An increase of this magnitude, if enacted, would have threatened the economic well-being of many drivers. In an effort to prevent this from happening, they decided to engage in collective action. Within two to three hours of the government announcement, they blocked all intersections in the country and paralyzed transportation for two full days.

This event was sociologically interesting in several respects. It indicated, for example, that the legitimation crisis of the Hungarian government is not restricted to the ruling coalition, but in fact encompasses the entire political system. The cabdrivers chose to express their dissatisfaction in the form of an act of civil disobedience because they did not have enough confidence in parliamentary representatives to support their interest.

Although members of parliament were reluctant to show solidarity with the drivers' cause, the general population certainly was not. According to a small telephone survey conducted by the Hungarian Public Opinion Research Institute a day after the strike, 60 percent of the population gave unconditional support to the cabdrivers, and another 25 percent expressed sympathy with their cause. This is not entirely surprising given that spokespersons for the drivers successfully reframed the particular interests of the drivers as a much broader national cause. Specifically, they argued that the government was using the Persian Gulf crisis, as well as the resulting increase in prices, to boost its tax revenues from the sale of gasoline. They were also quite successful at convincing people that this strategy was unwise economically because its inflationary results could have disastrous effects in an economy already bordering on hyper-inflation. With the doubling of gasoline prices, they argued, about half of all cabdrivers would go out of business, the relative size of the proletariat would expand, competition for work would increase, and all would suffer from the inflationary effects of fuel price increases.

In the end, the dispute came to a halt in a negotiated settlement. In an uncommon alliance, the trade unions and representatives of the Chamber of Commerce joined forces against the government (or, to put it more generally, against the new political class) and forced a compromise. The price of gasoline was liberalized, and the amount of tax on each gallon was set at a fixed amount (rather than as a percentage). With the absorption of world market prices, government and its negotiating partners finally agreed on a modest price increase.

One of the most positive results of the cabdrivers' blockade was a major restructuring of the political parties. SZDSZ, under the leadership of Kis, once again made a cautious opening toward the center-left. Restructuring also took place on the political Left; Pozsgay exited from MSZP and announced his intention to form a "national center" political party.[18] Upon being freed from Pozsgay, MSZP held a national congress and formulated an unambiguously social democratic program. MDF also responded to the crisis with a major reorganization; populists within the party expressed dissatisfaction with Antall for pushing the party too far Right and argued for a political program that would recapture the left-populist vote. It is clear from these reorganization efforts that the political class in Hungary is beginning to learn the rules of electoral politics; politicians are starting to think in terms of constituencies and not in terms of ideologically inspired political programs. Moreover, they are also showing concern about low electoral turnout and formulating policies that they hope will capture the support of the silent majority.

The cabdrivers' blockade during the last week of October showed that the electorate in Hungary is far from apathetic. If they stayed away from the election booths, it was not because of lack of interest in politics, but because they simply did not see any of the political parties offering a desirable alternative to communist rule. This silent majority could go in different directions politically. From this point of view, the presidential elections in Poland during December 1990 were of utmost importance. Mazowieczki, who represented a sober version of liberal economic policies, suffered a humiliating defeat and finished only third in the first round of the elections, being beaten by an unknown Polish emigree from Canada. In the second round, Lech Wałęsa secured roughly 75 percent of the votes, and he did so with a largely Peronist program. He promised security, law and order, and also strong leadership.

In sum, there is a large social democratic constituency in Hungary around which a possible challenge to the dominant Christian nationalist regime could emerge. During the electoral campaigns of 1989 and 1990, however, the interests of this constituency remained unarticulated for a number of generally institutional reasons. The future of Hungarian politics depends on whether these institutional problems can be corrected. If the necessary center-left force fails to emerge, the dominance of the Christian nationalist forces is likely to last a long time. If a major crisis evolves due to the explosion of unemployment, for example, or unbearable increases of social inequality, there is considerable chance that a right-wing force could rise to power in Hungary, a force even further to the right than Antall's regime. This force could then fill the gap that the potential center-left parties failed to occupy during the elections.

Notes

This chapter was completed while the second author was the 1990–91 Annenberg Fellow in the School of Humanities and Sciences at Stanford University; support through a postdoctoral research grant from the Hoover Institution is also acknowledged. We are grateful to Éva Fodor, David B. Grusky, Tamás Kolosi, György Lengyel, John W. Meyer, Marc Ventresca, and Bruce Western for their helpful comments.

1. It is noteworthy that the "eastern region" of central Europe (represented by Romania, Bulgaria, and Serbia) followed a different path to postcommunism. As late as October 1990, countries in this region were still governed either by communists or successors of the old communist elite. Such differences in the developmental trajectories of the two regions may be coincidental. At the same time, we are impressed by the eerie continuity between these

patterns of development and a long-standing division in this region along the lines of Western and Eastern Christianity.

2. This statement was made by the president of the American Council of Learned Societies at a conference held in Budapest during the summer of 1990.

3. Gyula Benda, *Magyarország Történeti Kronológiája* (The chronological history of Hungary) (Budapest: Akadémiai Kiadó, 1983), pp. 810, 954, 1023.

4. Róbert Manchin and Iván Szelényi, "Theories of Family Agricultural Production in Collectivized Economies," *Sociologia Ruralis* 25 (1985): 260.

5. See Zygmunt Bauman, "Officialdom and Class: Basis of Inequality in Socialist Society," in *The Social Analysis of Class Structure*, ed. Frank Parkin (London: Tavistock, 1974); George Konrád and Iván Szelényi, *The Intellectuals on the Road to Class Power* (New York: Harcourt, Brace, and Jovanovich, 1979); Iván Szelényi, "Prospects and Limits of the New Class Project in Eastern Europe," *Politics and Society* 15 (1986–87); Iván Szelényi, *Socialist Entrepreneurs: Embourgeoisement in Rural Hungary* (Madison: University of Wisconsin Press, 1988); and Szonja Szelényi, "Social Inequality and Party Membership," *American Sociological Review* 52 (October 1987).

6. See Tamás Kolosi, "Stratification and Social Structure in Hungary," *Annual Review of Sociology* 14 (1988): 405–19, and *Tagolt Társadalom* (Stratified society) (Budapest: Gondolat Kiadó, 1989); and Szelényi, "Prospects and Limits."

7. Alwin Gouldner, *The Future of Intellectuals and the Rise of the New Class* (Oxford: Oxford University Press, 1979).

8. Nicos Poulantzas, *Classes in Contemporary Capitalism* (London: Verso, 1978), pp. 209–23.

9. For examples of such conversions, see Elemér Hankiss, *Kelet-Európai Alternatívák* (East European alternatives) (Budapest: Közgazdasági és Jogi Könyvkiadó, 1989); Jadwiga Staniszkis, *The Dynamics of the Breakthrough in Eastern Europe* (Berkeley: University of California Press, in press); Erzsébet Szalai, "Az Új Elít" (The new elite) Beszélö 27 (1989); and Erzsébet Szalai, "Ismét az Új Elítröl" (The new elite revisited), *Élet és Irodalom*, December 8, 1989.

10. The extent of sale of public property to domestic and foreign owners is unknown, but it almost certainly under 10 percent of all formerly state-controlled assets.

11. Szelényi, "Prospects and Limits," pp. 124–29; István Gábor, "The Major Domains of the Second Economy" in *Market and Second Economy in Hungary*, ed. Péter Galasi and György Sziráczki (Frankfurt: Campus Verlag, 1985), pp. 133–79.

12. *Magyar Nemzet*, August 1, 1990, p. 5.

13. The data collection was supervised by Tamás Kolosi, director of TÁRKI. The questionnaire was administered as part of a larger survey sponsored by the International Social Survey Program. For greater details, see Tamás Kolosi, *International Social Survey Program: Hungary 1990* [MRDF] (Budapest: Social Research Informatics Society, 1990).

14. See, for example, Roberto Michels, *Political Parties* (New York: Free Press, 1966).

15. The precise wording of this question was as follows: "Mennyire ér-

deklödik ön a politika iránt?" (How interested are you in politics?). The full set of possible responses included: "nagyon" (very much), "melehetösen" (considerably), "nem nagyon" (not very much), "egy kicsit" (a little), and "egyáltalán nem" (not at all).

16. Juan Peron was elected as president of Argentina in 1946 largely by working-class support. In its centrist-authoritarian politics, Peronism brought together a unique combination of nationalist sentiments with right-wing social attitudes, as well as a strong sense of law and order and a positive orientation toward trade unions. For more details on Peronism, see Seymour Martin Lipset, *Political Man* (New York: Doubleday, 1960), pp. 173–75; and Giullermo A. O'Donnell, *Modernization and Bureaucratic-Authoritarianism* (Berkeley: Institute of International Studies, 1979), pp. 56–77.

17. Interview with János Kis, December 1989.

18. Pozsgay's new party will represent an alliance between the center-left and the nationalist center-right.

19. Voter turnout in the Polish elections was almost as low as in Hungary. On December 9, when Wałęsa was elected president, only 55 percent of the electorate turned up at the polls.

After the Golden Age

Is Social Democracy Doomed to Decline?

Wolfgang Merkel

With the temporary "blockage of the Keynesian coordination," the numerical decline of blue-collar workers, the growing differentiation among wager earners' rising social demands, and a shrinking ability of social democracy to shape the political discourse of reformism, progress, and modernity during the 1970s, the traditional favorable environment for social democratic politics and policies seemed to dissolve.

Considering these developments as if they occurred simultaneously and independently of specific national contexts, political and social scientists, liberals, Marxists, and the New Left simply subsumed them under a generally valid crisis theory. Value judgments and judgments of facts were confused, and empirical analyses of political scientists fell victim to ideologies or sophisticated general theories. As if a mysterious "invisible hand" conducted this Babel of voices, they seem to harmoniously spread the message of crisis, decline, and the end of social democracy.

The Neoliberal Voice. Not very cautious in its prophecies, the neoliberal voice predicts nothing less than "the end of the social democratic century."[1] The main argument is that, with the establishment of the welfare state, social democracy has already fulfilled its historical task. However, in having done so, it has overburdened the economy, weakening the self-regulative forces of the free market and the meritocratic incentives of citizens.[2] Social democrats overestimated the role the state can play in steering the economy and society. They have underestimated the paralyzing forces that "hypertrophic" state activities can have upon economic dynamics and welfare. "Big government" does not solve economic and social problems, it creates them. It crowds out resources from the market system while the overdevelopment of the welfare state makes people passive economic actors in the market system.[3] In sum, overly extensive state regulation disturbs the vital forces of the market system. The voices of neoconservatives (Michel Crozier et al.), supply siders (Arthur Laffer), monetarists (Milton Friedman), fiscal conservatives (Friedrich Hayek), or rational expectationists (James Buchanan) commonly argue that everybody would be better off if the state withdrew from the economy and investors were no longer restrained by disturbing interventionist or distributional regimes.

The Paleo-Marxist Voice. Whereas the liberal and neoconservative voice criticizes the "overstretching of the welfare state" and laments "too much state," orthodox Marxists complain about "too much market" in the social democratic state. The "collapse of Keynesianism" and the breakdown of corporatism since the economic crisis of the 1970s exhausted the limits of social democracy's reformist and electoral possibilities.[4] What has remained of its former self is "a ghost, a form of nostalgia. A nostalgia, ridiculous and poignant for something which once existed and will never exist again."[5] Having rejected the road to socialism, social democrats fell victim to their own attempt to administer capitalism more socially.

The Voice of Rational Choice. Social democracy as a "historical phenomenon"[6] has not simply failed due to deviations from a supposedly "correct line" or the betrayal of its leaders. It has rather been doomed because of rational strategic choices that leaders were forced to make facing specific "dilemma of electoral socialism."[7] When it appeared that workers never become a numerical majority in any society, it became clear that the mandate for the social democratic project— the emancipation of workers—could not be obtained from workers alone. Leaders of social democratic-socialist parties must seek support elsewhere in society, that is, they must continuously decide "whether or not to seek electoral success at the cost, or at least at the risk, of diluting class lines and consequently diminishing the salience of class as a motive for the political behavior of workers themselves."[8] Here the dilemma appears. To be electorally successful, social democratic parties cannot appeal to workers alone; they have to assume a "supraclass posture." In so doing they dilute their capacity to win workers as a class. Therefore, social democratic and socialist leaders are confronted with a persistent trade-off dilemma. They are condemned to minority status when they pursue class-only strategies, and they lose votes among the working class when they follow supraclass electoral strategies appealing also to the middle class. "Unable to win either way" is the quintessence of the electoral dilemma of democratic socialism.[9]

Przeworski and Sprague perceive social democratic parties as passive victims of an electoral trade-off: the more allies social democracy wins among the middle class, the more workers it will lose. However, the steepness of the trade-offs, that is, the "opportunity costs," vary with the strength of the unions, the existence of neocorporatist institutions, and Communist party competition for the working class vote. But these factors matter only temporarily, they do not alter the fundamental logic of the strict trade-off. Consequently, Przeworski and Sprague conclude, "Thus the era of electoral socialism may be over."[10]

A peculiar paradox can be detected in Przeworski and Sprague's explanation. On the one hand is epistemological elegance of the choice-centered perspective of methodological individualism; on the other hand, the rational choice approach does not protect Przeworski and Sprague from ultimately falling victim to a rather crude sociological determinism. Although the authors concede that electoral strategies and specific policies may make a short-term difference, they state that in the long run the fate of electoral socialism is determined by industrial change and a supposedly unchanging electoral dilemma. "Ultimately, it probably mattered relatively little whether socialist leaders did everything they could to win the elections. Their choices were limited." The authors' concession that "parties mold the 'public opinion,' . . . evoke collective identification, [and] instill political commitments"[12] has no bearing on their final conclusion.

Neither the neoliberal, the Marxist, nor the rational choice assumptions of the "voices" are sufficient or appropriate to justify their prophetic predictions and deterministic conclusions. Their common weakness is the static perception of social democracy as a political actor and the inherent tendency to neglect varying political institutions, socioeconomic contexts, and cycles as nationally differing "opportunity structures" for political choices. On the one hand, they provide a detailed and pervasive analysis of the dynamic change of the economic, social, and political environment since the mid-seventies.

On the other hand, they consider the social democratic parties simply as passive victims of a changing world, thereby neglecting their revisionist capacity to reassess values, strategies, and policies in the light of these changes to reshape the conditions for their political survival and success.

Two approaches that avoid such fallacies of a priori exclusions of possible relevant independent variables and deterministic conclusions, whether motivated by ideology or the intellectual esthetics of theoretical monism, have been presented by Gösta Esping-Andersen and Fritz Scharpf.[13] The "enlightened sociostructural" analysis of Esping-Andersen's "Politics against Markets" shows in the example of Scandinavia that social democratic parties are not simply doomed to sociostructural change, but have choices that have a decisive impact on their success or failure. Specific adjustments of policies to the changed environment, writes Esping-Andersen, can help create and strengthen the alliance between blue-collar workers and the middle class, possibly a winning social coalition. State policies that modify the mechanism and outcomes of the market are still at the core of these adjustments.[14] Fritz Scharpf's "neoinstitutional" approach links politics and policies to varying institutional opportunity structures. If social democratic parties succeed in designing their policies appropriately according to relevant institutions and power relations in state and society, they do not have to renounce political values and goals, not even under the auspices of a world economy dominated by monetarism and supply-side economics, as the social democratic governments of Austria and Sweden have demonstrated. A part of my own study will take patterns from the two studies of Esping-Andersen and Scharpf in order to link the nationally differing opportunity structures to the rise, resilience, or decline of social democratic parties and policies. Against the background of these considerations, I will investigate the question of the supposed decline of social democracy on three levels: (1) the electoral evolution of social democratic parties in western Europe since 1945; (2) the social democratic participation in government after 1945; and (3) the economic and social policies of social democratic governments during the 1980s.

Social Democratic and Socialist Parties at the Polls

The following analysis of the postwar electoral trends of social democracy is on a highly aggregate level. Nevertheless, I will present the first empirical evidence of how dubious it is to speak of a general and irreversible "decay," "decline," and "crisis" of social democracy. To test the decline hypothesis for the "post golden age" of social democracy (after the first oil price shock) I will divide the postwar period into two phases: 1945 to 1973, the golden age of social democracy, and 1974 to 1990, the so-called "decline period" (Table 1).

In order to control and specify the findings of these two periods, I will compare the electoral results of a narrowly defined golden age from 1960 to 1973, when the postwar economy was reconstructed and most West European countries experienced their "economic miracle," with the electoral results from 1980 to 1990, when according to the decline hypotheses the crisis of social democracy should have advanced still further.

The figures of Table 1 can only be read as a classical falsification of the decline hypotheses as far as the electoral level is concerned. The average of the national electoral results of all West European social democratic and socialist parties (excluding the parties of Iceland and Luxembourg due to the small size of the two countries) for the total postwar period has been 31.2 percent. During the golden years from 1945 to 1973 social democratic parties polled 31.7 percent, only 0.5 percent more than throughout the whole postwar period. Even if one compares the electoral average of the golden years in the narrow definition (1960 to 1973, 31.8 percent) with the total postwar average, the result does not change. These findings are confirmed when the electoral data of the good years (1945 to 1973) are compared directly with that of the decline period, when social democratic parties gained 31.5 percent (1974 to 1990) or 31.5 percent (1980 to 1990) of the popular vote; 0.2 percent can hardly be interpreted as an irreversible decline. Since the mid-seventies, when political science literature on the crisis of social democracy began to boom, no measurable general decline occurred in the electoral level. On the contrary, social democratic parties reached their electoral peak in 1983, when the demise of social democracy should have been particularly visible. It is not the decline that must be explained, rather it is the striking stability of the social democratic vote, as Klaus Armingeon convincingly points out.[15]

To explore the reasons for the stability of the social democratic vote on a less aggregate level without referring simply to all single cases, it might be useful to group the social democratic parties under different subtypes and to examine those groups of social democratic parties specifically. One possibility of classification has already been carried

Table 1. Electoral Share (%) of Social Democratic Parties at National Elections in Western Europe (averages)

	1945–90	1945–73	1960–73	1974–90	1980–90
Austria	45.2	44.2	46.3	47.0	44.6
Belgium	30.2	32.1	30.0	27.2	28.2
Denmark	36.0	37.7	38.7	33.3	32.2
Finland	24.8	24.8	24.0	24.9	25.4
France	21.7	17.5	16.8	32.3	34.7
Greece				35.8	42.2
Ireland	11.2	12.4	14.5	9.3	8.7
Italy	16.5	17.6	17.3	14.9	16.4
Netherlands	29.1	27.7	25.9	31.5	31.0
Norway	42.3	44.2	42.9	38.7	37.4
Portugal				30.6	27.2
Sweden	45.5	46.3	46.8	43.9	44.5
Switzerland	24.5	25.5	24.3	22.7	20.7
Spain				38.6	44.0
UK	41.5	46.0	45.1	34.3	29.2
Average (without Greece, Portugal, Spain)	31.2	31.7	31.8	31.5 (30.7)	31.5 (30.6)

Note: The following parties have been taken into consideration: Austria, SPÖ; Belgium, BSP/PSB; Denmark, SD; Finland, SDP; France, (SFIO)/PS; FRG, SPD; Greece, PASOK; Ireland, ILP; Italy, PSI/PSDI; Netherlands, PvdA; Norway, DNA; Portugal, PSP; Sweden, SAP; Switzerland, SPS; Spain, PSOE; UK, Labour party.

out along geographical lines.[16] Although such an attempt partially reflects common historical socioeconomic and sociocultural particulars of the national environment within which the parties must act, I will employ a more systematic approach. Modifying and extending an approach developed by Hans Keman[17] my typology is based on five criteria of classification: (1) type of relations between the social democratic party and trade unions; (2) fragmentation of the Left and the position of the social democratic party within the Left camp; (3) ideology as it is manifested in policymaking; (4) type and extent of governmental power (1974–89); and (5) governmental power quotient throughout the postwar period (1945–89).

Based on these five criteria I have constructed four "ideal types" of social democratic parties.

1. Labourist: the trade unions have historically preceded the party and still influence it strongly; there is hardly any competition at the Left; pragmatic ideological approach.

2. Pragmatic coalescent: dominance of the party vis-à-vis the trade unions and/or medium cooperation between party and unions; some competitions at the Left; pragmatic, social-liberal policymaking; medium "power quotient" (Table 4); and mostly compelled to govern in coalition governments.

3. Welfare Statist: close and equal cooperation between party and highly organized unions; some or strong competition at the Left; dominant political force, often governing in single-party governments.

4. Roman: little cooperation with only parts of the ideologically fragmented unions; strong competition at the Left; rapid change from radical ideological to rather pragmatic positions; rise from political inferiority to strong, respectively dominant positions since the mid-seventies; some characteristics still in flux.

According to the five classification criteria, West European social democratic parties can be subsumed under four ideal types (Table 2):

Table 2. Typology of West European Social Democratic Parties

CLASSIFICATIONS

1. Party-Trade Union Relations:
A trade unions have historically proceeded the party and are still influential
B dominance of the party vis à vis the trade unions and/or medium cooperation
C close cooperation between trade unions and party without dominance on either side
D (little) cooperation with only parts of the ideologically fragmented unions

2. Position at the Left (Camp):
A hardly any competition at the Left
B some competition at the Left
C strong competition but the Socialist party is still the strongest party on the Left

D strong competition and Socialist party is the minor party of the Left

3. Ideology (Related to Policymaking):

A pragmatic labourist position giving priority to high wages

B social-liberal, pragmatic position

C strongly committed to full employment and universalistic welfare state

D radical ideological position (Marxist, anticapitalistic, leftist-socialistic)

4. Type and Extent of Governmental Power (1945–90):

A high (alternating single party governments)

B medium (coalitions governments)

C dominant (single-party governments or hegemonic force in coalition government)

D low (junior partner in coalition government; opposition)

5. Governmental Power Quotient of Postwar Period (1974–90):

A high

B medium

C dominant

D low

	TYPOLOGY					
	1	2	3	4	5	Type
Austria	C	A	B	B	C	welfare statist
Belgium	D	B	B	B	D	pragmatic, coalescent
Denmark	C	C	B	C	B	welfare statist (weak)
Finland	B	C	B	B	C	pragmatic, coalescent
France	D	D/C	B/D	D	B	Roman
FRG	C	B	B	D	B	pragmatic, coalescent
Greece	D	C	D	D	A	Roman
Ireland	A	A	A	D	D	labourist (weak)
Italy	D	D	B	D	D	Roman
Netherlands	B	B	B	D	D	pragmatic, coalescent
Norway	C	C	C	C	C	welfare statist (strong)
Portugal	D	C	B	D	B	Roman (weak)
Spain	D	C	D/B	C	D	Roman
Sweden	C	C	C	C	C	welfare statist (strong)
Switzerland	B	A	B	D	B	pragmatic, coalescent
UK	A	A	A	A	A	labourist

Note: A (Labourist): Ireland, the UK; B (pragmatic, coalescent): Belgium, Finland, the FRG, the Netherlands, Switzerland; C (welfare statist): Austria, Denmark, Norway, Sweden; D (Roman): France, Greece, Italy, Portugal, Spain.

type A (Labourist): United Kingdom and Ireland; type B (pragmatic, coalescent): Belgium, Finland, the Netherlands, Switzerland, and West Germany; type C (welfare statist): Austria, Denmark, Norway, and Sweden; and type D (Roman): France, Greece, Italy, Portugal, and Spain. The electoral results of these four groups (Table 3) reveal that rather different developments have taken place since 1945. Due to the disastrous electoral defeats of the British Labour party during the 1980s, the labourist group (type A) lost substantial votes during the decline phase compared to the golden years (-7.4 percent) and the total postwar period (-4.6 percent).[18]

Distinguished from this decline pattern, the average electoral outcome of the pragmatic, coalescent social democratic parties (type B) proved to be extraordinarily stable. The combined vote of this group shows almost identical results for all three periods. While the Belgian and Swiss social democrats had to accept a minor decrease of their electoral shares, the German SPD and the Dutch PvdA could increase their average vote for the decline period. The electoral results of the Finnish social democrats has remained stable for all periods since 1945.

The parties of the welfare statist type (type C) suffered minor electoral erosions. Compared with the total postwar period (-1.6 percent) and the golden years (-2.4 percent), these parties have been confronted with a slight melting off of their unusually high electoral plateau during the period of decline. If one looks closer at this group, Danish, and perhaps Norwegian, social democrats can easily be defined as the losers. Whereas it is probably too early to interpret the losses of Norway's DNA at the 1989 elections (-6.5 percent) as a stable trend (the DNA's main competitor, the Conservative party, lost with -8.3 percent even more votes), Danish social democrats suffered a continuous electoral decline from 1979 until 1990, when a dramatic vote swing stopped it. The Danish social democrats polled 37.4 percent and increased their electoral share by 7.5 percent compared to the electoral results of 1988. The Danish example shows that downward electoral trends are by no means irreversible and cannot be explained simply by the general decay of social democratic policies or the supposed inherent contradictions of the welfare state as such. But social democratic voters have become much more volatile.[19] This volatility and erosion of the SD electorate can partially be attributed to a "pervasively liberalistic welfare state that enhances social stratification

Table 3. Electoral Share (%) of Social Democratic Parties Classified by Typological Groups (Averages)

	1945–90	1945–73	1974–90
A. Labourist			
UK	41.5	46.0	34.3
Ireland	11.2	12.4	9.3
Average	26.4	29.2	21.8
B. Pragmatic Coalescent			
Belgium	30.2	32.1	27.2
Finland	24.8	24.8	24.9
FRG	37.3	36.3	38.8
Netherlands	29.0	27.7	31.5
Switzerland	24.5	25.5	22.7
Average	29.2	29.3	29.0
C. Welfare Statist			
Austria	45.2	44.2	47.0
Denmark	36.0	37.7	33.0
Norway	42.3	44.2	38.7
Sweden	45.5	46.3	43.9
Average	42.3	43.1	40.7
D. Roman			
France	21.7	17.5	32.3
Greece	17.2	—	35.8
Portugal	—	—	30.6
Spain	—	—	43.9
Average	19.5	17.5	35.9

and cleavages cutting across class lines" and a relatively weak performance in controlling the business cycle.[20] This made Denmark's social democrats much more vulnerable to and dependent on economic and sociocultural changes and cycles than their sister party in Sweden. Finland's move toward a more universal welfare model since the late seventies has not caused electoral backlashes for Finnish social democrats (which I still subsume under the "pragmatic coalescent type"), the main proponents of the improvement of the Finnish welfare state.[21]

The minor electoral losses of the welfare statist social democracies and the Anglo-Saxon labour parties have been compensated for by the rise of the new socialist parties in southern Europe and France.[22] They are the "winners" of the 1980s. In particular, the renewed Parti Socialiste Français (PS), the Panellino Socialistiko Kinima (PASOK), and the Partido Socialista Obrero Español (PSOE) "created" and extended their electorates with breathtaking rapidity. The electoral appeal of the French, Spanish, and Greek socialists to large segments of the middle class shows that the social democratic parties are not irrevocably doomed due to Przeworski's dilemma, that is, electoral socialism is confronted with the apparently impossible task of appealing to the working and middle classes simultaneously. Moreover, French socialists benefited from the institutions of the Fifth Republic, the wear of the bourgeoise parties during the economic crisis of the 1970s, and the rapid decline of the Communist party. Greek and Spanish socialists, also enjoying the luck of being in opposition during the economically difficult 1970s, could profit in particular from the extreme fluidity of the electorates of postauthoritarian regimes.

All three parties campaigned successfully with the suggestive slogan of change, aiming at the political, economic, and social dimension as well. At a time when the end of the "social democratic century" was already proclaimed, the socialist parties of southern Europe won their elections with programs entailing all the classical elements of social democratic policies.[23] But there is a border case (Portugal) and a deviant case (Italy) in this group. After remarkable successes in the immediate aftermath of the Portuguese revolution (1975, 40.7 percent) and erratic electoral results at the end of the 1970s and the beginning of the 1980s, the electorate of the PSP, one of the most conservative socialist parties of western Europe, was almost halved in 1985 (20 percent) and 1987 (22.3 percent).[24] In contrast to its Southern European sister parties, which stayed in opposition during the 1970s, the PSP was paying the price for the mere fact that it stayed in power during that difficult decade. Discredited by unsuccessful economic crisis management, Portuguese socialists proved to be unable to present themselves as a credible force of economic and social reforms at the beginning of the 1980s. Italian socialists represent the deviant case within the Roman type group; they are still the minor force of the Left.

However, it can be argued that the proper Social Democratic party in Italy has become sociostructurally and programatically the Partito Comunista Italiano, which emblematically changed its name to Democratic Party of the Left (PDS) at the beginning of 1991. Taking the socialists and communists together, the democratic Italian Left no longer represents an exceptional case.

No general decline of social democracy has occurred since the early 1970s. Two groups lost votes, the labourist group heavily, and the welfare statist group slightly, not extraordinary considering the high vote level of the latter. The pragmatic, coalescent group maintained its electoral share, while Southern European socialist parties became strong and even dominant political forces. Moreover, there seems to be more evidence that Danish, West German, and Norwegian social democrats, Portuguese socialists, and the British Labour party suffered electoral losses due to their incumbency during the economically difficult years of the late 1970s rather than to sociostructural change and a shrinking working class or pursuing anachronistic social democratic policies.[25]

Strengths and Weaknesses of Competitors of Social Democracy

Strength and weakness of social democratic parties is closely interrelated with the strength, weakness, cohesiveness, or fragmentation of their competitors in the respective party systems. In other words, what matters is the relative strength of social democratic parties compared with the strength of their main competitors. In this regard a good deal of the dominant position of the Scandinavian social democratic parties can be attributed to the marked heterogeneity of their bourgeois opponents throughout the postwar period.

With the exception of Denmark (1982–89), bourgeois parties failed to establish a durable block capable of pursuing concerted political action. The bourgeois governments of Sweden (1976–82) and of Norway (1981–86) failed, not least as a result of such heterogeneity.[26] The same holds true in the Spanish case. Due to the erosion and complete dissolution of the heterogenous UCD, the socialists' bourgeois predecessor, the bourgeois camp is fragmented into two bigger national (PP and CDS) and some minor regional parties. Because these parties are not only incapable of forming an alliance, but are also unable to agree to any concerted action with the communist opposition, they have proven to be far from a challenge to the hegemonial position of the socialist party during the 1980s.[27] The fragmentation of the conservative forces (RPR and UDF) turned out to be conducive to the recovery, stabilization, and return to power of French socialists too, as the presidential and parliamentary elections of 1981 and 1988 proved.[28] While in Sweden, Norway, Finland, Spain, and France the fragmentation of their political opponents turned out to be a source of strength, the Labour party in Great Britain, the SPD in West Germany, and, to some extent, PASOK in Greece did not enjoy such favorable competitive situations. The bourgeois camp in their countries is much more cohesive and able to gain stable parliamentary majorities, either as single parties or durable coalitions.

Even at an aggregate and formal level it can be demonstrated that the degree of fractionalization of the competitors of social democracy has not diminished since 1974. By employing Rae's fractionalization index Klaus Armingeon has shown for twenty-one party systems within the OECD that the fractionalization of all nonsocial democratic parties has indeed slightly increased from 0.61 during the golden years (1945–73) to 0.66 for the decline period (1974–88).[29] These findings have been confirmed by my own computations for the sixteen West European party systems here under consideration: the fractionalization of competing parties has risen from 0.64 (1945–73) to 0.66 (1974–88). Although these differences are too small to support the thesis that the opponents of social democracy have been weakened, they are even more inadequate to prove the opposite.

The Social Democrats in Government

If neither a general decline of social democracy at the electoral level nor a strengthening of its opponents in terms of political cohesiveness can be observed, does more evidence support the decline hypothesis at the level of government power? In order to compare governmental power during the periods under investigation I computed a "power quotient," which, with slight modifications, is based on calculations that Anton Pelinka has done previously.[30] Depending on the mode of government, I attributed a certain amount of points per year to social democratic parties. At the level of governmental power there has been no decline since 1974 (Table 4). On the contrary, the power quotient for the total decline period from 1974 to 1990, and from 1980 to 1990 as

Table 4. Governmental Power of Social Democratic Parties
(power quotient, 1945–90)

	1945–90	1945–73	1960–73	1974–90	1980–90
Austria	2.5	2.2	2.3	2.9	2.5
Belgium	1.2	1.4	1.2	0.8	0.7
Denmark	2.3	2.8	3.0	1.6	1.0
Finland	1.7	1.7	1.1	1.8	2.7
France	1.0	0.6	0.0	1.8	2.7
Germany	1.0	0.6	1.3	1.5	0.7
Greece	0.8	—	—	2.3	3.5
Ireland	0.2	0.1	0.1	0.5	0.4
Italy	0.5	0.4	0.6	0.7	1.0
Netherlands	0.8	0.9	0.3	0.7	0.3
Norway	3.1	3.4	1.8	2.6	1.8
Portugal	0.5	—	—	1.3	0.7
Spain	0.9	—	—	2.4	3.6
Sweden	3.5	4.1	4.1	2.6	3.0
Switzerland	0.9	0.8	1.0	1.0	1.0
UK	1.8	2.5	2.0	1.5	0.0
Average	1.4	1.7	1.4	1.6	1.6

Note:
5 points: exclusively social democratic governments with parliamentary majority
4 points: exclusively social democratic governments without parliamentary majorities (minority cabinets)
3 points: social democrats as the dominant partner in a governing coalition
2 points: social democrats as equal partner in a grand coalition
1 point: social democrats as junior partner in a governing coalition
0 points: social democrats in opposition

well, are 0.3, respectively 0.2 points higher than for the golden years or the whole postwar period.

If one looks in more detail at the evolution of the governmental power of social democratic parties according to the four groups, the figures reflect a similar picture to that of the electoral level. The two labourist parties of group A have been confronted with a marked decline of power during the 1980s. The parties of group B could maintain their position. They could even slightly increase their governmental share during the period from 1974 to 1990 due to their good performance during the 1970s, thus compensating for minor losses during the 1980s. A visible decline can be observed for group C. Departing from an extraordinarily high power level during the golden years welfare statist social democracies suffered a decay of governmental power after 1974. This decline was primarily caused by the erosion of the dominant position of Danish and Norwegian social democrats. Although Norwegian social democrats returned to government during the second half of the 1980s, Danish social democrats lost the election in 1982 and went into opposition for the rest of the decade. Although it is too early to interpret these losses as a stable trend, there were some indications at the beginning of the 1990s that the parties of the welfare statist type would lose their once-hegemonic or dominant positions.

The rise of the Southern European socialist parties since the mid-1970s lead to continuously increasing governmental power. Spanish socialists became the hegemonic political force in their country, and the Parti Socialiste Français stabilized its position as the strongest party in France. Due to political scandals Greek socialists lost the dominant position they held throughout the 1980s but despite the scandals they still polled around 40 percent of the electoral votes at the end of the 1980s. Only the socialist party of Portugal declined to a second-order party after a brief interlude in government from 1983 to 1985.

Thus, even at the level of governmental power there is no general trend of decline. The visible decline of the Anglo-Saxon labour parties and slight erosions of the welfare statist social democracies have taken place at the same time, while the power of the pragmatic coalescent social democratic parties has slightly increased and Southern European socialism has risen to a major or dominant role in these countries.[31]

Social Democratic Policies during the 1980s

At the level of economic and social policies only actual policies and not party programs will be compared.[32] This implies a specific selection of cases to be analyzed. Only the policies of those parties that stayed in government during the 1980s can be included into this policy analysis. The two Anglo-Saxon labour parties and, with the exception of the Finnish socialists, all social democratic parties of the pragmatic, coalescent type will be excluded from the comparison.[33] In terms of governmental power these two groups can be called the losers of the 1980s. The Danish social democracy cannot be analyzed because it

Table 5. Governmental Power According to the Four Typological Groups

	1945–90	1945–73	1960–73	1974–90	1980–90
A. Labourist					
UK	1.8	2.5	2.0	1.5	0
Ireland	0.2	0.1	0.1	0.5	0.4
Average	1.0	1.3	1.1	1.0	0.2
B. Pragmatic, coalescent					
Belgium	1.2	1.4	1.2	0.8	0.8
FRG	1.0	0.6	1.3	1.5	0.7
Finland	1.7	1.7	1.1	1.8	2.0
Netherlands	0.8	0.9	0.3	0.7	0.3
Switzerland	0.9	0.8	1.0	1.0	1.0
Average	1.1	1.1	1.0	1.2	1.0
C. Welfare statist					
Austria	2.5	2.2	2.3	2.9	2.5
Denmark	2.3	2.8	3.0	1.6	1.0
Norway	3.1	3.4	1.8	2.6	1.8
Sweden	3.5	4.1	4.1	2.6	3.0
Average	2.9	3.1	2.8	2.4	2.1
D. Roman					
France	1.0	0.6	0.0	1.8	2.7
Greece	0.8	—	—	2.3	3.5
Portugal	0.5	—	—	1.3	0.7
Spain	0.9	—	—	2.4	3.6
Average	0.8	0.2	0	2.0	2.6

was in opposition. The Portuguese and Italian socialists cannot be taken into consideration either because the first governed only for two years (1983–85) in a "grand coalition" and the latter, although it remained in power throughout the 1980s, has always been the junior partner in a five-party coalition. Therefore, it is impossible to attribute specific policies or the government's performance as a whole to the PSP or PSI.

Only the dominant governing socialist-social democratic parties during the 1980s remain: the Swedish, Norwegian, Finnish, and Austrian social democrats, as well as the socialists of France, Greece, and Spain. These parties can be distinguished in two groups according to the typology of social democratic parties I have developed, the periods in which these parties came to power and could entrench their policies, institutions and values, as well as some similarities of economic, social, and political environments. The groups are: (1) established, dominant social democracy (welfare statist types), such as Sweden (SAP), Norway (DNA), Austria (SPÖ), and Finland (SPF),[34] and (2) new, dominant socialist parties, such as Spain (PSOE), Greece (PASOK), and France (PS).

The explanandum is, have these parties pursued social democratic policies during the 1980s, and which causal factors created the divergence or convergence of the actual policies pursued? In other words, what is in the "black box" that separates the declared programmatic intentions from the output of policies?

Considering the logic of the neoliberal-neoconservative paradigm of the overburdened economy and the hypertrophic state activities of social democratic welfare regimes, one could expect the most rapid erosion in those countries where the "sclerosis" through statist regulations has progressed the most: the Nordic countries and, with minor reservations, Austria.

Marxists would expect that the more class-oriented labor movements in France, Spain, and Greece (strong communist unions, relevant communist parties, and more radical socialist parties) could press for more progressive social reforms than the collaborative social democratic parties and unions in Sweden, Norway, Finland, and Austria. The rational choice plus sociostructural approach is more indifferent in the North-South comparison. In the long run, no social democratic and socialist party can escape the assumed electoral dilemma of needing support from workers and the middle class simultaneously. In the short run, one would expect that in unionized, neocorporatist countries, social democratic leaders would rationally choose policies designed to meet the needs of the middle class because the partially institutionalized loyalty of workers diminishes the probability of their electoral exit. However, the reality is much more complex and contradictory, and it largely falsifies the one-dimensional decline hypotheses.

If one disentangles the Keynesian welfare state at its two fundamental levels—state intervention in the sense of macroeconomic steering and policy regulation and welfare commitment to provide collective goods and monetary transfers[35]—one can draw several conclusions. The three Nordic countries represented a homogeneous sample in the 1980s, despite some gradual differences regarding the standards of social welfare. A retreat from the commitment to universal social welfare has not taken place there, nor has a breakdown or irreversible erosion of neocorporatist arrangements occurred. Even with respect to macroeconomic policies, the state still plays an important role. What changed during the 1980s was not the involvement of the state in steering the economy as such, but the mode and direction of state interventions. Particularly in Sweden (after 1982) and Norway (after 1986), state interventions shifted visibly in favor of the supply side, stimulating investments by specifically designed tax reliefs and subsidies. Although a rethinking of tax policies is occurring even among Scandinavian social democrats, tax reform in Sweden and Austria at the end of the 1980s did not mark a real supply-side U-turn. Certainly, Swedish social democrats reduced the marginal tax rates on personal income (as the grand coalition did in Austria), but the reinvestment of profits are still highly privileged while the withdrawal of profits are taxed away more than in most OECD countries. Moreover, new property taxes have been implemented and already existing property taxes increased in Sweden and Austria. Although the already existing supply-side elements of the tax system had been strengthened at the end of the 1980s, it would be misleading to equate those carefully balanced tax reforms with the ones implemented by the conservative governments of the United States, Great Britain, or West Germany during the 1980s.

The "end of the Keynesian coordination" turned out to be not as definite as some economists and political scientists suggested at the end of the 1970s.[36] Since the Finnish government turned its policies cautiously toward a more demand-oriented economic management, all three Nordic countries have pursued a fairly balanced mixture of supply- and demand-oriented policies. From this perspective, Sweden, Norway, and Finland in the 1980s should be termed "interventionist social welfare states" in order to differentiate them from the Keynesian welfare states of the 1970s.

Yet, in the longer run, the partial deregulation of financial markets could pose some restraints upon controlling the exchange rate in the future. Devaluations as a macroeconomic national instrument for restoring economic competitiveness can no longer be used as flexibly as in the past. The liberalization of credit markets could particularly reduce future capacity of the Norwegian state to direct the domestic economy, because the nationalized credit sector played a crucial role in past social democratic policies (credit socialism). Combined with the fact that the continuous flow of considerable oil revenues concealed the relative loss of competitiveness in manufacturing during the 1980s, the future of the Norwegian social democratic state could become more contingent. The enforced restructuring of the industrial sector stimulated by the social democratic government of Gro Harlem Brundtland at the end of the 1980s shifted the economic policies toward a stronger supply-side orientation. However, this restructuring period was neither accompanied by the state's retreat from economic intervention nor was it paralleled by a relative decline of wages and social welfare.

Some erosions of the social democratic model could possibly loom for the future in Norway, and even the Swedish model came under certain stress at the end of the 1980s. However, the main features of development in the three countries since the mid-1970s contradict the undifferentiated decline hypotheses. In each of the three countries a consolidation or even enlargement (as in Finland) of the welfare state has taken place; the unemployment rate (1980–88, 3.3 percent) has been considerably lower than the average rate within the OECD (7.7 percent) or EC (8.8 percent). On the contrary, welfare and tax policies have been coordinated to enhance both economic growth and social equality. The high level of income tax and tax reliefs for reinvestments contributed to the high rate of capital accumulation. A considerable part of nominal wage increases was taxed away by the progressive income tax and transformed into financial surplus of the public sector to support productive investments of the corporate sector and finance social welfare.[37] The tax system did not simply favor corporate profits, but was specifically designed to stimulate investments in the most productive enterprises. The Finnish move toward these policies[38] also underlines the argument that neither the welfare state nor its most comprehensive social democratic version, the welfare-interventionist state (or Keynesian welfare state), is condemned to perish by virtue of its supposedly inherent contradictions.

This does not imply that Scandinavian social democracy has not changed. However, incremental changes in the level of macroeconomic management did not alter fundamental politics and policies during the 1980s. In particular, these changes did not diminish the social welfare commitments of the three social democratic parties to provide collective goods and transfer payments on a high level and universal base.[39] Moreover, the fact that the Swedish social democrats in 1985 and 1988 and the Norwegian Labor party in 1985 won elections with rather traditional welfare campaigns points to the maintenance of social democratic values and policies in these countries.[40] While the Finnish welfare state expanded during the "critical" seventies and eighties, Norway and Sweden did not experience a crisis in their welfare states, but only the end of linear expansion. Austria's social democrats face deeper problems, however. The obsolescence of "Austro-Keynesianism" and the privatization and "marketization" of the nationalized sector have already shown some negative consequences for the goals of full employment and social equality.[41] The PSOE has not found functional equivalents for the important role that both Austro-Keynesianism and the nationalized industries played in its social democratic concept.[42] Because Austrian social democrats have had to govern with the conservative Austrian People's party (ÖVP) since 1986, the temptation to look for market solutions could be strong. However, even in the case of Austria, it remains to be seen whether the trend to more market, less state, and less social equality is irresistible, or whether a new turn will occur if the business cycle continues upward, industrial restructuring is completed successfully, and the decline of the ÖVP continues.

Failure and Success of Southern European Socialism

The "southern group" is more heterogeneous than the northern. True, all three socialist parties entered government at the beginning of the 1980s with radical (PS and PASOK) or moderate (PSOE) social democratic programs.[43] When in power, the differences among socialist governments in France, Greece, and Spain became more pronounced, however. The Parti Socialiste, PASOK, and Spanish socialists did not try to establish the ideal social democratic steering mix of state-market neocorporatism. Each socialist government followed its own bias.

State interventions of the PASOK government into economy and society did not decrease during their eight years in power, yet after four progressive years, these interventions have scarcely been linked to left-ist or progressive goals after 1985. They often have followed a traditional Greek set of paternalistic and clientelistic practices. French socialists also relied heavily on the state, particularly in the first phase of the Mauroy government. But their statist approach from above prevented them from fully recognizing the importance of the active involvement of social partners in the planning and implementation of reform policies; an oversight that led Mark Kesselman to call the "Mitterrand experiment" a "socialism without workers."[44] Moreover, technocratic preferences induced the PS to underestimate external constraints upon managing a medium-sized open economy within the international capitalist world economy. The conclusions the Parti Socialiste drew after its first term in power can best be seen in the moderate social democratic government of Michel Rocard, who gives the market absolute priority for the allocation of economic resources but uses the fiscal state for cautious improvement of social welfare. Without proposing the renationalization of industries privatized by the Chirac government, the PS gives priority to selective industrial interventions, even after 1988. Its continuing commitment to more social justice is demonstrated in the measures of the Rocard government to increase minimum social benefits and to improve education for the underprivileged while implementing a wealth tax for the rich.

The Spanish socialist government, however, has been from the beginning very much aware of external and internal economic constraints, particularly in the perspective of EC membership and the creation of a single European market in 1992. This attitude led them at times to an uncritical emphasis on the market and a lack of willingness to use existing space for state interventions in order to steer the economy and society along the lines of more social equality. The attempt to instrumentalize socioeconomic pacts unilaterally in favor of investors underlines PSOE's market bias.

As moderate the reform outcomes of the socialist parties in France, Greece, and even Spain may have been, however, they had some social welfare impact on their societies. In particular this holds true in the Greek case (a health policy, gender equality, new pensions for agrarian employees, and extension of public services), but it can also be maintained for France (Auroux laws, the rise of minimum wage, and social transfers for persons with low incomes). Spanish socialists are beginning to improve Spain's health service and the pension system.

The Established Social Democracy and
Southern European Socialism

How is one to explain these divergent developments? More specifically, how is one to explain the relative stability of established social democratic policy in Sweden and (with some reservations) Norway, the social democratization of Finnish policies throughout the 1980s on the one hand, and Austria's beginning departure from its social democratic past on the other? What about the only moderate success and partial failure of socialist parties in southern Europe to implement progressive-reformist policies.

Przeworski and Sprague's sociostructural hypothesis can scarcely contribute an answer to these questions. As far as the three Nordic countries are concerned, the losses of Norwegian social democrats in the 1989 elections do not indicate the end of the northern social democratic parties as dominant political actors nor can incremental changes of their economic policies be interpreted as unequivocable signs of a supposedly irreversible decline of social democratic policies.

The actual shrinking of numbers of blue-collar workers and their progressive differentiation did not simply develop into electoral losses for social democratic parties or a shift away from social democratic policies. Przeworski and Sprague's "iron law"—"the more allies social democratic parties win among the middle strata, the more workers they will lose"—was broken by the influence of organizations, institutions, cultural values, policy legacies, economic performance, and the competitive situation in the party system. That is to say, actors and structures functioned as intervening variables in a process in which ultimately they were not supposed to appear.[45]

Given these concrete structures, values, and actors that determine the fate of social democratic parties, a more contingent and open scheme has considerable explanatory advantages with respect to deterministic "iron" laws derived from one, supposedly unavoidable, electoral dilemma. The configurative framework I apply here contains four sets of variables: economic factors (GDP per capita, economic competitiveness, and size and function of the nationalized sector); societal factors (the role of the middle class, type of industrial relations, and the type of the welfare state); factors of political power (the power quotient, the type of governing coalition, the fragmentation of the oppo-

Table 6. Economic, Social, Institutional, and Political Conditions for Government Policies during the 1980s

	Economic Competitiveness	Industrial Relations	Type of Welfare State
Austria	medium	high centralization/ neocorporatist	bourgeoise
Finland	medium	high centralization/ neocorporatist	bourgeoise/ universalist
Norway	medium	high centralization/ neocorporatist	universalist
Sweden	high	high centralization/ neocorporatist	universalist
France	medium	low centralization/ conflictual	bourgeoise
Greece	low	low centralization/ paternalistic/ conflictual	marginal
Spain	low/medium	medium centralization/ cooperative, 1976/ 1986, conflictual	marginal

*Power quotient: given points divided by years in government
 Points: Exclusively social democratic governments: 4 points for each year in government; Social democrats as dominant coalition partner: 3 points for each year in government; Social democrats as equal partners in a grand coalition: 2 points for each year in government; Social democrats as junior partners in a small coalition: 1 point for each year in government

sition, and the relevance of the leftist opposition); and the time factor. These variables seem to me of particular relevance in explaining the different development of social democratic policies in northern and southern Europe during the "supply side decade" (in Dahrendorf's term) of the 1980s (see Table 6).

Economic Level and Competitiveness

Medium-high economic competitiveness[46] in Sweden and Finland, successful adaptation to the new conditions of the international economy, and good economic performance during the 1980s set the base for

| Power Quotient* | | Single-Party government/ | Fragmentation | Relevance of the |
1945–88	1980–88	Coalition government	of the Opposition	Leftist Opposition
2.5	3.1	single-party government coalition government[1]	medium	irrelevant
1.8	1.9	coalition governments[2]	high	high
3.0	2.0	single-party government[3]	high	low
3.5	2.1	single-party government[4]	high	low/medium
1.0	2.1	coalition government[5] single-party government	medium	medium
0.7	3.2	single-party government	medium	medium
0.6	2.8	single-party government	high	low

[1]1970–83, single-party government; 1983–86, small coalition; 1986– , grand coalition
[2]1980–87, small coalitions; 1987– , grand coalition
[3]Minority governments
[4]Minority cabinets with parliamentary support of the Communist party, and to a minor degree of the Center party and the Millieu Partiet
[5]1981–84, coalition with Communist party; 1984–86, single-party government with parliamentary majority; 1988– , minority cabinet

the maintenance and corresponding extension of social welfare. The delayed economic restructuring in Norway and Austria caused comparative decline of competitiveness in those economies. This posed some problems for the goals of full employment and redistribution of their social democratic parties in the second half of the 1980s. However, the high GDP per capita, particularly in the Nordic countries, provided a favorable material base for collective social welfare.

All three southern European socialist governments had to cope with the legacy of a highly uncompetitive economy (Greece and Spain) and a relatively uncompetitive one (France, with regard to the United States, Japan, and West Germany). The imperative to modernize economies left little room for distributional maneuvers and social welfare. Therefore, throughout the 1980s all three socialist governments were more constrained by the international economic environment than their sister governments in northern Europe. Moreover, the fact that Austria and the Nordic countries do not belong either to the EC or the EMS and have, therefore, enjoyed greater autonomous room for maneuver in managing their economies can be interpreted as a comparative advantage with regard to southern European EC members. This advantage becomes evident if one looks to the deteriorating trade balance between Spain and Greece and the rest of the EC. This negative development could not be compensated for by net transfers from EC funds to both countries. But the French socialist government also payed its price for being a member of the EC and EMS. During the first phase of expansive Keynesianism in 1981 and 1982 much of the domestically generated demand flew off to West Germany. One year later when the Mauroy government tried to solve France's balance of payment problems its choice to regulate exchange rate policies was clearly restricted by EMS membership.

Size and Function of the Nationalized Sector

Nationalization did not matter, at least not in the sense of being conducive to achieving social democratic goals for a more egalitarian society with universal social welfare, full employment, and new forms of work organizations or economic democracy. The French leftist government was unable or unwilling to use the extended nationalized sector for such social democratic goals. Nationalization under Mitterrand remained basically an act of symbolic politics. The Greek socialists succumbed to the temptation to use the nationalized sector for clientelistic purposes and statist-authoritarian measures concerning the regulation of strikes. The PSOE government had to cope with the legacy of an indebted and highly unproductive nationalized sector. Only the rationalization and the privatization of some parts of the nationalized industry and services took a heavy burden away from the annual state budget.[47] Austrian social democrats used the nationalized sector too long and too extensively to hide redundant workers. When they had to restructure nationalized industries during the 1980s state-owned firms lost their defensive employment function. The whole concept of Austro-Keynesianism became particularly vulnerable since the SPÖ had failed to develop functional equivalences for the macroeconomic functions of the nationalized sector. However, the example of Norway demonstrates that an all-inclusive negative judgment of experiences with extended nationalized sectors runs the risk of an undue generalization. Norway's Labour party succeeded in using the largely nationalized credit sector (credit socialism) in order to steer the economy and society more along the lines of their own social democratic criteria. And even Statoil, Norway's large state-owned oil company, produced relatively more revenues for the government than private oil companies in Great Britain. But despite the single exceptions of Norway and Finland, the comparison of all seven cases indicates that the "functional socialism," as Gunnar Adler-Karlsson terms it, of Sweden, with its small but efficient nationalized sector, turned out to be less vulnerable to supply-side imperatives of the 1980s than did those policy designs that tried to instrumentalize the nationalized sector as an important element of their macroeconomic management. Again, these outcomes raise considerable doubts about the rationale for nationalization as an essential element of progressive reformist policies in advanced industrial societies.[48]

The Role of the Middle Class

Like their Northern European sister parties, Southern European socialists need the votes of large segments of the middle class to gain electoral majorities. But in contrast to the economically and socially more advanced welfare states of northern Europe, the middle class in southern Europe is aware of employment opportunities and provisions of the welfare state, simply because it is not as developed in the North. A universal welfare program and economic democracy would not have much appeal for the new rising middle classes in southern Europe, who are more interested in immediate private consumption than collective welfare provisions for the future. Furthermore, under the economic conditions of the first half of the 1980s, the middle class realistically perceived the creation of a strong tax and welfare state as a zero-sum game in which they would have to contribute more than they could win in the short and medium term. In addition to the external factors, this led socialist governments to meet the challenge of productivity, even at the expense of traditional social democratic goals. This is particularly evident for the PSOE government, but to a minor degree also valid for the French socialists after 1983 and PASOK after 1985.

Although the easy times of neocorporatism seem to be over, the leadership of the highly centralized and organized trade unions of all four countries of established social democracy could still "convince" their membership that concerted wage bargaining works for the advantage of all. The return of the Swedish unions and the employer association SAF to centralized wage settlements in 1988 is only one indicator that erosions of institutions and arrangements have not been irresistible, but can also be reversed. The still-close cooperation between the unions and the Social Democratic party in government has enabled a coordinated economic strategy. Hence, in times of economic restructuring a more equal distribution of social costs has been achieved in Sweden than in most of the other OECD countries.

Despite some differences among the three Southern European countries, industrial relations in France, Greece, and Spain are much more decentralized, fragmented, and conflictual than in the North. A concerted economic strategy was impossible, with the temporary exception of in Spain, because neither PS, PASOK, or PSOE have the same organic relationship with the trade unions that their established sister parties in northern Europe do. Nor are they exclusive agents of organized labor, and organized labor in southern Europe is not as strong, united, and representative as it is in northern Europe. In this sense, Southern European socialist governments enjoyed a greater degree of "relative autonomy"[49] from the interests of the workers than did the social democratic governments of Sweden, Norway, Finland, and Austria. This autonomy has been enhanced by the fact that socialist parties in Greece, France, and even Spain draw a smaller part of electoral support from the working class than do their sister parties in the North.

Type of Welfare State

The policy legacy of an extended welfare state as provider of social welfare *and* as employer of a considerable part of the work force is an important factor for the electoral success of social democratic parties in the three Nordic countries because social democratic parties are most closely associated with the maintenance of such a welfare state. The Swedish model of the welfare state (and with some reservation those of Norway and Finland, too) with its high standards satisfies not only the needs of the lower-income groups but also of middle-class clientele. The fact that the welfare systems in Sweden, Norway, and Finland are not primarily based on monetary transfers but also provide a wide set of public goods and services renders the state's position as an employer important for many voters while reducing neoconservative and neoliberal attacks on social democratic welfare policies. Certainly neopopulist flash parties like the Norwegian Progress party could gain some electoral support as in 1989 on the base of antitax and antiwelfare campaigns. But they are too weak to change the course of traditional full-employment and welfare policies. Policy proposals which do not give priority to the issues of full employment and social welfare still tend to be electorally "punished" in Sweden and Norway. In having succeeded in maintaining a broad consensus for this universal type of welfare state, social democrats have established an important cornerstone for the reproduction of their own political power.[50]

The institutions of and social demands for welfare states in Greece, Spain, and even in France are much less developed. The marginal (Greece and Spain) and the continental, mainly insurance-based welfare state in France[51] are only of minor importance as employers. The standards of many social services are too low in Greece and Spain to be attractive to the middle class who are often not eligible for them anyway. When the economic circumstances of the early 1980s apparently demanded a choice between productivity and redistribution, governments could opt more unilaterally for productivity without having to fear mass voter defections. This was particularly significant in Spain but also occurred in varying degrees in France (1983–84) and Greece (1982 and 1985). However, the medium to high standards of social transfer payments in France shows in this and several other respects that France must be considered geographically, socially, and politically a border case between the Southern European and the Northern European groups.

Political Variables

Because political variables, governmental power, fragmentation and weakness of opposition parties, and relevance of the leftist opposition are similar in both country groups, or even favorable to the socialist parties of southern Europe, it seems reasonable to conclude that they have played only a minor role in the divergent policies of social democratic and socialist governments. This consideration is by no means based on a crude economism, but rather stresses the accumulation of unfavorable economic and societal constraints on progressive reform policies in southern Europe. Particularly in Spain, and to some extent in Greece, the political elites paid more attention to political questions of transition to and consolidation of democracy than to the modernization of the economy or the creation of a welfare state.[52]

The Time Factor

The most important factor for the policy differences among the established social democracy of the North and the "new socialist hegemons"[53] of the South can be seen to be in the different periods when northern Europe's social democrats and southern Europe's socialists came to power. PS, PASOK, and PSOE entered government at the beginning of the 1980s, when external economic constraints and the state of the domestic economy (policy legacy in Spain and Greece) did not allow for much more than the modernization and restructuring of economy, state, and society—modernizations that had taken place in northern Europe decades earlier. The social difference between the modernization policy of Southern European socialists and the redistribution policies of the social democrats during the fifties, sixties, seventies, and eighties is essentially due to the different moments of opportunity, when parties could entrench themselves and their political goals in domestic sociopolitical systems.

In periods of difficult economic growth, and without a macroeconomic strategy that ensures production and redistribution simultaneously, the lack of competitiveness in their open economies did not allow for a genuine leftist alternative to actual policy formation of a temporary preference of production with regard to redistribution. From this perspective, the socialist governments of southern Europe followed the logic of national competitiveness on domestic and export markets; a logic that cannot be disregarded even by leftist reform-oriented parties. In southern Europe, one can argue that the absence of all those organizational, institutional, and timing factors, which ensured the maintenance and resurgence of social democracy in the three Nordic countries, have essentially been the cause for the failures of leftist-reformist policies. However, this does not imply that many progressive goals of the socialist governments of France, Spain, and Greece simply fell victim to the unfavorable economic, social, and institutional environment. Sometimes they also failed because of ill-designed policies or the omission of strategic reforms. The neglect of a tax reform that ensures simultaneously the accumulation of private capital, high investment rates and the fiscal resources for social welfare, and failure to stimulate more cooperative relations among state, capital, and labor are certainly among the most serious failures in this regard.

Conclusion

The divergent evolution of social democratic politics and policies during the 1980s were empirical arguments against strict laws predicting the irresistible decline of the "historical phenomenon"[54] of social democracy. The data of the electoral evolution since 1945 unequivocally demonstrate that no general decline of social democratic parties has occurred in western Europe. Even the data concerning the participation of social democratic parties in government must be read as a falsification of the decline hypotheses. More specific analysis at the basis of typological differentiation of the social democratic parties reveals that a considerable decline occurred in only two parties of the labourist type and slight erosions of the full-employment social democracies. But this statement is only valid since 1980; it holds true for neither the total decline period since 1974 nor for the two other types of social democratic parties, pragmatic, coalescent and ambivalent, during both decline phases. Moreover, at the beginning of the 1990s, eleven of sixteen West European social democratic parties were in power—more than at any other time since World War II.

At the more substantial level of concrete policies the situation is more ambiguous and modifies some of the findings on the quantitative level. The social policies of Nordic social democratic governments proved to be fairly resilient despite some changes of macroeconomic management and minor electoral erosions during the 1980s. However, the loss of governmental power of Norway's social democrats in 1989 and beginning signs of a possible departure from social democracy in Austria cast shadows on this positive balance.

The changes in economic policies of the four established social democratic governments in the 1970s and 1980s can neither be compared with the retreat from the concept of revolution during the first two decades of the century nor with the abandonment of the pursuit of socialism by parliamentary means in favor of the commitment to employment, efficiency, and social welfare after World War II. The retreat of social democratic governments from single modes of state intervention in the economy (the economic dimension) did not negatively affect the provision of social welfare (the social welfare dimension) in northern Europe. Nor can it be interpreted as a third change of fundamental social democratic paradigms in this century or as signs of the end of the social democratic century.

Ironically, amid the predicted decline phase of social democracy young socialist parties of southern Europe were elected and have become—with the exception of Portugal—dominant political forces in their countries throughout the "Schumpeterian decade," in Dahrendorf's term, of the 1980s. However, the moderation of these once leftist-socialist parties on the way to, and finally in, power did not convert them automatically into social democratic parties. Whereas the Spanish socialists have undergone a liberal metamorphosis, PASOK has developed into a statist party with strong clientelistic elements. Only the French Socialist party has changed its policies toward a moderate social democratic direction even though its party structure and links to trade unions remained untypical. This is not surprising, because many variables that constitute the environment of policymaking (higher developed and more competitive economy, higher development of the welfare system, and an efficient state apparatus in France) enabled a more balanced combination of economic restructuring and social welfare in France than in Greece and Spain. By the end of the 1980s the policies of the PS resemble those of the social democratic parties of the pragmatic, coalescent type. In other words, French socialists have become a border case between the northern and southern group. The social direction of further development of PASOK and PSOE is still uncertain.

Concerning the future of this historical phenomenon, there are reasons to take reversible patterns into account. Political parties are able to adapt to new circumstances in order to influence the conditions of their further existence and success. Therefore, it is likely that those social democratic parties that spent most of the 1980s in opposition can return to government under conditions of successful economic restructuring, an upswing in the business cycle, corrections of administrative deficiencies in the welfare state, and the wearing down of bourgeois parties in power. Belgian (1988) and Dutch socialists (1989) are examples.

To again take up the question of whether there has been a decline of social democracy, whether we face the end of social democracy, and if social democracy has a future, the decline, wherever it has taken place, has neither been general nor irreversible. The development must be differentiated into parties and policies, economic management and the provision of social welfare. National differences must also be taken into account. There are too many cases of resilience and resurgence of social democratic parties and policies, too many exceptions for even the most elegant general thesis to sustain. Nevertheless, the social democratic paradigm has become more heterogenous since 1974; in this sense, "social democracy has not one but several different futures."[55]

Notes

1. Ralf Dahrendorf, *Life Chances: Approaches to Social and Political Theory* (London, 1980).

2. Michael Crozier et al., eds. *The Crisis of Democracy* (New York, 1975).

3. Richard Rose, ed., *Challenge to Governance: Studies in Overload Polities* (Beverly Hills, 1980); OECD Economic Studies no. 4, *Special Issue: The Role of the Public Sector* (Paris, 1985).

4. Leo Panitch, "The Impasse of Social Democratic Politics," *Socialist Register* 22 (1985–86): 52.

5. Marcel Liebman, "Reformism Yesterday and Social Democracy Today," *Socialist Register* 22 (1985–86): 21–22.

6. Adam Przeworski, *Capitalism and Social Democracy* (Cambridge, 1985), p. 7.

7. Adam Przeworski and John Sprague, *Paper Stones: A History of Electoral Socialism* (Chicago, 1986), p. 55.

8. Przeworski and Sprague, *Paper Stones*, p. 3.

9. Ibid., pp. 3, 55–56, 58; Przeworski, *Capitalism*, p. 104; Adam Przeworski, "Class, Production and Politics: A Replay to Buroway," *Socialist Register* 19 (April–June 1989): 78–112.

10. Przeworski and Sprague, *Paper Stones*, p. 185.

11. Ibid., p. 126.

12. Ibid., pp. 125–26.

13. Gösta Esping-Andersen, *Politics against Markets* (Princeton, 1985); Fritz W. Scharpf, *Sozialdemokratische Krisenpolitik in Westeuropa* (Frankfurt, 1987).

14. Esping-Andersen, *Politics*, pp. 34–35.

15. Klaus Armingeon, "Sozialdemokratie am Ende?" *Österreichische Zeitschrift für Politikwissenschaft* 18, no. 4 (1989): 321–45, esp. 332.

16. Christine Buci-Glucksmann and Göran Therborn, *De sozialdemokratische Staat* (Hamburg, 1982).

17. Hans Keman, *The Development toward Surplus Welfare: Social Democratic Politics and Policies in Advanced Capitalist Democracies (1965–1984)* (Amsterdam, 1988), pp. 32 ff.

18. Although the two Labour parties of Great Britain and Ireland do not constitute a real group, it is worthwhile to note that the two non-European Labour parties of Australia and New Zealand, which perfectly fit into the laborist group, did not suffer a visible electoral decline. Australia's turnout was 45.7 percent (1945–90), 46.5 percent (1945–73), 45.7 percent (1974–90), and 47 percent (1980–90). For New Zealand the totals were 44.5 percent (1945–90), 45.8 percent (1945–73), 42 percent (1974–90), and 43.4 percent (1980–90).

19. Diane Sainsbury, "Scandinavian Party Politics Re-examined: Social Democracy in Decline?" *West European Politics* 7 (October 1984): 67–102.

20. Esping-Andersen, *Politics*, pp. 149, 244.

21. Jukka Pekkarinen, "Corporatism and Economic Performance in Sweden, Norway, and Finland," in *Social Corporatism and Economic Performance*, ed. Jukka Pekkarinen, Matti Pohjola, and Bob Rowthorn (Oxford, 1992).

22. I am fully aware that France is not geographically, economically, or socially a "true" Southern European country, but rather a border case between North and South. However, since the French Socialist party shares more characteristics with Southern European socialism than with northern social democracy I subsume it under the heading of Southern Europe.

23. Dahrendorf, *Life Chances*; David S. Bell and Byron Criddle, *The French Socialist Party: The Emergence of a Party of Government*, 2d ed. (Oxford, 1988); Howard R. Penniman, ed., *France at the Polls, 1981 and 1986* (Durham, 1988); Christos Lyrintzis, "Between Socialism and Populism: The Rise of Panhellenic Socialist Movement," Ph.d. thesis, London School of Economics, 1983; Michaelis Spourdalakis, *The Rise of the Greek Socialists Party* (London, 1988); Richard Gunther, Giacomo Sani, and Goldie Shabad, *Spain after Franco: The Making of a Competitive Party System* (Berkeley, 1988); Wolfgang Merkel, "Sozialdemokratische Politik in einer postkeynesianischen Ära? Das Beispiel der Sozialistischen Regierung Spaniens (1982–1988)," *Politische Vierteljahresschrift* 30 (December 1989): 629–54.

24. Bernd Rother, *Der verhinderte Übergang zum Sozialismus* (Frankfurt, 1985); Tom Gallagher, "Goodbye to Revolution: The Portuguese Election of July 1987," *West European Politics* 11 (January 1988): 139–45.

25. This argument is supported by the fact that most of the conservative governments that governed during the late 1970s lost votes and often their power. The most salient examples are France, Greece, Spain, and Sweden.

26. Jan-Erik Lane and Svante O. Ersson, *Politics and Society in Western Europe* (London, 1987), p. 229.

27. Mario Caciagli, *Elezioni e partiti politici nella Spagna postfranchista* (Padova, 1986).

28. Bell and Criddle, The French Socialist Party.

29. The fractionalization index measures both the number of parties and their size. Here, only the index of the competing parties of social democracy are computed by the sum of the squared vote percentages of the single opposing parties divided by the total vote of all nonsocial democratic parties.

This sum will then be subtracted from 1. For example, two opposing parties poll 20 percent and 50 percent of the vote. Together they gain 70 percent. The fractionalization index of the competing opponents is: $1 - <(0.20/70) + (0.40/70) > = 1 - <0.0816 + 0.3265 > = 1 - 0.4081 = 0.5919$. The maximal value of the Rae Index $= 1$, that is, if there is only one nonsocial democratic party, it approximates 0 the more competing parties with successively diminishing electoral shares exist. See Armingeon, "Sozialdemokratie," Appendix Table 2.

30. Anton Pelinka, *Social Democratic Parties in Europe* (New York, 1983), p. 80.

31. Tom Gallagher and Allan M. Williams, eds., *Southern European Socialism: Parties, Election and the Challenge of Government* (Manchester, 1989).

32. Programs of political parties in opposition and policies of parties in government fulfill different functions, face different constraints, and follow different logics. Considering these principal differences, a synchronic comparison between, say, a Spanish socialist party in power and the British Labour party in opposition becomes meaningless.

33. Although the Swiss social democrats stayed in government during the 1980s due to their consociational political system, they will be excluded from the comparison too. The system of the Konkordanzdemokratie and the minor role the SPS plays within the government make it extremely difficult to attribute certain policies to the social democrats.

34. To be sure, the Finnish social democrats that I have subsumed under the pragmatic, coalescent type can certainly not be described as dominant as the other three parties, not in the least because the communists played a more important role in the Finnish Left and the country as a whole. The facts that the SDP has mostly been the strongest party in the Finnish multiparty system throughout the postwar period (with the exception of 1954, 1958, and 1962) and their high power quotient highlight its persistent important position in postwar Finnish politics and justify the party's inclusion as a border case in the group of established, dominant social democracy.

35. Philippe C. Schmitter, "Five Reflections on the Future of the Welfare State," *Politics and Society* 16, no. 4 (1988): 503–16.

36. Michael Bruno and Jeffrey Sachs, *The Economic of Worldwide Stagflation* (Cambridge, 1985).

37. Katri Kosonen, "Saving and Economic Growth in a Nordic Society," in *Social Corporatism and Economic Performance*, ed. Jukka Pekkarinen, Matti Pohjola, and Bob Rowthorn (Oxford, 1992).

38. Pekkarinen, "Corporatism and Economic Performance."

39. Andrew Martin, "Restoring the Social Democratic Distributive Regime," unpublished paper, Cambridge, 1987; Jan-Otto Andersson, "Controlled Restructuring in Finland?" *Scandinavian Political Studies* 12, no. 4 (1989): 373–89.

40. However, the Norwegian social democrats lost 6.5 percent of their votes in 1989, still before they could harvest the fruits of their restructuring policies of the last two years. But the fact that the leftist-socialists won 4.6 percent and the main conservative opponent Höyre lost even more votes (-8.3 percent) qualifies the electoral defeat of the DNA as by no means disastrous.

41. Wolfgang C. Müller, "Privatising in a Corporatist Economy: The Politics of Privatisation in Austria," *West European Politics* 41 (October 1988): 403–56.

42. Georg Winckler, "Der Austrokeynesianismus und sein Ende," *Österreichische Zeitschrift für Politikwissenschaft* 17, no. 3 (1988): 142–66.

43. Criddle and Bell, *The French Socialist Party*; Lyrintzis, *Between Socialism and Populism*; Spourdalakis, *The Rise of the Greek Socialist Party*; Jose Maria Maravall, "The Socialist Alternative," in *Spain at the Polls*, ed. Howard R. Penniman and Eusebio M. Mujal-León (Durham, 1985).

44. Mark Kesselman, "Prospects for Democratic Socialism in Advanced Capitalism: Class Struggle and Compromise in Sweden and France," *Politics and Society* 11, no. 4 (1982): 397–438.

45. Although Przeworski and Sprague acknowledge the role of coherent trade unionism, social democratic subcultural organizations, and neocorporatism in moderating the electoral trade-off, in the long run they consider these factors inadequate for preventing the irreversible decline of social democratic parties.

46. In small and medium-size open economies "economic competitiveness" is to be understood as the relative unit labor costs (cost side) and the export market share of crucial products relative to the degree of penetrability of the domestic market (output).

47. Merkel, "Sozialdemokratische Politik."

48. Anthony A. Crosland, *The Future of Socialism* (London, 1964); Peter Hall, "The Evolution of Economic Policy under Mitterrand," in *The Mitterrand Experiment*, ed. George Ross, Stanley Hoffmann, and S. Malzacher (Cambridge, 1987); Timothy A. Tilton, "Why Don't the Swedish Social Democrats Nationalize Industry?" *Scandinavian Studies* 59 (March 1987): 142–66.

49. David Cameron, "The Colors of a Rose: On the Ambiguous Record of French Socialism," Harvard University, Center for European Studies Working Paper (Cambridge, Mass., 1987).

50. Sainsbury, "Scandinavian Party Politics Re-examed"; Göran Therborn, *Why Some Peoples Are More Unemployed than Others* (London, 1986); Walter Korpi, *The Democratic Class Struggle* (London, 1983); Esping-Andersen, *Politics*; Gösta Esping-Andersen, "Equality, Efficiency, and Power in the Making of a Welfare State," unpublished paper, Florence, 1988.

51. Although France has to be subsumed under the ideal type of the "conservative," insurance-based welfare state (Manfred G. Schmidt, *Sozialpolitik: Historische Entwicklung und internationale Vergleich* [Opladen, 1988], p. 165), it also shows strong patterns of tax-financed social transfers; generous family allowances are certainly the prime example.

52. Salvador Giner, "Southern European Socialism in Transition," *West European Politics* 7 (April 1984): 138–57; Victor Perez-Diaz, *El retorno de la sociedad civil* (Madrid 1987); Tom Gallagher and Allan P. Williams, eds., *Southern European Socialism*.

53. Herbert Kitschelt, "Mapping the Course of the European Left," unpublished paper, Durham, N.C., 1988.

54. Przeworski, *Capitalism*.

55. William E. Paterson and Alistair H. Thomas, *The Future of Social Democracy* (Oxford, 1986), p. 16.

The West German Left in a Changing Europe

Between Intellectual

Stagnation and

Redefining Identity

Andrei S. Markovits

This chapter poses itself a straightforward task: to offer some answers about why the West German Left—with virtually no exceptions—reacted with despondency, often bordering on hostility, to the monumental events transforming east central Europe and the Soviet Union in 1989 and 1990.[1] To be sure, the West German Left was as surprised by the structural magnitude and alacrity of these epoch-making developments as the rest of the world. Nobody foresaw the appearance, let alone the far-reaching consequences of this *annus mirabilis*, perhaps not even the subjects of this historic change themselves. Moreover, it is no secret that the transformations in eastern Europe and the virtual disappearance of the Soviet bloc caused substantial crises of identity for virtually all left-wing movements and parties in the West. Most have responded with some ambivalence, perhaps even trepidations concerning their own future. But none seemed as reticent, skeptical, critical, even outright hostile regarding these events as the West German Left. One German observer astutely referred to this mood as an "anti-position."[2]

While there have been a number of excellent accounts of this anti-position and fine descriptions of its various manifestations, none of these contributions have attempted to provide a comprehensive analytic answer about why this has been the case.[3] This is precisely what this discussion attempts to do. Concretely, I will discuss a number of items that will demonstrate the uniqueness of the West German Left among its counterparts in the rest of the advanced capitalist world. As will be clear, all these items are linked inextricably to Germany's recent past, thus rendering the West German Left's particularly negative reactions to the events of 1989 and 1990 an integral part of modern German history. As such, the "Germanness" of these reactions cannot be denied.

The West German Left's Problems with Nationalism

If one had to point to perhaps the most consistent and arguably fatal Achilles heel of the European Left's strategic thinking over the last hundred years, it surely would have to be the Left's woefully inadequate understanding of nationalism as a major force and a powerful agent of collective identity. Hailing from the cosmopolitanism and international existence of the early socialists, as well as from Marx's correct assessment that modernization entailed an increasingly internationalized and global exploitation of labor by capital, leftist intellectuals by and large concluded that progressive politics had to be ipso facto international. Above all, international seemed always to mean a- or even antinational. Whereas the Left generally assumed identities derived from the "universalistic" realm of production to be progressive, it viewed identities stemming from the "particularistic" areas of geography and culture with suspicion. Most of the time the Left viewed the latter identities as a priori reactionary. Only in the context of Third World liberation movements did the Left ever accept nationalism as a legitimate and progressive expression of collective solidarity. Specifically, the Left accorded nationalism its *Salonfaehigkeit* mainly in the context of its struggles with the United States or its allies, that is, when forces confronting American and/or capitalist hegemony used nationalism in support of their cause. Whenever conflicts arose that involved the Soviet Union as a repressor, the Left either remained silent, sided with the Soviets, or—in its more liberal version—rallied to the cause of the oppressed, always emphasizing that the support accorded the anti-Soviet combatants was given for their lack of civil rights and autonomy, not their inability to express their national identity. This remained constant from the East Berlin uprisings of 1953, through the Hungarian revolt of 1956, the destruction of the Prague Spring of 1968, the various Polish incursions in the course of the 1970s, and Afghanistan in 1979.

In addition to these "generic" problems that virtually all lefts of the first world have exhibited for nearly a century, the German Left has had to confront additional complexities in its dealing with nationalism that reflect key peculiarities of modern German history. Unlike in the British, the French, and even the Italian Left, nationalism with all its complexities already played a crucial role in the debates of the nascent socialist movement in Germany. With the processes of state and nation building incomplete, socialist politics in Germany became inevitably intertwined with issues pertaining to them. Should one attain social and political progress via a unified national German state, even under the aegis of a semifeudal Prussia, as the Lassallians argued, or was it better for the Left first to support broad, progressive, bourgeois-led coalitions whose task it would be to topple the reactionary aristocracy before constructing a united Germany based on the parliamentary principles of liberal democracy?[4] Even though Bismarck's international and domestic triumphs rendered the debate moot by rapidly eliminating the second option, the role of nation and nationalism, as well as socialism's relations to them, had entered the Left's world on a permanent basis. The particular acuteness of this topic in the case of the German Left hailed from the fact that it had to confront two simultaneous problems in the complex formation of class and national identities. In contrast, socialist movements in western Europe were by and large "only" faced with one of these problems.

Nationalism most certainly did not endear itself to the German Left because even before the official institutionalization of the newly established nationalist German Reich, the state used the rhetoric of national interest to outlaw socialists. With nationalism becoming increasingly more rabid toward the turn of the century in circles generally hostile to the German Left, nationalism's ambivalence and its pejorative meaning grew for socialists. It also became a major topic of programmatic and strategic debates. How were class and nation to be reconciled by socialists? Could nationalism be progressive under certain circumstances? If yes, which ones, where and when? Although for obvious reasons, never as keenly debated by German socialists as by their Austrian comrades, Rosa Luxemburg's polemics on nationalism inside German social democracy simply have no West European counterparts.

Nationalism continued to matter to the German Left throughout the troubled Weimar years. While increasing its hostility to German nationalism, which by then had become the virtual prerogative of the reactionary Right, the Left made definite attempts to use nationalism for its own purposes as in the case of the communists' strategy of "national Bolshevism."[5] While this and similar experiments were simply no match for the Right, it is clear that nationalism played an existentially crucial—albeit largely negative—role in the German Left's identity during the Weimar Republic. The German Left's traditional aversion to nationalism received unprecedented support with Hitler's rise to power.

Hitler and Auschwitz not only changed German history but also all conventional parameters of nationalism. It is through the lasting legacy of this change that one must analyze the West German Left's uniquely troubling relationship to its own (i.e., federal republican) and German nationalism, as well as to nationalism in general. It is quite true that following the war, and well into the 1950s, it was the German Left—particularly the Social Democratic party—that pursued a strategy of a single German state. In marked contrast to Adenauer's policy, which aimed at Germany's integration into the West—even at the cost of unity—as the only possibility to overcome Germany's errand ways of the past and guarantee a prosperous and democratic future for Germany and Europe, the German Left believed that only a socialist Germany was a plausible guarantee against a recurring of fascism on German soil. This socialist Germany was to be demilitarized, pacifist, and not belonging to any political alliance. Because the Left's electoral bastions lay in what became the German Democratic Republic in October 1949, unification for the social democrats also had a pragmatic-instrumental dimension that should not be underestimated. Thus, although explicitly pro-unification and single-statist, the West German Left pursued these policies more in the name of socialism and a fundamental restructuring of class power in Germany than in the name of conventional nationalism. Paradoxically, those sentiments remained strong, although often subdued, in the officially two-statist Christian democratic Right.

With the "Westernization" of the Federal Republic's Left complete by the late 1950s, the existing two-state solution became one of the fundamental ideological pillars of the West German Left. Being a German nationalist in any way, shape, or form simply became unacceptable for any leftist. With the belated discovery of the Holocaust in the course of the 1960s, any kind of German nationalism was discredited in leftist circles. Indeed, it was during this time—and not immediately after the war—that much of the West German Left developed the notion that Germany's permanent division is one of the just costs exacted from the German people for Auschwitz. In no other West European Left did nationalism evoke such embarrassment and conflicted emotions as in the Federal Republic. Thus, it was de rigueur for West German leftists to root for Algeria in its soccer match against the Federal Republic at the World Cup in 1982. Similarly, one of the major cleavages between West German and French socialists was their different sensibility toward nationalism, particularly their own, but also—as we will see—those of eastern Europe and the Soviet Union. It would have been unthinkable for the West German Left to welcome the deployment of a German nuclear force as a sign of the Federal Republic's national independence even from the much-hated United States similar to the French Left's often enthusiastic approval of the *force de frappe*.

One of the major tenets of virtually all West German leftists was the complete acceptance of the German Democratic Republic as a legitimate German state. That this was the case is best illustrated by the Left's complete misreading of what exactly happened on November 9, 1989. Well into the winter of 1990—in some cases, such as major segments of the Green party, until the East German elections of March 18, 1990, and even until the first all-German Bundestag elections of December 2, 1990—the bulk of the West German Left simply refused to acknowledge the fact that an undeniable majority of East Germans wanted—for whatever reasons—to have their country join West Germany, thereby ending a forty-year episode that defined the postwar European order. All kinds of explanations for this were given by the West German Left, ranging from the evil machinations of Helmut Kohl to the slightly more elitist version that the East Germans obviously do not know what is good for them if they sell their souls for Western consumer goods. A discussion follows of whence this assessment of the German Democratic Republic by the West German Left.

The German Democratic Republic
and Real Existing Socialism

For the West German Left, the GDR's legitimacy hails from many sources. Foremost among them is the universally held view within the

West German Left that for all the GDR's shortcomings it—rather than the Federal Republic—represents a true break with Germany's fascist past.[6] By establishing the first socialist experiment on German soil under adverse domestic and international conditions, the GDR—in notable contrast to the FRG—came to terms with Germany's past simply by being socialist which, after all, was antithetical to capitalism, perhaps the single most compelling social arrangement favoring the rise of fascism. The establishment of socialism extended the GDR a "legitimacy bonus" in the eyes of the West German Left that the latter bestowed on few other countries outside the Third World. The GDR's dictatorial ways and bureaucratic repression, although meeting with the West German Left's disapproval, were simply no match for the system's true achievement, namely the abolition of private property. With this major step the GDR had obviously initiated a structural change that made it in the eyes of most West German leftists qualitatively superior to any capitalist society. Even compared to such social democratic success stories as Sweden, for example, the West German Left perceived the GDR as qualitatively more progressive. Of course it was flawed, but in its essence it was socialist, which was certainly not the case with Sweden. The GDR was socialist, and it was so on German soil: it embodied the legacy of Marx, Engels, Liebknecht (more son than father), Luxemburg, Thaelmann, and Brecht in a country where Hitler had ruled not long ago. The GDR, although deformed, did represent—in principle and structure at least—the good Germany.

The GDR's perception by the West German Left is linked inextricably to the latter's political fate inside the Federal Republic as well as to the developments of West German politics at large. As in so many other things in the Federal Republic, the major watershed in the perceptions of and relations with the GDR occurred in the late 1960s.[7] Until then, virtually all public discourse in the Federal Republic was engulfed by an anticommunism bordering on an article of faith if not outright hysteria. In no other European country did anticommunism play such a fundamentally system-affirming role as in the Federal Republic. Indeed, much of the West German Left—led by the pro-unity, one-statist Social Democratic party—shared this antipathy for everything communist throughout the 1950s and much of the 1960s.

Enter 1968: West German public life experienced a fundamental transformation "from above" as well as "from below" in both of which the GDR, communism, Eastern Europe, and the Soviet Union were to play decisive roles. As to the changes from above, the most important and lasting center on the Willy Brandt-initiated Ostpolitik, which in many ways has to be viewed as one of the decisive contributors to communism's collapse twenty years later. Secure in its explicitly reformist position in an increasingly prosperous Federal Republic, West German social democracy began a strategic initiative that completely contradicted its main tenets of the 1950s. Replacing their earlier anticommunism with an acceptance of it, the social democrats began pursuing relations with the GDR, thereby giving further evidence to their apparently final departure from a one-state solution and their legitimization of two sovereign German states. The essence of the SPD's policy was what its intellectual architect, Egon Bahr, called "Wandel durch Annaeherung" (change through rapprochement). Ostpolitik's dialectic could best be summarized by the following quotation from Brandt: "In order to shake up the status quo politically, we had to accept the status quo territorially."[8] Following initial opposition to Ostpolitik from West Germany's conservatives, this policy became a bipartisan pillar of the Federal Republic's relations with the GDR and all of eastern Europe, thus making Ostpolitik the most lasting and successful component of the social democrats' reform initiatives of the late 1960s and early 1970s.

As to the reforms from below, it was the West German student movement and the New Left that challenged virtually every convention and institution in the Federal Republic, including anticommunism and the postwar order. Critical of communism's reality in the GDR and eastern Europe, the New Left was equally vocal in its opposition to anticommunism's repression as part of the Cold War atmosphere that built the Federal Republic. Explicitly dismissive of the old Left's (i.e., social democracy's and communism's) bureaucratic, centralized, and heteronomous qualities, the New Left and its legacy nevertheless transformed the characterization and "anticommunist" into an epithet—a genuine Schimpfwort—in most West German intellectual circles by the mid-1970s. That the social democrats were not enamored with the rapidity and direction of the New Left's reforms and that they still feared being labeled "red lovers" in a society barely shedding its cold war past was best exemplified by their feeling compelled to pass the so-called "Radical Decree," which was to screen all applicants to the civil service for communists and other "enemies of the constitution."[9] There can be little doubt that the SPD-initiated Radical Decree was in good part a domestic pacifier for Ostpolitik.

The New Left's creative and euphoric movement phase of the late

1960s disintegrated in a number of directions by the early 1970s. Some new leftists began their "long march through the institutions," most notably the world of social democracy with its party, affiliated research institutes, and ancillary labor organizations. Others formed the core of a number of leftist organizations which—in opposition to the SPD and the establishment—adhered to a variety of orthodox Leninist positions. A minority even joined organizations close to the West German Communist party (DKP), which had been readmitted to the West German political scene in 1968 following a twelve-year constitutional ban of communism at the height of the Cold War. While these worlds were very different from each other and often consumed by bitter ideological rivalries, they also developed certain commonalities that clearly identified them as "the Left." One of the shared values in this milieu was never to criticize the GDR and other communist regimes in eastern Europe, even if one disapproved of certain concrete measures and policies. In this world of the post-1968 West German Left, "real existing socialism" was without any doubt preferable to any capitalist arrangement, hence worthy of at least tacit, if not explicit, approval. This led to the shameful situation in which the West German Left became perhaps the most solid Western supporter of the status quo in eastern Europe and the Soviet Union throughout the 1970s and 1980s, publicly and consciously forsaking the plight of opposition movements.

Examples abound. Unlike in France, and to a lesser degree in Italy, where Alexander Solzhenitsyn's *The Gulag Archipelago* caused considerable consternation and soul-searching among left-wing intellectuals, the West German Left's response was a scolding of its French comrades for drawing the wrong conclusions about socialism and the Soviet Union from Solzhenitsyn's book. Above all, the West German Left decried Solzhenitsyn's nationalism and criticized the French for overlooking such an obvious shortcoming in their effusive praise of the author which seemed part of the French intellectuals' zealous quest for the discovery of liberalism and the shedding of their Marxist past. Teaching about the Soviet invasion of Afghanistan was repressed in one of the trade union movement's most important youth education programs. The trade union's youth organization refused to condemn the Soviet invasion even though this condemnation was to have occurred in a balanced way by having the Central American involvement of the United States criticized in equally harsh terms. A leading member of the printing, media, and writers' union (currently IG Medien, formerly IG Druck und Papier) condemned union members who—as German authors—protested the dissolution of the Polish writers' union. He called them a "fifth column" that helped destabilize Poland by "offering resistance against the regime."[10] Others in this union called KOR, the organization of Polish intellectuals explicitly formed to help workers and closely associated with Solidarity, "a questionable organization which transforms Solidarity into a political resistance movement."[11] Many railed against the "Catholic-reactionary" nature of Solidarity, and one member even dared to compare Polish activists to Hitler's storm troopers, the SA.[12] It has been common knowledge that, in certain West German unions, members who tried to organize symposia in favor of dissident movements in eastern Europe met with massive resistance on the part of the union leadership and fellow unionists. That this tacit approval of the communist status quo reached the highest echelons of the social democratic hierarchy was best exemplified by that bizarre—although telling—coincidence of December 1981 when Helmut Schmidt spent a sequestered weekend tête-à-tête with Erich Honecker in the latter's country house in the GDR while General Jaruzelski's troops imposed martial law in Poland. Worst of all, Schmidt did not find the events sufficiently disturbing to leave his meeting with Honecker.[13] The East European dissidents' disappointment concerning this betrayal on the part of the West German Left runs deep. This sentiment was best conveyed by the Czech intellectual Pavel Kohut in his speech to guests gathered in Berlin for the celebration of Willy Brandt's seventy-sixth birthday: "You will have to analyze it yourselves why you dropped us in the 1970s, why you—instead of allying yourselves with the beaten—preferred the beaters, or at best stayed neutral."[14] There are no comparable feelings in eastern Europe with regard to any other Western Left.

West Germany's Special Relationship with the United States

As a consequence of the Third Reich's destruction and Germany's broken national identity ever since, the United States assumed a special role in the formation and weaning of the political reality known as West Germany, something the United States has not replicated anywhere else in western Europe and perhaps not even in Japan due to that country's continued cohesion as one sovereign entity. The special texture of German-American—as opposed to British-American, French-American, or Dutch-American—relations clearly lies in the broken nature of Germany's national identity and historical legacy. For just as in West Germany, so, too, has the United States continued to exert a hegemonic authority in military and political relations with respect to virtually all West European countries since the end of World War II. Again, in a clear parallel with the German situation, the United States emerged all over western Europe as the first and foremost economic and cultural power since 1945. And yet, American missiles and Coca-Cola embodied a very different symbolic—thus political—texture in West Germany compared to any other West European country. Both have been appreciated or rejected by different people at different times in France, Britain, or Italy; in no instance, however, did American missiles or Coca-Cola play a key part in the post-World War II identity formation of the French, British, or Italians. One could take or leave either (as in the case of the French, who decidedly opted for Coca-Cola and spurned American missiles as early as 1986) or both without any of the choices implying something beyond the manifest nature of the choices themselves. In other words, in contrast to the West German case, there never existed a meta level of understanding and experience beyond the manifestly political and cultural in America's relations with the countries of western Europe. Without a doubt, the creation of the Cold War and Germany's position as a frontline state in an antagonistically divided Europe made American penetration of the Federal Republic's political, military, economic, and cultural life a lot more pronounced than anywhere else in the West. But more than geography, it was the broken continuity of German history and the ensuing uncertainty of German national identity that lent the United States willy-nilly a role in West Germany's post-1945 existence that was unique. The United States has been qualitatively different toward the Federal Republic than toward any other political and military ally, just as Americanism as a sociocultural phenomenon has meant different things to post-World War II Germans than to other Europeans.

As already mentioned, nowhere in Europe was the belief in the evils of communism as essential to the formation of postwar political identity as was the case in the Federal Republic. Indeed, this commonly shared distrust and hatred of the Soviet Union and communism created an important bond between the United States and the Federal Republic, and formed a major pillar of what was to become the much-vaunted "specialness" of German-American relations. It bears mention, of course, that this "special" relationship was from its very inception profoundly unequal in America's favor, which is not to say that West Germans did not derive major benefits from it on all levels. But therein lay many of the problems that have since emerged. Had the United States only been repressive and exploitative with respect to the Federal Republic, the Germans would not have developed conflict and ambivalence toward the United States and Americans. A relatively straightforward aversion would have arisen with little need for explanation and analysis. The United States, however, resembles a rich uncle with annoying foibles, much generosity, and definite demands, who is admired and needed by an initially poor, young, and talented nephew. The nephew may even appreciate the uncle and emulate him. But would he love him? Would he accept him without resistance and resentment, always knowing—and being reminded of—the uncle's initial generosity with material and spiritual support? Would there not be constant jockeying for more control on the part of the uncle and greater autonomy on the part of the increasingly independent nephew? It is in this dynamic, unique to German-American relations in the context of postwar European history, that anti-Americanism attained a special quality in West Germany.[15]

Nowhere has this assumed a more pronounced and acute reality than in the Federal Republic's leftist milieu.[16] For the West German Left, America is a priori politically dangerous and morally reprehensible by virtue of its power as the leading capitalist actor in a capitalist-dominated world. The West German Left sees the United States as dominating, domineering, and intimidating due to its might and its willingness to use it without much restraint. By being the world's leading capitalist power, the United States—for the West German Left—cannot but be imperialist, thus predatory, bellicose, and brutal. In addition to a structural critique of the political and economic arrangements in the United States and profound skepticism with respect to America's very existence, the West German Left also paid considerable attention to particular American policies it saw as prima facie evidence for America's unsavory role in the world. Beginning with the Vietnam War and continuing with American assistance to Israel and U.S. involvement in Central America, the West German Left had ample opportunities to have its general views about America empirically corroborated. Yet the Left's anti-Americanism attained a different quality in the course of the early 1980s. Starting with the neutron bomb debate in the late 1970s and accentuated by the deployment of intermediate-range nuclear missiles in 1983, the West German Left began to see the United States as an evil and dangerous occupying power whose reckless policies were to lead to Germany's physical annihilation.[17] The victims of American aggression metamorphosized from Salvadorean peasants to German housewives. Whereas in its pre-1980s anti-Americanism the West German Left viewed the Federal Republic as a quasi junior accomplice to the United States in the two countries' joint quest to exploit the Third World, Germany (not just the Federal Republic) had in the Left's eyes joined the Third World as one of America's most threatened victims at the height of the Euromissile debate; as graffitti on a Frankfurt wall opined, "The FRG = El Salvador."

In this context the West German Left added yet another favorable dimension to its already relatively benevolent picture of the Soviet Union and its East European allies. While still scorned for its bureaucratic centralism and excessive heteronomy, the Soviet Union was perceived by the Left in the Federal Republic not only as a socialist country but also as a peaceful, defensive, and reactive global power that naturally had to arm itself in its legitimate defense against the American aggressor.[18] Only very unusual West German intellectuals such as Peter Schneider, who have explicitly used the events of 1989 and 1990 to come to terms with their own past as leftists, publicly confessed their bewilderment and shame when the Kremlin, following Gorbachev's accession to power, openly admitted to having deployed its own intermediate-range missiles as part of a premeditated offensive strategy against the West.[19] This revelation should come as no surprise because the Soviet Union consistently escaped rigorous criticism by the West German Left well before the Euromissile crisis.

The German Left's Excessive Etatism

In its communist as well as social democratic version, the German Left has traditionally exhibited a greater degree of "state fixation" than any of its West European counterparts.[20] Developing without the substantial anarchist and anarcho-syndicalist traditions of the Latin lefts and not sharing the British labor movement's autonomy in civil society, the history of the German Left has been linked inextricably with a strong state on virtually all levels: the state as creator of a nation, repressor, provider of welfare and protection, regulator and mediator among groups and classes, initiator of political reforms, and guardian of an acceptable industrial relations system. In the realms of the political economy—in notable contrast to issues pertaining to civil liberties—the West German Left has by and large continued to view the state as good. One can detect a clear liking for a "verstaatlichte Gesellschaft" (a state-dominated society) that by and large enjoys a preference over any other social arrangement in West Germany's leftist milieu.[21] This state fixation has led union politics in the Federal Republic—certainly not a key carrier of progressive causes in the country—to be among the most juridified anywhere in the advanced capitalist world.[22]

One of the corollaries of this state fixation has led to a deep-seated suspicion of the market. Crudely put, much of the West German Left adheres to the notion of "state good, market bad," regardless of the issues involved. If the state remains associated with solidaristic measures and a structural propensity to foster collectivism, the market is seen as the state's exact opposite, undermining all solidarities and encouraging privatization. Above all, the market is associated with the furthering of individual choice and liberty, certainly among the most disdained concepts inside the West German Left. Thus, it should have come as no surprise to Petra Kelly of the Green party that few of her party colleagues and comrades in the West German Left supported the Chinese students who dared challenge the Chinese communist regime with that ultimate bourgeois symbol, a replica of the Statue of Liberty.[23] Kelly compares the West German Left unfavorably to the Italian, which did in fact demonstrate on behalf of the Chinese students' quest for liberal reforms in China. Much more characteristic of the West German Left's antipathies toward any movement clamoring for individual liberties is the opinion of a leading intellectual and veteran of the West German student movement of the late 1960s: "We don't have a clear picture . . . what did the demonstrators mean by democracy? Did they have a clear program? One also has reservations about becoming engaged on behalf of the movement, since photographs from China showed violent students and demonstrators indiscriminately attacking tanks, vehicles and soldiers with rocks and rods." Another leading leftist simply resorted to racism and the worst kind of "First Worldism": "What were the first three men called who were executed? One cannot even remember their names."[24]

None of this is to say that the West German Left will be spared soul-searching discussions in the coming years about socialism and its own past as it transforms itself from the West into the German Left. These will be trying times for many individuals and a collective that deserves enormous credit for having made the Federal Republic by far the most humane, enlightened, and democratic polity that ever existed on German soil. At this early juncture one can detect the roots for the following contradictory but also complementary lines of argument.

Total denial. Socialism is superior to capitalism. The Soviet Union and its East European allies were socialist, regardless of their shortcomings. They were thus superior to the West in every possible way. Everybody will soon realize that the Soviet Union and eastern Europe will be governed by various forms of neofascist and ultra-nationalist regimes beholden to crude consumerism and a market capitalism creating hitherto unprecedented social inequality, economic hardship, and ethnic strife. Only socialism, whose defeat is temporary, could prevent these countries from returning to barbarism. This openly Stalinist whitewash that continues to sing the unmitigated praises of real existing socialism represents the voice of a small minority within the West German Left.[25]

Partial denial. Much more prevalent are various interpretations that admit to some problems but continue to extol the socialist "project" and the moral—if not economic and political—superiority of socialism. The number of themes comprising partial denial is best characterized by the following quotation: "What did not exist does not necessarily have to be wrong; and: The opposite of something wrong need not by necessity be right."[26]

The first part of the statement denies that socialism ever existed anywhere in the world, most certainly in the Soviet Union and eastern Europe. Whatever system ruled those countries—Stalinism, bureaucratic repression, state-led accumulation, modernization from above, or a deformed workers' state—it most certainly was *not* socialism. Hence, as the Greens' Jutta Ditfurth argued at a panel discussion at the Humboldt University in East Berlin, there simply is no need to reexamine socialism's validity as a model because it was not socialism that was defeated in eastern Europe and the Soviet Union because these systems were never socialist.[27] This exoneration of socialism is extremely widespread in virtually all facets of the West German Left.

It is often accompanied by a quasi-religious extolling of socialism, not so much as a political and economic reality but as a moral mission. As a leading West German leftist intellectual told me, "one is simply a more righteous person if one is a socialist." It is interesting that people with such views continue to seek making socialism into an orderly "science" superior to capitalism's chaos even though none of science's most elementary qualities (such as falsification, for example) and all of religion's (unquestioned adherence to dogma) pertain to their political approach and general Weltanschauung.[28]

The second part of the quotation warns against any extolling of capitalism simply by virtue of socialism's ostensible failure. This faute de mieux embracing of capitalism as the lesser of two evils—understandably so prevalent among East European and Soviet intellectuals[29]—need not worry the author of those lines in the German case. Most German leftists have remained completely immune to capitalism's lure throughout these momentous events and will hardly concede anything positive to it in economics or politics. Much more prevalent, however, will be the debate concerning the next line of argument.

The frenzied search for the elusive "third way." Everyone seems on a treasure hunt for the elusive "third way" combining the humane collectivism and solidaristic protection of the socialist model with the efficient accumulation and allocation, plus the individual liberties, of a market-dominated capitalism. A number of points constantly appear in this ubiquitous debate. First, there is a woeful absence of empirical examples. With the Yugoslav economy in total shambles and the country on the verge of political disintegration, no one extols the Yugoslav model as the much-vaunted panacea along the third way. Second, there is still the assumption that real existing socialism—of the GDR variety in particular—created a certain solidarity among people, and a serenity and humaneness in interpersonal relations that ought to be reintroduced into the brutal, commodified, and rat-race-dominated West with its individualistic and pushy *Ellenbogengesellschaft* (elbow society). Third, everyone wants to go "beyond social democracy." Systems such as Sweden's or Austria's for example are always mentioned in a "yes, but" mode. Of course the Federal Republic—let alone any other Western country—never serves as a model for anything. Finally, there still continues the search for the all-encompassing solution, the total transformation of politics and economics, the definitive answer, the new—and completely moral—human being.

The latter point is particularly surprising as well as disappointing coming from a Left that has arguably included perhaps the most effective and powerful new social movements anywhere in the world. It may go to show that despite these movements' insistence on being neither Left nor Right but ahead—in other words in being quintessential representatives of postmodern politics—they are actually much closer to the traditional Left than they might like to admit. The greenish subculture of the Federal Republic maintained a surprisingly reddish hue over the years. Despite the many postmodern claims to the contrary, Socialism with a capital S still possesses a powerful spell over the German Left.

Instead of its moping, it behooves the German Left to rejoice about the following immense improvements in European and global politics to which paradoxically—perhaps even unbeknown to itself—it contributed through its activism of the 1970s and 1980s: the end of the Cold War, meaning the beginning of an era of true peace and integration in Europe, not just an extended cease-fire; the end of Germany's division; the long-overdue liberation for the Left of having to bear the millstone of Stalinism and Soviet-style despotism around its neck whenever the word *socialism* is mentioned in any context; and the extension of liberal democracy from Portugal to the Ural Mountains for the first time ever in European history.

Thus, the German Left should forget about salvaging anything "socialist" from eastern Europe and the German Democratic Republic. Those who argue that these societies were not socialist should be consistent: they really weren't. Contrary to widespread belief among the West German Left, almost everything in the GDR turned out disastrously, including the much-vaunted day-care centers.[30] The solidarity in the GDR was based on shared misery and scarcity, exactly the opposite of the socialist view that envisions the creation of a solidarity based on personal choice and abundance. Above all, the Left in the Federal Republic should give itself credit for having created 1968, which has proven to be so woefully absent in the world of real existing socialism. Instead of living socialism (small s) through the emancipatory struggles that transformed the Federal Republic and other Western societies from below, the GDR and its East European cohort were decreed Socialism (capital S) from above, which led to a wholesale state-run "emancipation" that treated citizens like wards, thereby amounting to no emancipation at all. Consider how *salonfaehig* racism, anti-Semitism, sexism, authoritarianism, and all other bad "isms" remained through forty years of real existing socialism after the Left had made them all but unacceptable—although far from nonexistent—in the West, including the Federal Republic. The Left in Germany has to come to the bitter realization that the GDR and real existing socialism have bequeathed nothing positive for the Left at all. Sad—and incredible—as this may sound, the experiences of the Soviet Union and eastern Europe can only serve as negative examples and warnings for Western leftists in their continued legitimate and necessary struggle to improve the human condition. If anything, the long-overdue Leninist debacle will soon enhance the validity of socialism as an emancipatory project. No one can tell if socialism will ever become the hegemonic system of an advanced industrial economy with a democratic polity. It is perhaps better that way.

Notes

1. Here, the West German Left comprises all Old Left groups to the left of the Social Democratic party (SPD) such as the Deutsche Kommunistische Partei (DKP) and the broad legacy of the '68ers and the New Left. Thus, it includes all the factions of the Green party ranging from the "fundamentalists" on the party's rejectionist or maximalist wing through its mediators in the middle, the so-called "Aufbruch" group, to the party's accommodationists, the "realists." The West German Left also encompasses all facets of the so-called "new social movements" (feminists, peace activists, antinuclear demonstrators) who defined the agenda of progressive politics in the Federal Republic throughout the late 1970s and much of the 1980s. Finally, I also count a good part of the West German trade union movement and the Social Democratic party as belonging to the Left. Definitely as a consequence of 1968 and its subsequent legacies, a number of trade unions such as IG Metall and IG Medien—those I have elsewhere termed *activists*—have been very much part of all aspects of leftist politics in the Federal Republic. The same pertains to the left wing of the SPD.

2. Sven Papke, "Links und kleinmuetig?" *Gewerkschaftliche Monatshefte* 41 (July 1990): 463–74; Papke uses the wonderful German term *Missmut*, best translated as ill-humoredness, despondency, sullenness, and discontent, as a section heading for the part of his discussion in which he describes the concrete reactions by the West German Left to the events of 1989 and 1990. He also uses the phrase *Noergelei der Intellektuellen*, which could be translated as the grumbling, grousing, or nagging, in short *kvetching*, of intellectuals. The title of Papke's essay translates as "left and dejected."

3. In addition to Papke's fine piece, see Walther Mueller-Jentsch, "Entzauberung eines historischen Projekts: Der Sozialismus ist im Osten gescheitert und im Westen von der Zeit ueberholt," *Frankfurter Rundschau*,

August 1, 1989; Norbert Roemer, "Politik sozialer Partnerschaft—Stellung-nahme zur gewerkschaftlichen Sozialismus-Debatte," *Gewerkschaftliche Monatshefte* 41 (April 1990): 217–25; Wolfgang Kowalsky, "Zur Kritik linker Deutschlandpolitik," ibid., pp. 226–32; and above all Peter Schneider, "Man kann ein Erdbeben auch verpassen," *Die Zeit*, April 27, 1990, and reprinted in *German Politics and Society* 20 (Summer 1990): 1–21.

4. Werner Conze and Dieter Groh, *Die Arbeiterbewegung in der nationalen Bewegung: Die deutsche Sozialdemokratie vor, waehrend und nach der Reichsgruendung* (Stuttgart: Klett, 1966). This debate is somewhat reminiscent of the dependencia controversy of the late 1960s and early 1970s in which the issue was also the establishment of progressive politics in the Third World, mostly Latin America: Should progressive forces in these countries advocate the forging of interclass, that is, national, alliances in order to diminish these countries' dependence on the neoimperialist First World, even if these alliances include openly reactionary elements such as Junkerlike landholders for example? Or should progressives advocate a social revolution at home first in order to eliminate the domestic forces of reaction before embarking on the larger national mission of dealing with the outside world? It is not by chance that the German situation evokes this debate because Germany exhibited characteristics in its state and nation-building that resembled those often encountered in the Third World.

5. Louis Depeux, *National Bolchevisme: Strategic communiste et dynamique conservatrice* (Paris: H. Champion, 1979).

6. To emphasize the structural characteristics and capital-dependent nature of the Nazi regime, as well as to show the ubiquity of many of its features, the West German Left has consistently preferred to refer to this epoch in German history by the generic "fascist" instead of the specific "National Socialist" or "Nazi." I have argued elsewhere that this seemingly innocuous semantic issue served the West German Left as a convenient distancing mechanism from the particularities of the Nazi—that is, German—as opposed to the generally fascist crimes. This has had deleterious effects on the West German Left's understanding of Jewish nationalism and the state of Israel. See Andrei S. Markovits, "Germans and Jews: An Uneasy Relationship Continues," *Jewish Frontier* (April 1984): 14–20.

7. It might be a consequence of personal bias, but I for one am convinced that it would be virtually impossible to exaggerate the importance of 1968 as a watershed for virtually every development in the Federal Republic's private and public life. If one had to summarize the difference between the FRG and the GDR in one word, I would not hesitate for one second in affirming "1968." It is not by chance that a former head of the conservative Konrad Adenauer Foundation referred to 1968—disapprovingly one might add—as a much more decisive caesura in recent German history than 1945.

8. Willy Brandt, *Begegnungen und Einsichten: Die Jahre 1960–75* (Hamburg: Hoffmann und Campe, 1976), p. 642.

9. For a fine study on the Radical Decree, see Gerard Braunthal, *Political Loyalty and Public Service in West Germany: The 1972 Decree against Radicals and Its Consequences* (Amherst: University of Massachusetts Press, 1990).

10. As quoted in Schneider, "Man kann ein Erdbeben auch verpassen," *German Politics and Society,* p. 6.

11. Ibid.

12. Ibid. Everything that I wrote about the West German Left's view of nationalism in the First World and eastern Europe pertains a fortiori to religion. Religion to most leftist intellectuals in the Federal Republic is little more than the "idiocy of rural life" and "false consciousness" that conceal the "objective interests" that define the essence of politics. As such, religion—together with nationalism—is merely a sleight of hand by the ruling classes, which leftists correctly perceive and then dismiss as obfuscation. With certain exceptions such as Latin America's "liberation theology" and the beginnings of the Shiite revolution against the dreaded Shah of Iran and his secret police (Savak), German leftists have continued to feel uncomfortable when religion enters politics. They thus risk misinterpreting its position in a country's political landscape and branding it "reactionary" much too prematurely. I will never forget the numerous discussions I had with West German leftists inside the SPD, the trade unions, the Green party, and any of the many "new social movements" who refused to support Solidarity in Poland because they found it "reactionary" by virtue of the central role the movement accorded to Catholicism. One person made it clear to me that the Left could not support anyone who—like Lech Wałęsa—had pictures of a Madonna (in this case of Czestochowa, not of Hollywood) on his office wall.

13. Friends who attended a demonstration on that Sunday in Frankfurt protesting the imposition of martial law in Poland were surprised by the low turnout in a town known for its political activism and social engagement on the part of its sizable and readily mobilized leftist subculture. Excepting some anarchists and Trotskyites, the bulk of the Left stayed home, which certainly would not have been the case had the demonstration involved Nicaragua or El Salvador.

14. As quoted in Schneider, "Man kann ein Erdbeben auch verpassen," *German Politics and Society,* p. 8.

15. Much of this analysis relies on previous research on German-American relations as well as Americanism and anti-Americanism in the Federal Republic. See Andrei S. Markovits, "Anti-Americanism and the Struggle for a West German Identity," in *The Federal Republic of Germany at Forty,* ed. Peter H. Merkl (New York: New York University Press, 1989), pp. 35–54, and "On Anti-Americanism in West Germany," *New German Critique,* no. 34 (Winter 1985): 3–27.

16. For a particularly egregious example of this attitude and conviction, see the journal *Prokla's* editorial "Aufgeklaerte Blindheit; Plaedoyer fuer einen linken Antiamerikanismus," 19 (March 1989): 2–10.

17. The usage of language associated with the Holocaust was unmistakable. Thus, judging by the West German Left's rhetoric, Americans were ready to do unto Germans what Germans had done unto Jews in the Holocaust.

18. Jeffrey Herf, *Soviet Power, German Neutralism and the Politics of the Euromissiles* (New York: Free Press, 1990).

19. See Schneider, "Man kann ein Erdbeben auch verpassen," *German Politics and Society,* p. 4.

20. On the useful concept of the German Left's—particularly social democracy's and the labor movement's—state fixation, see Bodo Zeuner, "Solidaritaet mit der SPD oder Solidaritaet der Klasse? Zur SPD-Bindung der DGB-Gewerkschaften," *Prokla*, 6, no. 1 (1977): 1–32.

21. On the issue of "verstaatlichte Gesellschaft," see Christianne Reymann, "Fuer manche Linke bricht ein Haus aus Selbsttaeuschung zusammen," *Frankfurter Rundschau*, October 21, 1989.

22. On how juridification has on the one hand helped West German labor attain many important reforms and positions of power while at the same time stymieing its radical potentials, see Andrei S. Markovits, *The Politics of the West German Trade Unions: Strategies of Class and Interest Representation in Growth and Crisis* (Cambridge: Cambridge University Press, 1986).

23. Petra Kelly, "Wiegen die Menschenrechtsverletzungen Pekings weniger schwer?" *Frankfurter Rundschau*, August 3, 1989.

24. Ibid.

25. For a representative statement see Hermann L. Gremliza, "No Deposit, No Return," *Konkret*, December 1989, p. 8. Parts of the Hamburg Left have developed in this direction. In addition to *Konkret's* repeated voicing of this opinion of total denial, the view is also voiced by former Green superstars Rainer Trampert and Thomas Ebermann.

26. Karlheinz Hiesienger, "Wider die Politik persoenlicher Denunziation," *Gewerkschaftliche Monatshefte* 41 (July 1990): 459.

27. In mentioning the well-known Ditfurth incident, Peter Schneider comments, "Wonderful. Our images intact, we can carry on as usual. Exhibiting the same determination, a young SA-fascist could have said in 1945: The collapse of the Third Reich does not effect me in the least, since true fascism has not even begun to be implemented anywhere in reality." Schneider, "Man kann ein Erdbeben auch verpassen," *German Politics and Society*, p. 10.

28. Steffen Lehndorff, a supposedly converted, that is, "critical" West German communist, is still trying to make Marxism into a better science. See Steffen Lehndorff, "Fuer manche Linke bricht ein Haus aus Selbsttaeuschung zusammen," *Frankfurter Rundschau*, October 21, 1989. Schneider demonstrates impressively how any kind of challenge to existing beliefs, any kind of admission of error, or any kind of opinion change, have negative connotations in German culture in general, and its leftist subset in particular. German culture, writes Schneider, frowns on inconsistency; one should not change one's mind. In the leftist milieu such concepts as *revisionist, renegade*, or *deviationist* are full of religious meaning. Schneider, "Man kann ein Erdbeben auch verpassen," *German Politics and Society*, p. 3.

29. For understandable reasons of the dialectic at work, Margaret Thatcher has become the new heroine in certain intellectual circles in eastern Europe and the Soviet Union. While this is not a pleasant prospect, there is little chance that it will endure to the point where Thatcherism will become the main mode of rescuing these countries out of their current misery.

30. We know from a number of sources that the GDR's day-care centers were immensely authoritarian in terms of imposing very early toilet training on children and requiring them to become obedient to the party's wishes and commands.

The Socialist

Discourse and

Party Strategy in

West European

Democracies

Herbert Kitschelt

The objective of this chapter is to show that the electoral decline of most European socialist and social democratic parties—two labels I will use synonymously—in the 1980s was not purely a matter of social circumstances and tactical miscalculations, but was rooted in fundamental premises of socialist ideology itself. The extent to which socialist parties have been able to question and to modify these premises provides a partial explanation for the fortunes of these parties. In other words, a study of West European socialism in the 1980s cannot simply assume that all parties that run under socialist labels represent the same substantive policies and programs. What is at stake in the transformation and decline of European socialism is not just the survival of an organizational shell associated with a particular "brand name," but the meaning of socialist party programs, organization, and strategy.

The most prominent explanations of socialist party decline in the 1980s ignore or only implicitly take into account the ideology and the moral-intellectual discourse in these parties. In the first part of this chapter I will sketch some of these explanations, including my own. Yet ultimately I will argue that the analysis of common ideological premises in socialist thinking on which I subsequently focus provides critical insights into why socialist parties have encountered difficulties to adapt to a changed political climate in the 1980s. Intellectual traditions in national political cultures and the peculiar alternative models of the good society that are controversial between parties in competitive democracies contributed to the differential intellectual mobility of socialist parties in the 1980s.

Given the small number of socialist parties and countries that can be compared, it is ultimately impossible to determine exactly what percentage of the variance in the observed party performance is explained by sociological conditions, constraints of the party systems, the organization of the parties, and political ideology. Yet in the absence of clear rules of attributing causal effectiveness to each set of variables, a satisfactory understanding of socialist party dynamics should engage in a multilevel analysis that includes the political activists' cognitive and normative frameworks that shape their orientation as well as the institutional conditions impinging on their strategic choices.

Explaining European Socialism

With some simplification, the 1980s were an era of strong socialist party resurgence across southern Europe, where the Spanish, French, and Greek parties controlled government power for much of the decade and less powerful socialist parties in Italy and Portugal participated in governments. In contrast, in central and much of northern Europe, socialist parties either stagnated or suffered severe electoral setbacks. The average electoral performance of the parties in the 1980s, compared to the 1970s, declined most in Austria, Britain, Denmark, Norway, Switzerland, and West Germany. In Belgium, Finland, the Netherlands, and Sweden, the parties held steady or slightly improved their support.[1]

To some extent, the electoral fortunes of socialist parties had nothing to do with their strategic appeals and policy outlook, but were a consequence of "economic fate." Where socialist parties held government office during the economic crisis period from 1974 to 1982, they usually suffered during the recovery period from 1983 to the end of the decade. This economic explanation, however, has only limited power in cross-national comparison. Not all elections were fought over economic issues. Socialist parties in office lost support at very different levels of economic misery (unemployment, inflation, low growth). Conversely, southern socialist winners in the 1980s often stayed in office, even though economic misery indices remained seriously high and improved only slightly. Voting behavior is not sufficiently explained by the electorate's myopic rationale of "punish or reward past government performance," but is shaped by voters' long-term experiences with socialist parties and expectations created by these parties.[2]

Voters' long-term expectations are especially influenced by parties' success in building egalitarian welfare states based on the provision of services, rather than on the payment of transfers proportional to contributions.[3] Moreover, socialist parties are more successful where they have built up a large public employment sector for social services because it is in the economic self-interest of public employees to vote for the party that defends their concerns best. Nevertheless, such institutions and policy strategies have only moderate explanatory power for the electoral performance of socialist parties in the 1980s. Encompassing egalitarian welfare states with large civil sectors, such as in Sweden, may have slowed and delayed the decay of the traditional social democratic appeal, but, taken by themselves, have been unable to inspire a new enthusiasm for socialist politics.

In a similar vein, conventional sociological explanations for the decline of socialist parties cannot cast light on the national variation of socialist party fortunes in western Europe. The proportion of blue-collar workers in the occupational structure, particularly that of "productive" occupations in extractive and manufacturing industries Marxists have focused on as the core of the working class, has declined everywhere, but in some countries socialist parties have overcome this adversity by appealing to new electoral constituencies, primarily white-collar employees of lower status.

Efforts to blend sociological and political choice arguments in reconstructing illuminate the course of socialist parties, such as in the highly provocative and analytically impressive writings of Adam Przeworski, remain, in the last instance, unconvincing.[4] According to this approach, socialist parties can appeal primarily to productive blue-collar workers based on their class identity, but, by choosing this strategy, are forced to sacrifice the votes of potential external allies who can be won over only with cross-class messages. Alternatively, the parties may appeal to a cross-class alliance, but therefore disorganize the working class and reduce the socialist parties' backing among blue-collar workers. The tragedy of socialism in capitalist democracy, then, is its inevitable decline due to the shrinking size and proportion of the working class and the inexorable trade-off between workers and allies that makes it impossible for socialist party leaders to increase their potential electorate beyond a definite limit ("carrying capacity") in order to make up for lost workers.

This orthodox interpretation of socialist class strategies has little actuality for a discussion of socialist parties and visions in the late twentieth century. There can be little doubt that the decline of the blue-collar working class has also reduced the electoral attractiveness of party appeals to class unity, yet general trends in the socioeconomic composition of socialist party support, taken by themselves, throw little light on the varying electoral performance of socialist parties and on their political discourse in western Europe.[5]

On the electoral level, the 1970s and 1980s may have brought an end to the trade-off between working class and allied support for socialist parties.[6] Instead, working-class and allied support for socialist (and communist) parties change in parallel movements at least as often as in trade-offs. Leftist parties opting for a class-based strategy often lose both working-class and allied support. Conversely, cross-class appeals have often helped the Left in both constituencies, even in countries where class models of electoral support detected earlier sharp trade-offs.[7]

These changes suggest that the content of socialist programs is not sufficiently characterized by the distinction between pure class and cross-class appeals. What mobilizes a class and its potential allies may change with the societal context, as does the existence or strength of a trade-off between workers and allies.[8] For each historical instance, we must ask the questions, What is the "classness" of class strategies? How are socialism and class interrelated in the intellectual appeal of socialist parties? In other words, we must analyze the discourse of socialist parties. By discourse, I mean the set of key organizing principles and axiomatic propositions that drives the programmatic vision of socialist parties and is invoked by socialist politicians to propose solutions for concrete policy problems in the economic, social, or cultural realm.

Two other explanations of socialist party performance in the 1980s at least implicitly refer to the parties' political discourse. They analyze how well parties were able to respond to new demand functions in the electorates. Were socialist parties able to redesign their discourse in order to tap new demands and interests? An increasing proportion of the electorate casts its vote according to the prospects a party can credibly offer for future change. Voters assess a party's prospects in light of its programmatic appeal and strategic stance, not just its past record in office. It is true that parties cannot choose positions at liberty because they are bound by a history in which they have acquired control of certain issues and voter concerns and lost other issues to competing parties.[9] Nevertheless, parties are able to adjust their stances to new challenges in the electoral arena that originate in changing voter demands and new strategies of competitors.[10] The socialists' electoral performance then depends on their ability to match new competitive environments with appropriate strategies.

In the 1970s and 1980s, socialist parties saw themselves confronted with two major new challenges to their traditional concerns, managing the capitalist economy and providing a social safety net for all wage laborers through comprehensive welfare state policies. On the one hand, the increasing openness of world markets for manufacturing products, services, and finance undermined domestic capacity for macroeconomic regulation and forced governments to offer internationally competitive levels of profitability and risk to increasingly mobile private capital investors, thus undermining goals of economic redistribution and domestic stabilization.[11] I will call this development the challenge of market efficiency. On the other hand, growing affluence and improving education have heightened sensibilities to the unintended and intangible material and moral externalities of a capitalist market economy and Keynesian welfare state. These externalities primarily accrue outside the realms of production and distribution in the spheres of social consumption and reproduction. Protest movements have attacked the consequences of the productive use of space and natural resource (such as environmental degradation and decline of urban living conditions). At the same time, movements have also focused on the constitution of social identities in advanced capitalism and have targeted the "moral externalities" of centralized bureaucratic welfare states as their point of attack. All these movements call for more decentralization and participation in political and corporate decision making as well as an autonomous civil society beyond market and bureaucratic regulatives, an opportunity to form spontaneous voluntary associations around a variety of economic, social, and cultural purposes.[12] I will call protests against the material and moral externalities of advanced capitalism the left-libertarian challenge because its supporters call for restraints upon capitalist markets as well as bureaucratic governance.

In the transition from the 1970s to the 1980s, socialist electoral performance was a function of the intensity of the left-libertarian and market efficiency challenges and the strategic flexibility of the parties to cope with the new demands. If party politicians are rational electoral vote maximizers, they will transform their appeal and assume electoral positions designed to satisfy these new demands to the extent that they have become pressing in a country. The challenge of market efficiency has affected all European economies to a considerable extent. Whether socialist parties face strong incentives to address the challenge, however, depends on their competitive position in the party system. Two conditions increase the likelihood of a response. First, where the right of the party system is consolidated around a single bourgeois party, it will be able to present a clear-cut economic policy alternative that responds to the challenge of market efficiency. Under these circumstances, socialists may be more compelled to develop a response than where they encounter a highly fragmented, internally diversified nonsocialist party camp. Second, socialists may sense the need to respond to the new challenges most intensely where socialist parties are actually or potentially in a pivotal position in the process of coalition and government formation. Here, small voter shifts translate into large changes of power over political office and policy. The other new demand pattern, the left-libertarian challenge, is a function of (1) a country's social structure; (2) its mobilization of left-libertarian protest movements and public opinion in the 1970s and 1980s; and (3) the emergence of a significant left-libertarian party competitor that cuts into the socialists' electoral support.

I have developed measures for gauging the intensity of left-libertarian and market efficiency challenges in European democracies elsewhere.[13] Here I will outline the logic of my argument and in Table 1 introduce the cases of socialist parties I claim to fit my theory. Within each configuration of challenges, the electoral success of parties depends on their ability to respond to the new demands in their party program and strategic choices.

Socialist parties have performed least well, where they have faced both demands at the same time (cell 1). Under these circumstances, the pressure for innovation may be too great to handle in the relatively brief time span of a decade. Moreover, the demands to meet the challenge of market efficiency and the left-libertarian challenge may be at least partially incompatible. For example, it is difficult to work out a compromise between business calls to relieve business from government regulation and the exigencies of implementing a tighter environmental policy.

Table 1. The Strategic Position of European Socialist Parties and Their Electoral Performance

Market Efficiency Challenge	Strong: consolidated bourgeois parties; (B) socialists close to pivotal position in party system	Weak: fragmented bourgeois parties; socialists remote from pivotal position in party system
Left-Libertarian Challenge Strong: Significant left-libertarian movements and significant left-libertarian parties	CELL 1 *Gain: N/A †Preservation: Sweden ‡Loss: Austria, Norway, West Germany	CELL 2 Gain: N/A Preservation: Finland, the Netherlands Loss: Denmark, Switzerland
Weak: Insigificant left-libertarian movements and parties	CELL 3 Gain: France, Greece, Spain, (Italy) Preservation: N/A Loss: Britain, Portugal	CELL 4 Gain: N/A Preservation: Belgium Loss: N/A

*Gain: Socialist parties win more than an average of 3 percent in national elections during the 1980s compared to the 1970s.
†Preservation: Gains/losses ≤ 3 percent in the 1980s.
‡Loss: Socialist parties lose more than 3 percent in the 1980s.

Too, in countries where the left-libertarian challenge outweighs the market-efficiency challenge, socialist parties have not performed well (cell 2). In the Netherlands, socialists indeed primarily addressed left-libertarian themes through much of the 1980s, but therefore isolated themselves in a political ghetto from which they emerged only in the late 1980s with a more balanced approach. Conversely, in Denmark socialists had abandoned left-libertarian topics and were squeezed between a strong left-libertarian party and a fragmented field of bourgeois parties.

In at least six countries, the challenge of market efficiency has considerably outweighed the left-libertarian challenge, with Italy probably being a mixed case that is hard to classify (cell 3). In most of these cases, socialist parties have indeed responded vigorously to the dominant challenge and moved toward economic austerity and modernization policies. The most glaring diverging case is the British Labour party, where an electorally adequate response failed to emerge.[14] In the fourth cell of the table, Belgium is the country where socialists have experienced fairly mild market efficiency and left-libertarian challenges. Here, even without major policy initiatives, the socialists have performed moderately well.

What accounts for the failure or success of parties to act electorally rational on the new constraints and opportunities in their environment? The traditional ideological alternatives debated in a country make a difference in the capacity of socialist parties to behave electorally rational. For now I wish to introduce another, although related, answer: party organization does matter. Party organization, of course, to a considerable extent represents petrified ideology, as studies of the continuing divergence of organizational patterns along ideological lines demonstrate.[15] Where party elites have gained strategic flexibility and are not tied down by an entrenched mass organization, concerns with market efficiency are most likely to gain strategic importance. Where small party organizations are susceptible to the influx of new activists with innovative ideas, radical appeals of the traditional or libertarian Left and, under certain circumstances even demands for more market-oriented policies, may win the day. Socialist parties have the least capacities to take on new challenges where neither leadership nor party militants are empowered to stake out new courses beyond conventional visions of socialist politics. This situation occurs in traditional social democratic mass membership parties with strong patronage networks, party bureaucracies, decentralized recruitment procedures for public office, and close linkages to powerful labor unions. Such parties are like huge "tankers," in Peter Glotz's term, that turn around very slowly.

Although organizational analysis throws light on the micro-logic of decision making in socialist parties, it does not reconstruct the process and content of political reasoning in these parties that eventually lead to a new strategic stance. This process of reasoning is not simply determined by societal challenges and organizational patterns, but also by the discursive universe in which party activists can place themselves. In order to illustrate this hypothesis for different socialist parties, I will first reconstruct an ideal type of the traditional socialist discourse.

The Socialist Discourse and Its Alternatives

Contemporary West European socialism and social democracy is a descendant of what became between 1860 and 1914, in the aftermath of Marx's overwhelming theoretical contribution, the dominant organizational form and outlook of Northwest European socialist parties.[16] Although social democracy has distanced itself from Marxian socialism and attenuated its objectives, it still has followed a grammar of problem solving in its political visions that bears close elective affinities to the older, more principled criticism of capitalist society. Although modern social democracy does not subscribe to a socialist transformation of society to the extent Marxian socialism advocated, its methods and objects of social change are still rooted in this tradition. It has followed Marxism in the commitment to strengthening centralized mechanisms of political administration as a key method of improving the organization of society. In this respect, socialism in the modern age is sharply set apart from its two main competitors, each favoring a different principle of social organization.[17] On the one hand, liberalism recommends the market and voluntary contracts among individuals as the primary social institution to which others (state, family) are subsidiary; on the other, paternalist or egalitarian-anarchist modes of communitarianism advocate a social organization based on primary groups with shared values and beliefs, direct contact among all participants, and generalized reciprocity.[18]

The preference for centralized social organization and statist control is evident in at least three major accomplishments of contemporary social democracy. First, social democrats have everywhere advocated and expanded the modern welfare state, a safety net that protects wage earners from the greatest vagaries of the labor market through a system of universal insurances (such as old age, sickness, and unemployment) and an increasingly large network of public services such as public education, child- and health-care facilities, and housing.[19] Second, this accomplishment is intimately linked to the arrangement of centralized, and often legally formalized, patterns of interaction among the peak representatives of business and labor at the factory, the corporate, and the national economic levels. Representatives of both sides are hierarchically organized so that they can make credible mutual commitments and enter compromises even against the resistance of some of their grass-roots clienteles. Finally, the preference for peak-level negotiation is predicated on the experience of the socialist party mass organization in which discipline and central control always counted more than critical debate and participatory democracy.[20]

In these accomplishments, West European socialism and social democracy are distinct from several other types of socialism. First, in contrast to East European Marxism socialism that followed the blueprint of a completely administered society, West European socialism begrudgingly conceded the continued necessity of markets and wholeheartedly accepted bourgeois democracy, although it has rarely taken the initiative to introduce markets where other institutions prevailed or to advance the theory and practice of democracy beyond its bourgeois-representative form. Social democracy has given up the claim to organize the totality of society based on central organization but has failed to construct a positive vision of social reform that would not revolve around centralized administrative interventions. Because of its concessions to nonsocialist forces, the innovations that socialist parties have made in capitalist society often have proven extraordinarily successful, as the widespread acceptance of the welfare state demonstrates. Therefore, the decline of contemporary social democracy is a consequence of its extraordinary success in bringing about broad improvement of life chances, yet also of its inability to look beyond these accomplishments. In contrast, the collapse of real, existing eastern socialism is not a consequence of success, but of utter failure.

Second, West European socialism and social democracy have displayed a strand of participatory, communitarian, and anarchist visions of socialism that survived well into the twentieth century in Spanish or French anarcho-syndicalism. Historically, the anarchist vision is associated with craftsmen in decentralized shops and with first-generation peasant workers who still recall the experience of the rural village community. For this reason, these conceptions of socialism have held out more in agricultural societies and in industrial systems dominated not by the large Fordist factory organization, but smaller craft production.[21] In addition to anarchism, these currents called for decentralized workers' cooperatives and industrial democracy, for example in British guild socialism, Scandinavian "functional socialism" (e.g., in the work of Ernst Wigforss), and the consumer cooperatives' movement in a number of countries. Although these tendencies had considerable impact until the first decade after World War I, they became dormant at least until the 1960s, when demands for participatory democracy and grass-roots control of economic and political affairs reemerged, but primarily outside the working class and the social democratic parties that generally remained rather hostile to bottom-up forms of democratic input.[22]

The key principles of what became the dominant socialist discourse in Western democracies thus are (1) the priority of collective choice over individual choice and group consensus; (2) an egalitarian provision of life chances within the framework of centralized societal concertation; and (3) an emphasis on collective problems of production and distribution over private and personal concerns of consumption and reproduction. Even in its attenuated, more flexible social democratic and democratic socialist version, this discourse promotes social equality more than freedom of choice and fraternity. At least three intellectual principles can be held responsible for this commitment. These principles originate in Marxian socialism but are still embodied in sublime ways in the social democratic discourse. The principles address the classical questions of philosophy: What can we know? What shall we do? What can we hope for? All three answers, however, entail ambiguities and implications that have provoked the criticism of socialist programs.

What can we know? The transition from communitarian, participatory socialism to an order governed by centralized mechanisms of collective coordination was facilitated by a realist and positivist epistemology that can be detected in Marx, but even more clearly among his most influential successors, Engels and Kautsky. Society is governed by universal laws that can be deciphered by scientists just as the laws of nature. Socialists are the first to grasp social laws correctly because the advancement of capitalism itself makes it possible to gain valid insights into the nature of its organization, as well as that of all preceding social orders. Socialists are also the only group with no stake in the defense of the existing capitalist order, a stake that gives rise to ideologies that systematically distort the ability to grasp the laws of social development. Socialist claims to knowledge of societal laws, in turn, suggest a technocratic and vanguardist reading of political practice. Political leaders, guided by scientific insight, can command mass discipline and deference as long as conditions to understand the laws of society scientifically are absent. As a consequence, socialist parties did not engage in Lenin's "democratic centralism," but rather in a "social democratic centralism" that produced highly concentrated, disciplined party machines.[23]

What shall we do? For socialist theory, the problem of the good and just society primarily concerns how to appropriate the means of production and distribute the products. Although eventually in communism the problem of justice is said to disappear with the advent of the age of abundance, under conditions of moderate scarcity a just socialist order will establish common property in the means of production and distribute goods contingent upon individual contribution.[24] The just order is possible because of the development of the means of production and mastery of nature. It is necessary because of the internal contradictions of other forms of social order, such as capitalism, which are not able to use or develop the means of production as well as the socialist alternative will when common property and central planning prevail. Because socialism has focused on the control and distribution of the means of production, social democrats have been more concerned with distributive questions than on social organization of production and consumption.[25]

What can we hope for? Socialist thinking has not answered the quest for ultimate ends by reference to a transcendent otherworldly realm, but by a social anthropology that also underlines the centrality of work and of relations of production in society. Human beings are defined by their capacity for conscious purposive action and seek their self-realization in creative work. Whether these capacities will be realized, however, depends on social institutions. According to Marx, empirical individuals are "ensembles of their social relations." Thus human self-realization hinges on the historical possibility and necessity that social institutions generate preferences and orientations in individuals to create new institutions permitting more self-realization. In this vein, Marxist anthropology is not only centered around the production process, but it also justifies the priority of society before the individual. The latter is a derivative of social relations, and individual spontaneity is conditioned by society itself. This approach can be read as a justification of the centralized management of social relations, particularly when combined with a technocratic epistemology.

Of course, other arguments and voices in Marxist texts suggest a more participatory, anarcho-syndicalist reading of social self-organization.[26] Such tendencies, however, remain ambiguous and ultimately inconsequential. As is well known, Marx himself never clarified his vision of a socialist order beyond dark allusions to a system of production run by "freely associated men," "consciously regulated by them in accordance with a settled plan."[27] Here, as well as in Lenin's later compilation and elaboration of Marx's and Engels's statements on socialism and the state, it is quite clear that the socialist order will be one in which material equality among all human beings should be a cornerstone of liberty and self-realization. At the same time, however, there is strategic ambiguity about the mode of governance under which equality and freedom should be realized. Market exchange is discarded as the anarchy of an outmoded capitalism. Yet it remains unclear how central planning, or formal bureaucratic organization, should be made compatible with the communitarian, almost anarchist, view of popular participation in all collective decisions as the benchmark of socialist society.[28] These essential ambiguities between a more centralist and statist conception of the good social order and a more direct democratic mode of organization were ultimately settled in favor of the centralist, technocratic alternative in the history of socialist theory and practice. In East European socialism, this vision was driven to its logical conclusion. In West European welfare states, it led to a more measured realization of welfare states, accompanied by private markets and representative democracy yet also inspired by a technocratic belief in the centralized management of human affairs.

In the 1970s and 1980s, this intellectual vision and practice came under siege from a variety of quarters, although social democracy had already weakened and abandoned some of the strong claims of the Marxian socialist tradition. This applies, for example, to the Marxist epistemology discarded in favor of a logic of piece-meal reform and technocratic intervention, yet with strong managerial and centralist undertones. Nevertheless, enough elements of the original socialist discourse have remained intact to make socialists vulnerable to attacks from both market liberals as well as left-libertarians who revive the anarchist option of decentralist self-organization. There are three critical claims.

1. The socialist discourse has tended to neglect what precedes (nature, the organization of production) and follows the process of appropriation and distribution (consumption, social reproduction). For market liberals, the socialist discourse fails primarily by not examining the supply side of the economic process, the incentives and in-

stitutions that permit efficient production. For advocates of the new social movement, the socialist discourse is limited by its treatment of nature and social consumption in socialism. For Marx, as well as his social democratic successors, nature is primarily a raw material, a natural laboratory for human creativity and, in fact, eventually itself a product of human labor and social institutions, as Marx emphasizes in the German Ideology.[29] In a similar vein, styles of social consumption and of aesthetic enjoyment, as well as patterns of human reproduction (gender relations), have played a subterranean, rarely emphasized role in socialist discourse.[30]

2. As a consequence, "relations of production" are privileged in comparison to "relations of social recognition."[31] There is no account of the formation of individual and collective identities, not even of class, and of individual and collective orientations in the socialist discourse. For liberals, Marx does not provide an adequate reconstruction of human self-interest and autonomy in society. For new social movement advocates, the nature of social community and of the social construction of use values must be explored.[32]

3. Because individual autonomy and relations of mutual recognition among members of society are not placed at the center of the analysis, socialist discourse has been unable to develop a satisfactory theory of political democracy that would be premised on the tension between individual and collective decision making. In many respects, the insistence on planning has induced socialists to follow Rousseau's lead in constructing the fiction of a General Will that reconciles individual and collective preferences and supersedes the aggregate of the empirically heterogeneous and contradictory individual preferences. For liberals, this solution becomes implausible once the Condorcet-Arrow problem is realized that it is impossible to aggregate diverse individual preference rankings into a consistent, stable collective welfare function within a democratic framework. For left-libertarian activists, the problem is rather that of an inevitable trade-off between technocratic planning and grass-roots participation. It is probably one of the major shortcomings of the socialist discourse that it has contributed very little to the development of democratic theory and the introduction of new democratic practices.[33]

I cannot discuss here in detail why the social democratic discourse and its practical correlate, the centralized, universalistic, corporatist welfare state most developed in those Western democracies governed by socialist parties for extensive periods, lost appeal during the 1970s and 1980s. Behind the challenges of market productivity and left-libertarian politics are complex changes in the industrial and occupational structure of modern capitalism, preference changes due to the increasing popular material affluence and education, and new grievances created by the successful abatement of existing social ills.[34] In response to the challenges of economic productivity and left-libertarian politics, and in light of the exhaustion of the conventional social democratic discourse and methods of problem-solving, it is no longer possible to build a political strategy around one dominant principle of social organization, be this the market place (liberalism), the community (anarchism or paternalism), or the state (socialism). What is needed is a creative combination of different modes of social organization, the political ability to redesign markets, communities, and state organizations to meet popular preferences. In other words, the opportunity for a successful postsocialist reconstitution of socialist parties may have to be sought in a different combination and equilibrium among individual autonomy in market transactions, the spontaneous constitution of collective identities in primary groups or voluntary associations, and centralized social management through public and private bureaucracies. In this equilibrium, political democracy must also be developed in a multiplicity of institutions and forms of influence that social democracy has neglected in the past.

Two arguments support this proposition. First, the social democratic discourse is not exhausted because everything it stood for and all the institutional changes it helped to introduce have been questioned or rejected. Quite to the contrary, at least the most far-reaching social democratic accomplishment, the universalistic welfare state, enjoys broad popular support, particularly in those countries where it has been implemented in the most comprehensive way. Misgivings about the welfare state tend to be greatest where it is least comprehensive and thus most likely to divide the haves and have-nots along the lines of particularistic interests.[35] As a consequence, social democrats are not challenged to abandon past accomplishments, but to redesign statist institutions to accommodate for the demands of economic efficiency, individual choice, personal autonomy, and participation.

My second argument derives from social theory. Liberalism, communitarianism, and socialism, as theories of modern society, originate in time periods that precede the sharp differentiation of society into semiautonomous cultural spheres of life with institutions governed by their own logics of operation and specified media of communication. Although all three basic theories negatively or positively refer to the division of labor, the qualitatively different internal constitution and rationality standards of the economy, politics, education, religion, science, and many other fields of human activity have been insufficiently appreciated by them. Only in the early twentieth century, beginning with Max Weber's work on the differentiation of autonomous rationalities in a multiplicity of life spheres, has social theory discovered the full impact of the process of modernization on the increasing autonomy of areas of social life, or subsystems as they are sometimes misleadingly termed.[36] In highly differentiated societies, no single mode of social organization (such as centralized planning or market exchange) can provide a master key for resolving conflicting claims and popular demands in all or most areas of social activity.

As a consequence, social democratic discourse can no longer build on a simple universal formula of justice, but must find different normative principles and rules of prudence guiding political programs for the multiplicity of spheres of life.[37] For social democracy to regain political momentum, it must find creative solutions to the problem of combining markets, communities, and centralized concertation. In the past, social democrats have heeded this imperative by purely defensive postures of granting concessions to liberalist calls for more markets and communitarian demands for voluntary association. The real challenge, however, is for social democracy to identify, on its own, where and how different modes of social organization can be employed. My claim is not simply an abstract demand imposed on social democrats, but reflects a sense of crisis in the socialist discourse that is articulated by social democrats themselves. In almost fifty interviews with Swedish and Austrian social democrats in spring 1990, one red thread that ran through all reflections on the status of parties was the necessity for liberation from treating statist modes of social problem-solving as the master key for social reform and the need to recognize the multiplicity of organizational forms in society that need to be combined in new and intelligent ways by the social democratic parties of the future.[38]

Models of the Postsocialist Discourse

The search for new combinations and intermediate institutional forms combining elements of markets, community, and central administrative control thus derives from the pitfalls of generalizing or at least prioritizing a single organizational form compared to all others. The main objective of the traditional social democratic discourse, realized to a considerable extent in the practice of the Keynesian welfare state, was to provide basic equality, security, and liberty to all citizens. At the same time, the realization of this social democratic objective has brought about new privileges and inequalities, primarily through the growth of a large sector of public employment enjoying protection from market competition and a stronger position with respect to the employer than private-sector wage earners, new unforeseen consequences of growth (environmental pollution), new social grievances (the "coldness" of public agencies administering personal lives of clients), and economic rigidity. In light of these problems, I have proposed as an abstract meta-rule for the construction of social democratic programs to redesign the welfare state and address these grievances by new institutions that blend different principles of organization while preserving some of the essential gains of the old socialist program. This rule, however, cannot generate specific political programs. A new postsocialist discourse cannot be spun out of simple general formula, but requires in-depth analysis of individual policy areas and spheres of social life. Because society is highly differentiated, it has become impossible to write synthetic party programs that cover the totality of social organization in any other way than a rather disjointed, cumulative enumeration of the policy measures a party proposes.

The following four examples are issue areas where socialist parties might wish to reconsider conventional policy commitments. Then the problem of democratic participation can be discussed in light of a pluralist form of social organization and applied to the principles of socialist party organization, a prime area in which a centralist-bureaucratic approach has remained dominant in socialist thought and practice and has been attacked by the adversaries of conventional socialism.

1. Remove from the socialist agenda the nationalization of industry and industrial democracy as ends in themselves. With respect to the nationalization of industry, most social democratic parties have made considerable concessions to liberalism since World War II. Institutional control, not formal ownership, determines the allocative and distributive consequences of production. Nationalization has often been confused with the choice of a new noncapitalist allocation and

distribution principle. If nationalization does not change such mechanisms of allocation as competition and profit it may be a superfluous exercise. Nationalization should be considered then only where markets fail due to natural monopolies and externalities, or where nonmarket substantive standards of production can be explicitly justified. These justifications are rarely supplied.

Social democrats have been much less willing to reconsider industrial democracy as a mode of corporate governance that can replace capitalist control of investment.[39] On the one hand, as long as corporations are immersed into competitive markets, it is not clear how workers' self-management could lead to systematically different investment decisions than those of firms under managerial control, even if we assume that worker-controlled firms are as efficient and have as much access to capital markets as capitalist firms. On the other, if workers' self-management is an end in itself and a prelude to the abolition of competitive markets, thus replacing a formal logic of capital accounting with some kind of substantive rationality to bring about certain highly valued nonfinancial benefits, what are the losses due to economic inefficiencies, new inequalities, and rigidities in the economy that socialists are willing to bear? Such questions about the trade-offs between different objectives of industrial organization have not been sufficiently addressed in the socialist debate about workers' self-management and can open the door to a reconsideration of how markets, planning, and workers' control can be combined.[40]

2. Decentralize social services and create more consumer input. Both in public health care and the educational system, complaints about inefficiency, anonymity, and lack of consumer control and choice of service are commonplace.[41] To address these concerns, a revised socialist program on social services could call for competing, decentralized local agencies among which consumers can choose, thus introducing an element of competition into the public sector. In addition, public social agencies could confine themselves to a fixed floor of services and above that floor encourage individual initiative to establish voluntary self-help and consumer services with public subsidies and infrastructure (e.g., buildings). Decentralized public welfare systems would incorporate more regard for efficiency and solidarity while still preserving a certain level of equal treatment for all citizens.

3. Open a choice between work in formal labor markets and the informal sector. In capitalism and in socialism, paid labor in formal business organization is the only formally recognized contribution to

society. But the provision of many personal services by public bureau-cracies or private markets is often neither efficient nor particularly gratifying for producers and consumers, for example in child care, ed-ucation, care for the elderly, and cultural activities. Instead, public agencies could encourage initiatives outside the formal labor market through a wide range of measures, including some form of minimum income for every citizen, to open the choice between formal and in-formal sector activities.

4. Acknowledge that regulatory standards are not the only method of environmental protection. Fixed environmental standards have been neither particularly enforceable nor economically efficient (re-moving the most pollution with the least allocation of resources) pol-icy choices. Yet because it is impractical to let the value of the environment be established through free market transactions among polluters and conservationists, some form of political intervention re-mains imperative. Alternatives are pollution taxes, leaving it up to economic decision units to determine the indifference point between paying pollution taxes and installing pollution control equipment, and in some areas the circulation of pollution vouchers to firms.[42] Both environmental taxes and vouchers presuppose a central collective de-cision-making process that sets levels of taxation and the number of vouchers to be auctioned to polluters and thus implicitly imposes a value of the environment on individual producers and consumers. Yet at the same time, taxes and vouchers allow actors to make crucial choices on the way pollution can be fought best. Moreover, commu-nitarian demands for more local self-governance and participation may find their place in how vouchers and tax regulations are imple-mented.

The need to design organizational principles for different areas of social life may also stimulate a reconsideration of democracy in the socialist discourse. In practice, social democracy has opted for restric-tive forms of representative democracy and has mistrusted demands for decentralized, participatory decision making raised in increasingly vocal criticisms of bureaucratic socialism and Western centralized welfare states with corporatist policy management. Each institutional design of democratic participation has its own dialectic that often gen-erates different outcomes than its advocates intended.

The social democratic case against direct democracy is clear-cut. Even if we set aside concerns that direct democratic participation, such as referenda or town hall meetings, is often an inefficient form of social choice involving prohibitively high transaction costs and usually not yielding a collective welfare function consistent with most individuals' preferences, direct democracy is constrained by the initial resource endowments of participants (education, information, disposable time) and the differential willingness of citizens to commit time to collective decision making. As Weber has argued, direct democracy may lead to an informal and unaccountable rule of notables who have the greatest resources and motivation to participate.[43]

To fight the lack of equality in direct democracy, formal rules of delegation between constituency and representatives may restore influence to weakly endowed citizens with little time to participate in politics, while restraining that of individuals with a wealth of political resources. Formal systems of representation, however, remove the individual citizen several steps from the actual decision-making process and make it difficult to bring innovative impulses from the grass-roots level into key decision-making arenas. This, rather than simply an oligarchy of self-interested leaders, has been a continued problem of the internal governance structures in socialist mass parties, which have relied heavily on formal principles of democratic representation across a multilayered organization. As a consequence, both rank and file members and leaders often had little capacity to innovate.

Without return to direct democracy, the pitfalls of formal representative democracy can be avoided only by a plebiscitarian leadership democracy that removes the intermediaries between masses and top politicians. Max Weber was a representative of this position toward the end of his life. After chastising the German Social Democratic party for clinging timidly to formal democratic representation Weber argues in defense of a strong presidency: "May it [the Social Democratic party] consider that the much talked about 'dictatorship' of the masses indeed requires the 'dictator,' a directly elected trustee of the masses to whom the masses submit as long as he enjoys their confidence."[44] Plebiscitarian leadership democracy, however, raises the specters of demagogy, intolerance, political polarization, and ultimately the collapse of political democracy.

Each of the three modes of democracy has its strengths and drawbacks, and each shows a considerable affinity to one of the three key ideologies of the modern age. Communitarian anarchism favors direct democracy, socialist egalitarianism opts for formal democratic representation, and market liberals tend to advocate plebiscitarian leadership democracy.[45] Again, the dialectic of each form of decision making shows that no single procedure will lead to a "governance of the people," but that the future of democracy may need to be sought in the creative combination and counterbalancing of different modes of democracy in different decision-making arenas.

This thesis can be illustrated with respect to socialist party organization. The conventional socialist mass apparatus parties that still exist, to a greater or lesser extent, in Austria, Belgium, Italy, the Scandinavian countries, and West Germany, often limit the choices of both leaders and rank-and-file activists. In some of these parties, therefore, traditional socialist discourse had its greatest staying power, although several elaborate a pluralist view of social organization beyond the statist-socialist, market-liberal, or communitarian anarchist discourses. In other countries where the imperatives of market efficiency have left a strong imprint on socialist party strategy, their organizational form has moved toward a liberal conception of plebiscitarian leadership democracy (especially in Spain and Greece, and also to a lesser extent in France, Portugal, and Italy). The party leaders have been empowered, while party activists have remained powerless. In contrast, where leftist and libertarian calls for the rank and file's direct democratic involvement in party strategy have won the day, such as in the Dutch Socialist party and, in a more limited way, the British Labour party in the early 1980s, activists empowered at the expense of the leadership have introduced elements of a communitarian grass-roots democracy.[46]

Each of the pure models of party organization has contributed to the electoral defeat or stagnation of socialist parties in countries where constituency preferences and the exigencies of party competition call for "mixed" strategies appealing to market-efficiency, left-libertarian, and socialist-egalitarian values at the same time. Under these conditions, a party structure is most likely to yield a sufficiently complex programmatic and strategic choice that permits an interactive democracy empowering both leaders and rank and file by combining different principles of democratic governance.[47] Here, party activists can influence strategic choices, but leaders have the capacity to go beyond rank-and-file mandates and convince their following of new political courses of action. Interactive democracy combines elements of direct democracy with competition among party leaders. Among socialist parties, only the French Parti Socialiste appears to have moved toward a model of interactive democracy in spite of its plebiscitarian-charismatic leader. The party is divided into competing factions, each headed by highly visible personalities who vie for nomination to the highest office in the state, the presidency, and are surrounded by loosely organized clubs of supporters. At the same time, control over the nomination of parliamentary candidates is decentralized to the regional level. The relatively small size of the French PS, with a member-voter ratio of less than 2 percent, and its fluid internal organization at least in principle permit comparatively great leverage to grass-roots participants.[48]

Thus, postsocialist discourse that will command public attention in the future must acknowledge the existence and desirability of a plurality of modes of governance and related normative standards in society more than its predecessor did. The traditional socialist discourse about class, equality, redistribution, and collective choice thus will not be completely discarded, as communitarian anarchism or market liberalism would have it, but rather integrated into a new pluralist perspective on social order.

The Postsocialist Discourse and Conventional Socialist Parties

The redirection of the socialist discourse is not simply the imagination of a few political theorists, but rather a topic widely debated among socialist politicians and party activists. There is a general sense that the traditional reservoir of social democratic ideas is exhausted and that the political agenda has changed dramatically since the 1970s. In practice, however, these parties have been able to elaborate post-socialist discourses in different ways. The ability to change party appeals is influenced by electoral incentives to respond to the different intensity of market-liberal or left-libertarian challenges in individual European countries and by the organizational facilities that made it possible for such challenges to be articulated by party activists and leaders. But it is also important to appreciate the cultural environment in which new arguments could be integrated into political debates. Three groups of countries face different conditions that have made an appeal to left-libertarian or market-liberal theorems more or less attractive. First, some countries have a strong polarity between a paternalist authoritarian Right and a communist or anarchist Left. The second group of countries focus the main political debates around the poles of market liberalism and democratic socialism. Finally, there are countries in which a variety of ideological discourses have cross-cut each other.

My argument is that not simply objective facts such as levels of unemployment, economic growth rates, or environmental pollution determine the viability of a party's arguments to electoral constituencies, but that its rhetorical position within a context of arguments and experiences has influenced the party's electoral attractiveness.[49]

Paternalist Right versus Communist Left

This ideological space is primarily relevant in countries whose party systems are characterized by "polarized pluralism,"[50] such as Italy, France, and other countries that had similar configurations of political alternatives before sometimes extensive spells of nondemocratic rule. In all these countries, market liberal parties played a marginal role since at least the 1930s. Moreover, the natural place of socialists in the universe of political discourse had already been occupied by communist parties. Because of their dissociation from the conventional Left discourse and the unwillingness of nonsocialist parties to appeal to market liberalism, socialist parties did not find it difficult in the 1970s to assimilate communitarian arguments, primarily the theme of *autogestion* or workers' self-management, and then, in the 1980s, to appeal to market liberalism. At the same time, however, these parties dropped much of their commitment to communitarian demands and thus cut themselves off from contemporary left-libertarian movements.

The most clear-cut case for this strategy is Spain, where an authoritarian Right before 1977 rendered many elements of the traditional socialist discourse such as state enterprise thoroughly unpalatable. As a consequence, from the beginning of the PSOE's regeneration in the early 1970s, the party experimented with such new political terrain as a libertarian version of socialist discourse (that is, workers' self-control). Later the ideological disarray in the center and on the right of the party system made a move into the market-liberal direction very tempting.[51] State-centered industrial policy had been discredited by the experience of the nationalized industrial sector under Franco. Moreover, the weak electoral performance of the communists reinforced aversions against adopting the traditional socialist discourse in the PSOE. At the same time, left-libertarian politics attracted only limited support in a country that remained still far behind levels of affluence found elsewhere in Europe.

In Italy and France, the situation is more complicated because the left-libertarian challenge of social movements in the 1970s was stronger and/or state enterprise was not as discredited as in Spain. Nevertheless, a market-liberal perspective won the day in the socialist parties. During the 1980s, it thrived on the inability of the existing conservative parties to present a credible modernization program that decisively committed itself to market efficiency as the overriding political objective.[52] Nevertheless, this interpretation must be qualified in several respects. In Italy, the rhetoric of liberal modernization in the PSI is belied by the exigencies of a patronage-oriented socialist party apparatus and increasing competition among the former communist party, the radicals, and the socialists for left-libertarian votes. Both factors may constrain the programmatic flexibility of the Craxi-PSI in the future.

In France, the PS initially swallowed elements of the traditional socialist discourse, particularly the nationalization program, in order to maintain PCF support. This strategy was possible also because French state industry enjoyed a better reputation than nationalized industries elsewhere. Further, in the 1970s the French left-libertarian mobilization, for example the women's movement and ecologism, ran rather high and attracted socialist sympathies. The party's conference resolutions, containing numerous references to the women's movement and enabling it to co-opt important elements of the movement into the party,[53] the promises to reconsider the French nuclear program after a victory of the Left, and above all the magic formula of *autogestion*, were meant to build a bridge between the traditional socialist discourse and new orientations while simultaneously differentiating the PS from the PCF. As Gaffney's careful textual analysis of socialist discussions and party programs in 1974, 1975, and 1984 shows, by the mid-1980s the rhetoric of autogestion had yielded to a vague appeal to modernization and social progress that thinly veiled the overriding concern of the party with a strategy of market efficiency.[54]

In Spain, France, and Italy, the socialist discourse has been pluralized by injecting market-liberal elements into the conventional debates. In each party, socialist discourse had been weakened since the early 1970s, yet left-libertarian impulses have remained too peripheral to influence the search for a new appeal.

In a second group of countries, political discourse has always been structured around the polarity between market and state, free enterprise capitalism and the social welfare state. Regardless of whether the socialist Left has been hegemonic or marginal in these countries, and regardless of which organizational form and competitive position socialists have encountered, the Left has experienced great obstacles in moving beyond the socialist discourse. These conditions prevail primarily in Anglo-Saxon countries and in Scandinavia.

In Sweden, the SAP was able to model significant components of the political-economic fabric around its version of the traditional social democratic discourse. When the bourgeois opposition in 1976 took over government for the first time in more than forty years, it was compelled to appeal to the same economic themes that also had guided social democratic policy. Swedish social democracy has therefore been comparatively slow in responding to the market efficiency and left-libertarian challenges of the 1970s and 1980s. The major policy initiative of the SAP since 1970, the introduction of wage-earner funds, initially proposed by the main Swedish labor union LO in 1975, was firmly rooted in a centralist organization-centered socialist discourse, particularly the initial outline of the Meidner Plan, which envisioned a surcharge on corporate profits to be deposited in union-controlled central funds that would gradually acquire Sweden's productive capital. In the late 1970s and early 1980s, the plan triggered an unprecedented wave of market-liberal, but also left-libertarian protest action against the specter of a corporatist economy. Even when the social democratic governed drastically watered down the original proposal in 1983 by reducing the amount of revenue to be collected by the funds, decentralizing fund management to the regional level, partially removing them from the control of labor unions, and placing a cap on the proportion of capital the funds could hold in each company, the majority of social democratic voters and union members still did not support this proposal.[55]

At the same time, the SAP was slow in responding to the left-libertarian agenda that began to emerge with the struggle against nuclear power in the early 1970s. Not by chance, it was the small Communist party and the center party that saw a political opening and claimed the left-libertarian themes for themselves. The SAP has not regained the intellectual initiative on environmental issues since, although it has tried to adapt its policy to the exigencies of a continued strong environmental mobilization. In a similar vein, Swedish social democrats have also adopted only those elements of the feminist agenda that fit into the socialist discourse on equality and gender solidarity, yet not the feminism that insists on the self-organization of women, the right to be different from men, and the expression of a new communitarian culture.[56]

Only in the second half of the 1980s did programmatic change in the SAP begin to quicken. The social democratic party and government introduced measures to improve market efficiency and Sweden's international competitiveness, such as liberalizing the country's credit markets, decentralizing small nationalized industries, and creating competition in the telecommunications sector. Moreover, it tried to reach out to market-liberal as well as left-libertarian concerns with plans and measures to provide more local choice for citizens and competition among public-sector services. These efforts pinnacled in a new draft program for the party that put great emphasis on efficiency, individualism, and quality of life within the framework of basic socialist accomplishments.[57]

Conventional socialist discourse also stifled the intellectual creativity of the British Labour party in the 1970s and 1980s, a party never as dominant as its Swedish counterpart. Ideological frictions inside the party have essentially been limited to the polarity between moderate social democratic advocates of the Keynesian welfare state and radical proponents of anticapitalist reforms with the aid of nationalized industries, a substantial wealth tax, the abolition of private elite schools, and numerous other redistributive measures. A perusal of programmatic statements by the Labour party Left in the mid-1980s revealed no readiness to consider the new themes of left-libertarian politics. Ecology does not surface at all in either volume, and feminism appears only in the garb of equality oriented socialist feminism.[58] In the second half of the 1980s, after two consecutive defeats with a conventional leftist party program, the ideological pendulum in the Labour party began to swing back to the Right. Yet even then it was difficult to discern new policy departures beyond a middle-of-the-road approach to economic management that would point into the direction of a pluralization of the party's programmatic discourse and recognizing the challenges of market efficiency and left-libertarianism.

The socialist discourse has also stagnated in the small leftist groups in the United States where the hegemony of the market-liberal discourse has always prevented the establishment of a viable socialist party. An early consequence was the Left's withdrawal into a strict Marxist orthodoxy with a sectarian practice.[59] This theoretical orthodoxy, however, is itself a mirror image of and reinforced by the undisputed intellectual hegemony of market liberalism. The instrumentalist conception of material interests in Marxist political economy and historical materialism can be readily adapted to the language of neoclassical liberal economics. In this sense, the prominence of "public choice Marxism" in the United States, with its emphasis on the classical economic themes of the socialist discourse—class, property, and exploitation—follows directly from the sectarian marginality of the American Left.[60] In this situation, left-libertarian themes have been relegated to small communitarian-anarchist and "new age" groups that operate in an entirely different realm than the orthodox Marxist Left.[61]

A Plural Ideological Universe

Whereas neither the Southern European nor the Anglo-Saxon/Scandinavian hemispheres appear to have provided a hospitable environment for a postsocialist discourse, conditions may be more favorable in countries where the ideological terrain has always been contested from a multiplicity of perspectives. In Austria, Belgium, the Netherlands, Switzerland, and West Germany, socialist discourse was firmly encoded in the subculture of mass parties linked to an array of surrounding social, economic, and cultural associations, yet was never able to become the sole adversary of a market-liberal Right. Instead, religious-paternalist visions of the good social order, as well as ethnic, religious, regional, or linguistic particularisms, weakened the prominence of socialist and liberal-market thinking. The great ideological diversity may have provided more intellectual stimuli for redefining socialist parties' message. It has also enhanced more ideological uncertainties and insecurities about the appropriate programmatic orientation than in countries defined by more clear-cut polarities.

Contrary to Przeworski and Sprague's thesis that socialist parties are the least able to withstand the demise of the blue-collar working class in countries where workers hold particularistic loyalties based on collective identities other than class,[62] it is possible that the reverse holds true. The pluralism of political discourse in such countries facilitates intellectual innovation and efforts to promote a postsocialist decentering of traditional Left parties by incorporating demands inspired by market efficiency, social equality, and left-libertarian communitarian politics.

This process of intellectual experimentation has clearly gone farthest in the Netherlands and in West Germany, both countries which face a strong left-libertarian challenge. In the Netherlands, new party members were able to sweep away much of the conventional social democratic discourse by the early 1970s and blend its remnants into a left-libertarian appeal.[63] An intellectual and electoral weakness of this program, however, has been that it has adopted left-libertarian themes in so uncompromising a fashion that other concerns, particularly those of market efficiency, were insufficiently considered to build a growing electoral constituency.

A similar process of opening the party to innovative demands began in the West German SPD in the 1970s, but never led to a decisive breakthrough of left-libertarian forces. Instead, the party lingered in a protracted state of stalemate between market-efficiency-oriented technocrats, old social democratic stalwarts, and left-libertarian radicals who moved from the old socialist beliefs to a left-libertarian orientation.[64] Although this process has generated considerable strains inside the party, it has also promoted new ideas that envision a pluralization of modes of governance in a variety of social spheres. It has moved the party away from conventional social democratic economic policies.[65]

Similar efforts are under way in Austria, where, however, the rhetoric of class and economic modernization continues to play a dominant role, while the challenge of the libertarian Left is not quite as strong as in West Germany. Nevertheless, socialist party programs have begun to incorporate left-libertarian and market-efficiency concerns.[66] Just as in West Germany, however, the process of rejuvenation led to more political confusion and stalemate than the clear statement of a strategy. In Switzerland and Belgium, efforts to renew the parties remained comparatively modest. In Belgium, left-libertarian and market-efficiency challenges were probably too subdued to force the socialist parties to innovate. In Switzerland, the party is deeply divided between working-class traditionalists, based in Swiss labor unions, and left-libertarian academics.[67]

All socialist parties located in countries with diverse ideological traditions, however, struggle with the recalcitrance of their organizational form as an impediment to programmatic reform. These socialist parties have developed extensive mass organizations with rules of formal democratic representation and bureaucratic control that tend to disempower both leaders and rank-and-file activists. Well-entrenched conservative forces, particularly those organized around the linkage between party and associated labor unions, have been able to slow the process of innovation and prevent the parties from clarifying their intellectual agenda. Whereas in France, the party organization of the PS is probably most conducive to supporting a program and strategy based on a postsocialist pluralization of programmatic appeals, the universe of discourse in which it is placed has not been supportive of this option in the 1980s. In much of central Europe socialist parties face the inverse configuration: a conducive intellectual atmosphere yet a counterproductive party organization.

Conclusion

I have first argued that explanations of socialist party strategy and decline in western Europe are incomplete if they do not consider the ideologies and traditions of debate within these parties. I have then presented an ideal type of the conventional socialist discourse and distinguished it from other currents in the history of socialist movements. Against this backdrop, I have attempted to identify the weakness in the arguments advanced by proponents of conventional socialism. Then, I have provided several examples of how socialist parties might try to overcome the limitations of their programmatic vision by a pluralization of the organizational mechanisms—market, state, and community—they intend to employ in the reform of existing society. I have also submitted that social democracy may need to recast its notion of democratic institutions and participation, if it actively endorses a pluralization of organizational mechanisms in society. A possible consequence of this change is a reform of the old, mass party organization and its formal and centralized patterns of decision making.

The extent to which socialist parties have accepted the pluralization of society's modes of organization has been examined as it is evidenced by party programs, internal debates, and government policies. While there is a widespread sense of crisis among socialist militants that the conventional questions and answers of socialist politics—redistribution, equalization, and public planning through state agencies in conjunction with centralized associations representing labor and capital—no longer provide the vision socialist parties need to appeal to an important electoral constituency, there is much less unanimity about the new course socialist parties should seek. In fact, national peculiarities of the universe of political debate contribute to the explanation of how far individual parties have leaned toward new market-liberal or left-libertarian policies.

Although I have emphasized the cross-national variation of the programmatic discourse inside socialist parties, the intellectual and political forces that have undermined the conventional socialist discourse are likely to affect all socialist parties eventually. The strategy of Southern European socialist parties to adopt a market-liberal stance may therefore be just as much a transitory phenomenon as the efforts of Scandinavia and Anglo-Saxon parties to cling to the traditional socialist agenda. Eventually these parties will face the same predicament—strong market-liberal and left-libertarian popular demands— that already characterizes the situation of some continental European socialist parties. I would buttress this line of reasoning with an evolutionary argument that has become unpopular in the institutions-oriented political science of recent decades: Modern capitalism is running through a series of steps characterized by the peculiar challenges and conflicts all advanced industrial democracies essentially share in common. This evolutionary perspective does not deny that important variations exist among countries and regions, yet it insists on the similarity of basic tendencies that are historically well documented for the development of modern welfare states.[68] Whereas after World War II most Western democracies institutionalized the basic citizenship rights to which social democracy contributed so much, the arena of struggle has shifted to a qualitative politicization of production, in which the natural preconditions, institutional forms, purposes, and consequences of production itself become the object of political argument in ways quite different from what the older Marxian socialism, caught up in the question of formal property rights and distribution rather than focusing on the modes of regulation and control, led us to expect.[69] The intellectual reorientation of social democratic parties in the economically most advanced and politically most institutionalized welfare states is one indicator of the increasing politicization of production. Social democratic parties may have a future, but only if they go beyond the socialist discourse and focus on the preconditions and consequences of the production process itself.

Notes

1. Here I summarize central arguments I have developed theoretically and empirically elsewhere. See Herbert Kitschelt, *The Transformation of European Social Democracy* (forthcoming), especially chs. 3–5.

2. For this reason, statistical analyses of voting behavior usually find that prospective economic voting explains at least as much variance as retrospective voting. For European elections, see Michael Lewis-Beck, *Economics and Elections: The Major Western Democracies* (Ann Arbor: University of Michigan Press, 1988).

3. For an analysis of different types of welfare states, see Gösta Esping-Andersen, *Politics against Markets* (Princeton: Princeton University Press, 1985), and *The Three Worlds of Welfare Capitalism* (Princeton: Princeton University Press, 1990).

4. Adam Przeworski, *Capitalism and Social Democracy* (Cambridge: Cambridge University Press, 1985), and Adam Przeworski and John Sprague, *Paper Stones: A History of Electoral Socialism* (Chicago: University of Chicago Press, 1986).

5. The decline of the working-class purity of socialist parties has often been measured with the Alford index, which subtracts the percentage of all non-blue-collar employees voting socialist from the percentage of blue-collar workers supporting that party. The Alford index has fallen considerably in most Western democracies, such as Britain, France, Sweden, the United States, and West Germany. See Ronald Inglehart, *Culture Shift* (Princeton: Princeton University Press, 1990), p. 260. Most of the decline, however, is due to an increasing percentage of nonworkers voting socialist rather than a decrease of working-class loyalty.

6. For evidence supporting this argument, see Mark Lichbach, "Optimal Electoral Strategies for Socialist Parties: Does Social Class Matter to Party Fortunes?" *Comparative Political Studies* 16 (January 1984): 419–55, and Diane Sainsbury, "Party Strategies and the Electoral Trade-off of Class-Based Parties," *European Journal of Political Research* 18 (January 1990): 29–50. Lichbach and Sainsbury employ more reliable data sources than Przeworski and Sprague, who suggested the trade-off hypothesis in *Paper Stones*, and carry the analysis forward beyond the 1960s where Przeworski and Sprague's time series terminated.

7. For example, this applies to France and West Germany, where Przeworski and Sprague's calculations found a sharp trade-off.

8. Przeworski and Sprague do not engage in an analysis of what it means—in terms of party program, organization, and strategy—to pursue a class or a cross-class strategy in socialist politics. See, critically, Sainsbury, "Party Strategies." As a consequence, Przeworski and Sprague deem it unnecessary to study the actual appeals and strategies of the socialist and communist parties whose electoral performance and electorate they examine.

9. Ian Budge and Dennis Farlie, *Explaining and Predicting Elections* (London: Allen and Unwin, 1983).

10. A further option, of course, is that socialist parties choose new stances without external provocation. In all the cases I am examining, however, endogenous strategic change from a position of electoral strength is an empirically implausible explanation.

11. Cf. Fritz W. Scharpf, *Sozialdemokratische Krisenpolitik in Westeuropa* (Frankfurt, Main: Campus Verlag, 1987), ch. 11.

12. Johne Keane, *Democracy and Civil Society* (London: Verso, 1988).

13. Kitschelt, *The Transformation of European Social Democracy.*

14. The Portuguese case is more difficult to interpret than the British because of the instability of the Portuguese party system in the aftermath of the 1974–75 revolution.

15. Kenneth Janda and Desmond S. King, "Formalizing and Testing Duverger's Theories on Political Parties," *Comparative Political Studies* 18 (July 1985): 139–69; Herbert Kitschelt, *The Logics of Party Formation* (Ithaca: Cornell University Press, 1989), ch. 2.

16. For a reconstruction of the historical spread and the survival of marginalized socialist tradition, see the chapter by Geoff Ely in this volume.

17. It is not by chance that a distinction among three strands of normative political theory is also reflected in the division of three fundamentally different modes of social organization by positive theorists. One needs only to refer to Albert Hirschman, *Exit, Voice, and Loyalty* (Cambridge: Harvard University Press, 1970), Charles Lindblom, *Politics and Markets* (New York: Basic Books, 1977), who distinguishes between preceptorial, market-based, and hierarchical social organization, and (in organization theory) William G. Ouchi, "Markets, Hierarchies and Clans," *Administrative Science Quarterly* 25 (January 1980): 129–41.

18. For an elaboration of the difficult notion of community, see Michael Taylor, *Community, Anarchy, and Liberty* (Cambridge: Cambridge University Press, 1982), pp. 25–33. The leading contemporary proponent of neocommunitarian thinking is Alasdair MacIntyre, *After Virtue*, 2d ed. (South Bend: University of Notre Dame Press, 1984).

19. The first steps toward the modern welfare state were made by authoritarian statists such as Bismarck in Germany. Although the universalism of the social democratic welfare state differs from more selective, authoritarian welfare systems, both share the same spirit of central organization and management.

20. Therefore, this organizational pattern may be called "social democratic centralism," a terminology that shows the difference to Lenin's "democratic centralism" in a cadre party of committed professional revolutionaries and also the affinities to that model (hierarchy, discipline).

21. For an analysis of workers' consciousness contingent upon different social careers and factory experiences, see Charles Sabel, *Work and Politics* (Cambridge: Cambridge University Press, 1982).

22. Without being able to flesh this argument out here, the decline of cooperative socialism must be sought in the tension between the internal democracy of socialist production units and the exigencies of their continued exposure to the forces of market competition among these units. For further comments on this question, see my discussion of the nationalization of the means of production.

23. For this reason, in his classic *Political Parties* (New York: Free Press, 1962) Robert Michels was wrong to locate the origins of oligarchy in socialist parties primarily in the psychological drives of party leaders or the inefficiency of democratic participation. The political and epistemological discourse of socialists itself calls for working-class deference to political leaders. This is particularly clear in the pre–World War I German social democracy when Karl Kautsky's positivist Marxism was supreme.

24. Marx provides the most clear-cut statement on this question in *Critique of the Gotha Program*, see Karl Marx, *The Marx-Engels Reader*, ed. Robert Tucker, 2d ed. (New York: W. W. Norton, 1978), pp. 530–31.

25. This even applies to Marx's own analysis of work organization and technology in the transition to the capitalist factory. Although Marx in *Capital*, vols. 1 and 3 (New York: International Publishers, 1967) clearly emphasizes the context of power relations in which new productive equipment was put to use, he also suggests an internal logic of technical progress and work organization independent of the relations of production. He comments that the "realm of freedom" can begin only outside the "realm of necessity" in the production process.

26. This applies even to Lenin's *State and Revolution* (New York: International Publishers, 1971).

27. Cf. Karl Marx, *Capital*, vol. 1 (New York: International Publishers, 1967), p. 80.

28. Lenin's view in *State and Revolution* (p. 44) that the imperial organization of the German post office should serve as the model of socialist organization is particularly instructive.

29. Marx, *Marx-Engels Reader*, pp. 171, 176.

30. Jean Baudrillard, *The Mirror of Production* (St. Louis: Telos Press, 1975), esp. pp. 22–47.

31. Juergen Habermas, *Knowledge and Human Interest* (Boston: Beacon Press, 1973), and *Theory of Communicative Action* (Boston: Beacon Press, 1985).

32. This problem is most clear-cut, for example, in reconstructions of the process of class formation. See Ira Katznelson, "Working Class Formation: Constructing Cases and Comparisons," in *Working Class Formation: Nineteenth-Century Patterns in Western Europe and the United States*, ed. Ira Katznelson and Aristide Zolberg (Princeton: Princeton University Press, 1986), pp. 33–41, esp. 14–22.

33. For this reason, the crisis of social democracy converges with a renewed interest in democratic theory and experiments that began to grow outside social democracy since the 1960s. For a survey of the theoretical debates, see David Held, *Models of Democracy* (Stanford: Stanford University Press, 1987), ch. 8, and Keane, *Democracy and Civil Society*, chs. 4 and 5.

34. The literature on the transformation of modern capitalism is too large

and varied to list. Especially useful, however, are Russell J. Dalton and Manfred Kuechler, eds., *Challenging the Political Order* (Oxford: Polity Press, 1990); Ronald Inglehart, *Culture Shift in Advanced Industrial Society* (Princeton: Princeton University Press, 1990); Horst Kern and Michael Schumann, *Das Ende der Arbeitsteilung?* (Munich: Beck, 1984); Scot Lash and John Urry, *The End of Organized Capitalism* (Madison: University of Wisconsin Press, 1987); Claus Offe, *Disorganized Capitalism* (Cambridge: MIT Press, 1985); and Michael Piore and Charles Sabel, *The Second Industrial Divide* (New York: Basic Books, 1984).

35. For this reason, conservative governments have found it the hardest to alter the most universalistic social insurances such as pension systems, or, in the example of Britain, the national health service, whereas more particularistic systems that benefit circumscribed social groups are much more vulnerable.

36. The first profound exposition of this theme is without doubt Max Weber's *Zwischenbetrachtung* in his sociology of religion. See Max Weber, "Religious Rejections of the World and Their Directions," in *From Max Weber: Essays in Sociology,* ed. Guenther Roth and C. Wright Mills (New York: Free Press, 1958), pp. 323–59. Since that time, authors in diverse traditions from functionalist systems theories (Talcott Parsons, Niklas Luhmann), via critical theories of advanced capitalism (Juegen Habermas, Alain Touraine) and economic neoinstitutionalism (Albert Hirschman, Oliver Williamson) to cultural analyses (Daniel Bell) and post-structuralist thinking (Michel Foucault) have made the plurality of life spheres a keystone of their argumentation.

37. In moral theorizing, this is the key argument advanced by Michael Walzer, *Spheres of Justice* (New York: Basic Books, 1983).

38. A first detailed report on these interviews which, however, stresses more the organizational than the discoursive aspects of the social democratic crisis can be found in Herbert Kitschelt, "Social Democracy and Liberal Corporatism: Swedish and Austrian Left Parties in Crisis," paper presented at the annual meeting of the American Political Science Association, San Francisco, August 1990.

39. I am not concerned here with shopfloor participation in work conditions, which is nonproblematic not only from a socialist point of view, but also from that of many capitalist management theories. My concern is with strategic control over investment decisions.

40. For the most recent example, see Carol Gould, *Rethinking Democracy* (Cambridge: Cambridge University Press, 1988).

41. The ubiquity of these complaints has been analyzed by Albert Hirschman, *Shifting Involvements* (Princeton: Princeton University Press, 1981), pp. 42–45.

42. A problem with vouchers is that the spatial distribution of pollution is difficult to control. If all vouchers are bought up by one source of pollution (water, air), certain areas would be hit excessively by pollution, while others would remain almost pollution-free.

43. Max Weber, *Economy and Society* (Berkeley: University of California Press, 1978), pp. 289–90.

44. Max Weber, *Gesammelte Politische Schriften*, 4th ed. (Tuebingen: Mohr, 1980), p. 499.

45. See, for example, Joseph Schumpeter, *Capitalism, Socialism, and Democracy* (New York: Harper, 1950). The rejection of intermediary party organizations and the insistence on the direct linkage between citizen and elected representative is a common theme in liberal conceptions of democracy.

46. For a more detailed comparative analysis of organizational forms and power relations, see Kitschelt, *The Transformation of European Social Democracy*, ch. 5.

47. Leif Lewin, *Governing Trade-Unions in Sweden* (Cambridge: Harvard University Press, 1980).

48. For an analysis of power structures in the French PS, see David S. Bell and Byron Criddle, *The French Socialist Party: The Emergence of a Party of Government*, 2d ed. (New York: Oxford University Press, 1988), chs. 9 and 10. It must be acknowledged, however, that due to the extraordinary centralization of political power and the weakness of the French parliament, the organizational inclination of the Socialist party toward interactive democracy had little influence on actual socialist government policy.

49. This perspective is also suggested by Wessel Visser and Rien Wijnhoven, "Politics Do Matter, but Does Unemployment? Party Strategies, Ideological Discourse, and Ending Mass Unemployment," *European Journal of Political Research* 18 (January 1990): 71–96.

50. For the definition of such systems, see Giovanni Sartori, *Parties and Party Systems: A Framework for Analysis* (Cambridge: Cambridge University Press, 1976).

51. Cf. Richard Gunther, "Electoral Laws, Party Systems, and Elites: The Case of Spain," *American Political Science Review* 83 (September 1989): 835–58. For ideology and government practice of the Spanish socialists, see Richard Gillespie, *The Spanish Socialist Party: A History of Factionalism* (Oxford: Clarendon Press, 1989), and Allan M. Williams, "Socialist Economic Policies: Never Off the Drawing Board?" in *Southern European Socialism*, ed. Tom Gallagher and Allan M. Williams (Manchester: Manchester University Press, 1989), pp. 188–216.

52. The factional conflicts within the Italian Christian Democrats and the tension between Gaullists and Giscardiens demonstrate these obstacles clearly.

53. John Gaffney, *The French Left and the Fifth Republic: The Discourses of Communism and Socialism in Contemporary France* (New York: St. Martin's Press, 1989), p. 169; Vicki Randall, *Women and Politics: An International Perspective*, 2d ed. (Chicago: University of Chicago Press, 1987).

54. Gaffney, *The French Left and the Fifth Republic*.

55. See the opinion polls reported by Leif Lewin, *Ideology and Strategy: A Century of Swedish Politics* (New York: Cambridge University Press, 1988), pp. 291–96.

56. As Joyce Gelb writes on the importance of the socialist discourse in Sweden: "An equal-opportunities mentality pervades society and policy-making; the emphasis on sex neutrality coupled with cooperation has produced a system in which women's issues are no longer perceived as a problem and are almost wholly integrated into family and social policy. Nevertheless, thus far equality has been defined exclusively in male terms. As most Swedish women interviewed for this study agreed, gender-neutral policies in a society still highly stratified by gender end up by benefiting the already powerful—that is males." Gelb also quotes another study on Sweden, concluding that "'[q]ualitative' gender issues, unrelated to economic concerns, have been neglected in a system that defines equality almost exclusively in economic terms." Joyce Gelb, *Feminism and Politics: A Comparative Perspective* (Berkeley: University of California Press, 1989), pp. 176, 175.

57. Socialdemokraterna, *90-tals Programmet: En debattbok om arbetarroerelsen viktigaste fragor under 90-talet* (Stockholm: Tidens Foerlag, 1989).

58. Examples are David Coates and Gordon Johnston, eds., *Socialist Strategies* (Oxford: Martin Robertson, 1983), and James Curran, ed., *The Future of the Left* (Cambridge: Polity Press, 1984). The only exception is one article by David Held and John Keane in these volumes on the importance of a decentralized civil society for socialist democracy. Yet even that essay puts great emphasis on the Swedish Meidner Plan and the French proposals for autogestion as examples of a new departure. See also Sarah Perrigo, "Feminism and the Struggle for Socialism," in *Socialist Strategies*, ed. Coates and Johnston, pp. 178–208.

59. I am adopting here the influential argument by Louis Hartz, *The Liberal Tradition in America* (New York: Harcourt, Brace and World, 1955). Of course, I am not suggesting that ideology is the only or the sole decisive factor accounting for the absence of a strong Left in the United States. The heterogeneity of the American working class and the specific operation of American party machines in the nineteenth century have also played a role. See Aristide Zolberg, "How Many Exceptionalisms?" in *Working Class Formation*, ed. Katznelson and Zolberg, pp. 397–456. See also Daniel Bell, *Marxian Socialism in the United States* (Princeton: Princeton University Press, 1967).

60. Examples of this approach are found in Przeworski, *Capitalism and Social Democracy*, and John Roemer, ed., *Analytical Marxism* (Cambridge: Cambridge University Press, 1986). Not by chance, public choice Marxism has also found a warm reception in other countries operating on the discursive axis dividing socialism from market liberalism, such as Britain and Scandinavia.

61. Moreover, feminist and ecological themes have been more integrated into the American market-liberal and populist discourse than into socialism.

62. Przeworski and Sprague, *Paper Stones*.

63. Steven Wolinetz, "The Dutch Labour Party: A Social Democratic Party in Transition," in *Social Democratic Parties in Western Europe*, ed. William E. Paterson and Alastair H. Thomas (New York: St. Martin's Press, 1977), pp. 342–88.

64. Hermann Schmitt, *Neue Politik in alten Parteien* (Opladen: Westdeutscher Verlag, 1987).

65. One highly controversial proponent of this intellectual approach has been Oskar Lafontaine, the party's candidate for the chancellor's office in 1990, who started from a left-libertarian point of view and then attempted to build a programmatic consensus that recognized elements of market efficiency, social equality, and left-libertarian politics. See Oskar Lafontaine, *Die Gesellschaft der Zukunft* (Hamburg: Hoffmann and Campe, 1988).

66. Sozialistische Partei Oesterreiches, *Sozialdemokratie 2000: Vorschlaege zur Diskussion ueber die Zukunft Osterreichs* (Venice: spoe, 1989); Werner W. Ernst, "Zur Programmatik der spoe seit 1985," and Werner Pleschberger, " 'Modernisierung' als Perspektive der Oesterreichischen Sozialdemokratie," both in Peter Pelinka and Gerhard Steger, *Auf dem Wege der Staatspartei* (Vienna: Verlag fuer Gesellschaftskritik, 1988), pp. 176–96, 199–211.

67. Ulrich Kloeti and Franz-Xaver Risi, "Neueste Entwicklungen im Parteiensystem der Schweiz," in *Das oesterreichische Parteiensystem*, ed. Anton Pelinka and Fritz Plasser (Vienna: Boehlau, 1988), pp. 717–37.

68. Peter Flora and Arnold Heidenheimer, eds., *The Development of Welfare States in Europe and America* (New Brunswick: Transaction, 1981).

69. For an elaboration of this hypothesis, see Herbert Kitschelt, "Materiale Politisierung der Produktion," *Zeitschrift für Soziologie* 14 (June 1985): 188–208.

Toward a Postsocialist Politics?

A Historical Postscript

Konrad H. Jarausch

In East and West triumphalism about the demise of socialism has become widespread. While the *Wall Street Journal*'s crowing about the victory of the market over Marx was predictable, such gloating by better-informed academics is more problematic. Even the Anglo-German sociologist Ralf Dahrendorf conflates the fall of communism in the East with the demise of social democracy in the West. In *Reflections on the Revolution in Europe* he claims "unequivocally that socialism is dead, and that none of its variants can be revived for a world awakening from the double nightmare of Stalinism and Brezhnevism" (p. 42). More careful analysts like Wolfgang Merkel and Herbert Kitschelt have refuted such predictions empirically for western Europe in their contributions to this volume. They correctly point out that the case for the demise of socialism rests on the decline of the Labour party and a drop in Scandinavian electoral performance, while the new Mediterranean parties seem to be flourishing. In other Western countries there has been little loss of power and only some modification of policies away from redistribution toward competitive economics. Even though its evidence is suspect, the death of socialism rhetoric has be-

Instead of presenting additional research, these remarks offer concluding reflections on the preceding essays from a historical perspective. These ruminations are especially indebted to the helpful suggestions of Christiane Lemke and Gary Marks.

come so widespread as to assume a weight of its own and has begun to influence events as a kind of self-fulfilling prophecy.

The new orthodoxy that politics have entered a postsocialist era is not only false but also dangerous because it risks leaving capitalism unchecked. During the last century, socialism has served as a powerful critique of market systems (social justice) and as an alternative blueprint for organization (economic planning). The very success of the socialist challenge has ironically helped to stabilize capitalism. Only in developing countries from the Soviet Union to the Third World has Marxism supplanted capitalist economies with an industrializing dictatorship. The evident failure of communism has removed this threat in the East while the loss of nerve of democratic socialism is lessening the corrective in the West. Flush with triumph, many capitalists now advocate policies that are about to revive the old abuses of untrammeled competition, labor exploitation, and destruction of the environment. When the traditional abuses of "free enterprise" return, they are likely to generate a new set of strictures against it. Because conservative and religious spokespersons have largely made their peace with a system they once despised, it is not clear from what direction such an opposition might arise. If the Marxist legacy remains discredited, will these inevitable and necessary critiques of capitalism be recognizably socialist or assume some other, newer, leftist form?

The likely outcome of the crisis of socialism can only be discerned if its dimensions are fully understood. The relative unanimity about the existence of the predicament suggests that one important dimension is psychological. Although they were initially overjoyed about their civic revolutions, democratic socialists in eastern Europe were quickly disappointed by the masses' repudiation of their program. The first free elections in the East brought to power not reformers aspiring to socialism with a human face, but rather competing groups of liberal democrats demanding a return to parliamentary democracy and market economics, as well as Christian conservatives seeking to restore traditional values and national glory (see the chapters by Iván and Sonja Szelényi and Sharon Wolchik). Intead of taking credit for the overthrow of the post-Stalinist regimes through championing detente and civil rights, Western social democrats reacted despondently to the upheaval. Although most Western socialist politicians denounced the faults of "real existing Socialism" and wanted nothing to do with the repressive system, some radical intellectuals saw aspects of the East

European experiment as a potential alternative to welfare capitalism. When that other future suddenly collapsed, reactions in East and West ranged from total to partial denial, seeking to preserve the essential correctness of the socialist vision while blaming its faulty implementation for the unforeseen denouement (see the chapter by Andrei Markovits). In the minds of participants and commentators, the fall of communism turned into a broader rout of socialism from which the Left has yet to recover its feistiness.

More serious is the conceptual disarray of the Left. Bored by the normalcy of the welfare state, many Western intellectuals like to flirt with more radical social programs. During the glorious heyday of the East European revolution, reformist thinkers searched for a "third way" between the faults of classic capitalism and Stalinist communism. Even in its Austrian or Swedish manifestations, welfare capitalism did not seem attractive enough to many eastern critics. At the same time, the economic failure and political repression of communism required a fundamental reassessment first of Stalinism, then of Lenin's role, and finally of the entire Marxist legacy (see the chapter by Norman Naimark). The endless discussions about the third way remind one of an earnest search for the mythical continent Atlantis in the wide ocean: All participants know it has to be there somewhere between Europe and America, yet it cannot be found. At the bottom of this longing seems to be a widespread need for a utopian vision of society that makes present-day imperfections bearable and life meaningful as a quest to a higher end. Although there is much discussion about how to combine the best of the capitalist and communist worlds, it is not at all clear that any of the ingenious and verbally often convincing solutions will prove to be a compelling goal or present a viable strategy to get there. None of the market versions of communism have so far succeeded, and even the Swedish example merely redistributes the spoils of efficient capitalist production. Moreover, the most promising directions of direct democracy seem already occupied by the remnants of the civic movement and various single-issue opposition groups such as environmentalists.

These psychological and conceptual dilemmas could be ignored if the crisis were not also practical. Except for the SPD victory in the East German state of Brandenburg, the electoral prospects for democratic socialists in the East are dim because they have so far lost out even to the successors of the communists. They seem to have much difficulty building new organizations against the remnant of the renamed communist apparatus. Apparently the discrediting of Soviet compulsion makes it well-nigh impossible to organize broad popular sympathies for welfare state programs into an attractive party (see the Szelényi chapter). In the West the large and often successful socialist organizations face a difficult strategic choice between market and libertarian challenges (see the Kitschelt chapter). The Thatcher legacy as well as excessive welfare spending militate in favor of a fiscally prudent managerial socialism. The post-1968 environmental, feminist, and peace movements pull in the opposite directions of a more radical social activism. While the bourgeoisification of the traditional proletariat indicates the need for a white-collar strategy, the emergence of a new underclass of foreigners, drug addicts, and homeless demands an extension of the franchise and social services to that lumpenproletariat, most detested by the traditional working-class. No doubt, attractive individual candidates can overcome these practical handicaps with well-run campaigns, and the incompetence or corruption of conservative foes might help. But widespread despondency, intellectual confusion, and practical difficulties have created the feeling of a crisis that seems to bear out predictions of socialist collapse.

Does the malaise need to be fatal? The experience of previous socialist setbacks indicates that this is not necessarily so if the present problems lead to a profound reordering of priorities (see the chapter by Geoff Eley). As dogma, justifying the dictatorship of a party, Marxism is discredited. As a critical perspective on social inequality, Marx's ideas continue to offer stimulating insights. To regain its political relevance, socialism needs to find more convincing answers to its intellectual dilemmas. At the same time, organizational strategies have to be reconsidered fundamentally. Although one should not underestimate the constraints of tradition, the collapse of East European communism and the disarray of Western social democracy also provide an opportunity for at least a partial new beginning. What will it take to facilitate such a fresh start?

One prerequisite for renewal is a reconsideration of the liberal legacy in regard to economics. Because socialism rose as a protest against laissez-faire industrialization, accepting the market may prove difficult. Critics never tire of pointing out the irony that a purportedly materialist ideology was overthrown due to a failure in economic performance. Hailed as antidote to capitalist crises and insecurity, the planned economy of the East European states led to stagnation. Nikita

Khrushchev's predictions of burying capitalism by outperforming it can only evoke a bemused smile in the 1990s. While Stalinist planning seems to have been able to manage some degree of smokestack industrialization, bureaucratic socialism was unable to master the transition to the third phase of information technology. The priority of political theater over production and the heavy emphasis on distributive egalitarianism created an economy of scarcity supplemented and distorted by a black market. There is no need to rehearse the details of the economic ills of eastern Europe in order to point out that the transition to market pricing and competition appears to be politically difficult because its negative side-effects such as inflation and unemployment seem to precede its positive effect on growth. At the same time some Western socialists, especially in France, Spain, and Scandinavia, have also realized that there might be fiscal limits to the expansion of social services. Although not as oppressive, social democracy nevertheless also spawned a huge, nonproductive bureaucracy. While in East and West managerial socialists are turning to the market as a deus ex machina, its compatibility with the redistributive agenda remains somewhat unclear.

The collapse of communism in eastern Europe also suggests the need for a rethinking of the relationship to the democratic heritage. Because socialism originally grew out of radical democracy, by adding to demands for participation rights a social agenda as basis for their actual implementation, the recovery of the democratic impulse may prove easier than the revision of economic posture. Democratic socialism expanded the democratic legacy of liberté by stressing social égalité as well as emphasizing human fraternité as prerequisites. Because other parties occupied the constitutional and participatory platforms, social democracy in the West turned ever more exclusively toward economic redistribution, thereby encouraging state dominance. While the establishment of welfare bureaucracy had a benign intent, in practice it often served to reduce citizens to "cases" for social work, thereby shifting dependence from the landowner or capitalist to the administrator. In the East, the revolutionary struggle of a minority eventually reduced the concept of democracy in Lenin's understanding to a justification for the dictatorship of the proletariat—thereby in effect abandoning civil rights. Much of the civic movement was motivated by an understanding of the need to recover the heritage of citizenship rights as a basis for political freedom. Instead of taking participation for granted and concentrating on economic equality, socialists need to reaffirm and expand the democratic basis of politics in modern mass society.

At the same time, the crisis demonstrates the urgency of reordering traditional relations within the Left. After the Bolshevik revolution much socialist energy was taken up in the internecine struggle between communists and social democrats for control of working-class allegiances. Communist charges of "social fascism" against moderates and social democratic attacks on the "revolutionary adventurism" of the radicals prevented a common front against the larger danger of fascism and national socialism until it was too late. Although the clash between the evolutionary and revolutionary strands was politically understandable, both could claim allegiance to the Marxist message with equal justification; Karl Marx himself vacillated between both stances, depending upon contemporary political prospects. The result of the confrontation was, however, disastrous because it contributed to the polarization of the movement and made communists more extreme and moderates more timid, rendering both less creative in the process. The communist feud against social democracy and vice-versa eventually squashed the middle position of a radical but at the same time democratic socialism. The collapse of this antinomy in Europe should open the door to a freer reappropriation of the socialist heritage, allowing for the reemergence not only of the centrist strain, but also of non-Marxist positions like syndicalism (see the Eley chapter). It should also liberate the Left to return to its humanist agenda and concentrate on social problems instead of fighting itself.

Another major problem area that must be addressed is the nationalist challenge to socialist internationalism. One of the great strengths of the working-class movement had initially been the international solidarity against oppression that rejected chauvinism. The socialist anthem is entitled the "international," and there have been several organizational "internationals" as well as Cominterns. However, World War I demonstrated the practical weakness of transnational solidarity, because the majority of socialist parties endorsed their respective countries' policies. Although the Bolsheviks claimed a rather consequential internationalism, once in power they militantly defended the Soviet Republic and through Stalin's influence turned more Russian and eventually even imperialist. One of the great surprises of the East European revolution of 1989–90 was the emergence of virulent nationalism, long submerged under Soviet and great Russian hegemony. Even if anti-imperial movements had been both revolutionary and nationalist, socialism has not been able to define a constructive and convincing relationship to the nation, leaving it to be captured by rightist groups. In the West the socialist response to European integration has also been confused because it was originally construed as a capitalist enterprise, to be rejected out of hand. In the long run, internationalist ambivalence about nationalism will not be enough. Both a recovery of the democratic potential of nationhood as well as a willingness to engage in the emerging regional structures seem necessary in order to achieve reformist ends.

A final cluster of difficulties that needs to be confronted intellectually is the socialist stance toward war. Because the military and empire had been viewed as tools of internal and external repression, the Left initially rejected both. However, the social patriotism of World War I demonstrated the practical impossibility of pacifism. In spite of peace rhetoric, the Bolsheviks fought vigorously in the Russian civil war. As a result, the Left was confused about the fascist threat in the 1930s, with some wanting to stop Hitler and others clinging to peace. While Western social democrats reluctantly reconciled themselves to the need for some defense, a broad-based peace movement time and again questioned the need for military budgets and favored other priorities. In the East, military training in schools provoked resistance against the contradiction of "fighting for peace" in uniform through the slogan "swords into plowshares." Initially the end of the Cold War confrontation seemed to usher in a new age of disarmament, but the unexpected Gulf War reopened the military question. While the East has agreed to dissolve the Warsaw Pact, seen as Soviet military domination, there is much confusion in the West about defense of one's own country, within NATO, within NATO plus the UN, or even beyond that. Socialists will regain their credibility only if they can resolve the contradiction between an antinuclear pacifism, anti-Americanism, or third worldism and some form of collective security. Although the specific solutions are by no means clear, only convincing answers to these questions will restore the attraction of socialist ideas.

Along with intellectual renewal must come an organizational recovery. The discrediting of communism has largely removed the Bolshevik form of leftist politics from the European map, even if small successor parties struggle on and some future backsliding may occur, especially in the Soviet Union. A wave of renaming organizations indicates that only fresh parties, untainted by Stalinist corruption, will be able to capture some of the latent radical sympathies of East European populations. As some of the earlier chapters have indicated, Western disarray is more conceptual and psychological than electoral. In contrast to the East, some moderate restructuring is likely to suffice in order to regain the political initiative. But beyond the traditional patterns beckon new, sometimes appealing, sometimes frightening alternatives. The space opened by recent events creates an opportunity for some reshuffling of traditional patterns. Overcoming the crisis therefore will also involve a restructuring of the organizational form of socialist politics.

In the East the idealists among former communists are struggling to reintroduce liberal and democratic elements into Marxism-Leninism. They seek to recover the center-left tradition of the German independent socialists (USPD) that was crushed between the hard-line communists (KP) and the moderate socialists (SPD). In terms of individual thinkers, they are rereading Rosa Luxemburg and Antonio Gramsci to discover a revolutionary stance that does not end in dictatorship. While there is a deep reluctance to give up the socialist utopia and the dream of revolution, postcommunist intellectuals are striving for an oppositional mass politics that articulates the popular disappointments in the reconversion to capitalism. Purged of its Stalinist perversions and even of some Leninist legacies like dictatorship, the Marxist vocabulary can still function intermittently as critique of market abuses. But parties like the East German PDS are handicapped by a lack of credibility due to a large number of former apparatchiks who have learned nothing from their debacle. Although they are attracting a smattering of Western intellectuals driven by the hatred of their own system, these parties' vision of a socialist future remains clouded and indistinct. Hence successor parties are likely to function as a decompression tank, facilitating the transition for stalwarts of the former regime, rather than as the basis for a new advance. Embarrassed by the debacle of their shared vision in the East, Western communist parties grope for a new identity. Only when democratic socialists manage to distance themselves sufficiently from this tainted past are they likely to recapture their potentially considerable constituency (see the Szelényi chapter).

Although the obstacles are smaller, the direction of socialist renewal in the West is equally uncertain. In the rapidly developing countries of the Mediterranean rim, a plebiscitary socialism that combines growing organized labor with some market concessions still seems to be quite popular. In the postindustrial countries of central and northern Europe, the situation is more difficult because the traditional working-class basis is eroding with the growth of a service economy (see the chapter by Christiane Lemke and Gary Marks). A recovery requires the extension of the socialist appeal to the white-collar sector without losing the blue-collar union base. With strong telegenic personalities, social democracy might function as a largely deideologized *Wahlverein*, combining superior managing skills and some remnants of a social conscience. While the plebiscitary solution depends upon attractive personalities, the technocratic answer runs the risk of programmatic atrophy. Obviously, the incompetence of competing parties or the magnetism of a particular candidate like François Mitterrand may temporarily overcome this dilemma. But in the long run democratic socialism cannot win simply as welfare administrator and protector of clients' fresh demands. SPD success in recent German state elections in Hesse and Rhineland-Palatinate suggests the attractiveness of socialist criticism without yet indicating a way to win in national elections. While Western wealth has already contributed to relaunching socialist parties in the East, the organizational drift of democratic socialism does not provide a compelling model to imitate. In spite of the lack of clear direction, the prospects for the continued success of only somewhat modified socialist strategy in the West are better than the likelihood of neocommunist recovery.

A more interesting alternative is the ferment of the civic movement in the East and the green groupings in the West. Although drawing on older marginal traditions of protest, the advocacy of peace, environment, feminism, and direct participation forms a potentially powerful ideological cluster. In contrast to the dead weight of bureaucratic socialism, this congery draws strength from the freshness of its political style and the orientation toward citizens' participation. Unlike classical socialism, its basic concerns address the survival problems of postindustrial society rather than the chief defects of the industrialization process. Instead of promising material equality through government redistribution, the program of a civil society aims at empowering citizens and at implementing postmaterial values. In overthrowing the communist regimes from within and in halting many capitalist excesses, the related impulses of the Eastern civic revolution and the Western greens have already made a significant contribution to European development. However, their spontaneity has made for amateurish politics and incessant internal quarrelling that have time and again limited their electoral appeal to a minority, stamped by the generational experience of 1968. Although they have only been able to influence the public agenda as coalition partners of traditional socialists, they exert considerable power through the partial absorption of their platform by the larger parties. Facilitated by Oskar Lafontaine, their ideas have already helped revitalize the leviathan of German social democracy. Although it remains unclear whether civic movements and environmental groups will cooperate enough to prosper as an independent party, their intellectual impact is likely to continue to grow in the future.

A more frightening possibility is the potential rise of a national socialist populism, or Peronism. Especially in eastern Europe, it is not at all improbable that the postcommunist transition difficulties toward market democracy will lead to a combination of national pride and social concerns in some kind of new and explosive way. Most fascist and even some traditionalist dictatorships of the interwar period were based on a rhetorical reconciliation of these two potent political impulses. Sensitive observers like Timothy Garton Ash were among the first to sound the alarm about the return of nationalism in eastern Europe. While suppressed resentment against Soviet domination was bound to explode, national passions are proving divisive within countries such as Czechoslovakia or Yugoslavia and hamper regional cooperation toward recovery. Moreover, many East European citizens are not about to give up their egalitarian demands for cheap food, housing, and transportation; they only want to achieve them more quickly through capitalism. When disappointed, as they are likely to be, these expectations will facilitate the renewal of demonstrations and socialist impulses, if sufficiently distanced from previous communist rhetoric. Some commentators like Iván Szelényi have already interpreted the election of Solidarity leader Lech Wałęsa in Poland as a harbinger of a national populist trend. While a strong leader might help ease the inevitable transition pains, the antidemocratic legacy of such regimes before World War II makes one wonder how benign such a development might turn out to be.

Even if the ultimate shape is still unclear, the organizational renewal of socialism is already beginning. The contextual differences of parties in eastern and western, northern and southern Europe are so great that it is unlikely that one model solution to the crisis will encompass them all. At the beginning of the 1990s, the rebirth of a democratic form of communism seems difficult on anything but a limited scale. The problems inherent in the Leninist tradition are too severe and its debased Stalinist implementation has discredited the Bolshevik vision too drastically for neocommunism to achieve mass appeal on the European continent. The emergence of a populist form of nationalist socialism also seems unlikely to become the chief trajectory of socialist resurgence. Although it might generate much popular appeal in some East European countries, this unstable compound is unlikely to win many converts in the West. Hence the most promising directions seem to be the reinvigoration of social democracy and its challenge by a broader civic movement, based on an alternative vision. At present, it is impossible to predict the exact outcome of this contest, but the intellectual discussion in East and West is so vigorous that the prospects for a subsequent organizational revival seem quite promising.

Although history can take surprising turns, a longer time perspective suggests some tentative conclusions about the present predicament of socialism. In the wake of the collapse of eastern communism the psychological, conceptual, and practical disarray of the Left may yet prove disastrous in the West. Spill-over effects from the Soviet paralysis and the "death of socialism" rhetoric might initiate a downward spiral. But the shock of the current crisis may also prove salutary if it leads to a recognition of fresh possibilities. Old fixations such as the denigration of liberal markets and the celebration of central planning can now be overcome. Old deficiencies such as the lack of attention to democratic rights and excessive bureaucratization may now be remedied. Old blockages such as the anticommunism struggle or the proscription of democratic socialism are suddenly removed. Old blind spots like the relation to nationalism can now be illuminated in a European reformulation. Old ambiguities such as the socialist attitude toward war can be clarified through the end of the Cold War. On all these fundamental questions a searching debate has begun that is bound to help restructure organizational responses. Even if socialism might continue to have difficulties in finding a convincing posture in the communist debris of eastern Europe, Western social democracy looks too vigorous and broad-based simply to give up the fight. Moreover, newer participatory forms of leftist politics toward peace, the environment, gender, foreigners, and the state are challenging established forms. The outcome of all this ferment is not at all clear, but there is little doubt that through redefinition the recovery has begun.

In the words of Mark Twain, predictions of the demise of socialism are therefore greatly exaggerated. The collapse of communism does not mean that the world has entered a posthistoric era without further problems or confrontations, even if the comfortable Cold War struggle between East and West is hopefully a thing of the past. Instead of pulling democratic socialism down with it, the East European revolution has for the first time in more than half a century created an opportunity for spreading social democracy throughout the entire continent. In order to recapture the initiative, socialists cannot rely upon a politics of nostalgia that addresses the pressing problems of yesteryear (see the chapter by Wolfgang Merkel). In the neue Unübersichtlichkeit of the postmodern age, democratic socialism will only survive if it meets the challenge with more than electoral manipulation and renews itself intellectually and organizationally. The example of the civic movement of the East can provide a valuable stimulus that goes beyond the sometimes theatrical antics of the greens. Even if the aspirations of the Bürgerbewegung and some reform communists for a third way proved impractical, their focus on peace, the environment, gender relations, minorities, and direct participation defines the current problems more clearly than the agenda of classical, union-based socialism. In the end, even nonsocialists ought to be vitally interested in the renewal of social democracy because the health of capitalism has depended upon the vitality of the challenge to it. If the socialist critique were no longer to exist, one would have to reinvent it—in the interest of capitalist democracy.

Contributors

Christiane Lemke is a faculty member in the Political Science Department at the Freie Universität Berlin. She was DAAD German Studies Professor in the Political Science Department at the University of North Carolina at Chapel Hill (1988–91) and is currently Visiting Associate Professor of Government at Harvard University (1991–92). She has published several books and articles on German politics and society. Her most recent work includes *The Quality of Life in the German Democratic Republic* (coeditor, 1989); *Die Ursachen des Umbruchs: Politische Sozialisation in der ehemaligen DDR* (1991); and "Women and Politics in the New Federal Republic," in Barbara Nelson and Najma Chohdhury, eds., *Women and Politics World Wide* (forthcoming).

Gary Marks is Associate Professor of Political Science at the University of North Carolina at Chapel Hill. He is the author of *Unions in Politics: Britain, Germany, and the United States in the Nineteenth and Early Twentieth Centuries* (1989); coauthor of a forthcoming book entitled *Why Is There No Socialism in the United States? A Comparative Perspective*, with S. M. Lipset; and has written several articles on political economy in western Europe and the European Community. Among his current projects is a volume of recent research on democracy coedited with Larry Diamond. At the Center for Advanced Studies in Stanford in 1991–92 he plans to continue writing on the European Community and the future of the state in western Europe.

Geoff Eley is Professor of History at the University of Michigan, where he also directs the Program for the Comparative Study of Social Transformations. He is the author of *Reshaping the German Right: Radical Nationalism and Political Change after Bismarck* (1980; new edition, 1991); *The Peculiarities of German History: Bourgeois Society and Politics in Nineteenth Century Germany*, with David Blackbourn (1984); and *Wilhelminismus, Nationalismus, Faschismus: Zur historischen Kontinuität in Deutschland* (1991). He is presently completing a book on the European Left in the nineteenth and twentieth centuries.

Konrad H. Jarausch is Lurcy Professor of European Civilization at the University of North Carolina at Chapel Hill. He has written or edited a dozen books, including *The Unfree Professions: German Lawyers, Teachers, and Engineers, 1900–1950* (1960). With Volker Gransow he has just published a volume entitled *Die deutsche Vereinigung: Dokumente zu Bürgerbewegung, Annäherung und Beitritt* (1991). At the Center for Advanced Studies in Stanford in 1991–92 he hopes to complete an analysis of German unification.

Herbert Kitschelt is Associate Professor of Political Science at Duke University. He has published several books on energy technology policy, new social movements, and changes of party systems in Western democracies. His recent books include *The Logics of Party Formation: Ecological Politics in Belgium and West Germany* (1989) and *Beyond the European Left: Ideology and Political Action in the Belgian Ecology Parties* (1990).

Andrei S. Markovits is currently Associate Professor in the Department of Political Science at Boston University and a Senior Associate at the Center for European Studies at Harvard University. He is senior editor of *German Politics and Society* and author of numerous books, articles, and reviews on German and Central European politics and society. He has just completed *The German Left: Red, Green and Beyond* (forthcoming 1992).

Wolfgang Merkel is Assistant Professor at the Institute for Political Science, Heidelberg University. He is the author of *Vom Oppositionssozialismus zur Staatspartei: Die Sozialistische Partei Italiens unter Bettino Craxi* (1985) and *Prima e dopo Craxi: Le trasformazioni del partito Socialista Italiano* (1987); coeditor of *Die Politik zur deutschen Einheit: Probleme-Strategien-Kontroversen* (1991); and editor of *Socialdemocracia en Europa* (forthcoming 1992).

Norman M. Naimark is Professor of History and Director of the Center for Russian and East European Studies at Stanford University. He serves as Chairman of the Program Committee of IREX and is a member of the Joint Committee on Eastern Europe of the ACLS-SSRC. He is also on the board of editors of *East European Politics and Societies*. He is the author of books on Polish Marxism and Russian terrorism, and is currently working on a book-length study of the Soviet occupation of eastern Germany, 1945–49.

Iván Szelényi is Professor of Sociology at the University of California, Los Angeles and Corresponding Member of the Hungarian Academy of Sciences. He is coauthor of *The Intellectuals on the Road* to *Class Power* (1979) and author of *Urban Inequalities under State Socialism* (1983) and *Socialist Entrepreneurs* (1988). He has published articles in many journals, including the *American Sociological Review, American Journal of Sociology, Theory and Society, Politics and Society,* and *International Journal of Urban and Regional Research.*

Szonja Szelényi is Assistant Professor of Sociology at Stanford University and a 1990–91 Annenberg Fellow in the School of Humanities and Sciences at Stanford University.

Sharon L. Wolchik is currently Director of Russian and East European Studies and Associate Professor of Political Science and International Affairs at the George Washington University. She has written extensively on policy-making, gender issues, and political change in Central and Eastern Europe. She is the coeditor of *Women, State, and Party in Eastern Europe* (1985) and *Foreign and Domestic Policy in Eastern Europe in the 1980s* (1983). Her most recent book is *Czechoslovakia in Transition: Politics, Economics, and Society* (1991).

Index

Library of Congress Cataloging-in-Publication Data

The crisis of socialism in Europe / edited by Christiane Lemke and
Gary Marks.

p.   cm.

Includes bibliographical references and index.

ISBN 0-8223-1180-1. — ISBN 0-8223-1197-6 (pbk.)

1. Socialism—Europe—History—20th century.   2. Europe—Politics
and government—1945–   3. Socialism—Europe, Eastern—History—20th
century.   4. Europe, Eastern—Politics and government—1989–
I. Lemke, Christiane, 1951–   . II. Marks, Gary Wolfe.

HX238.5.C75   1992

335'.0094—dc20   91-14680

                                                            CIP